Certified Function Point Specialist Examination Guide

Certified Function Point Specialist Examination Guide

David Garmus

Janet Russac

Royce Edwards

CRC Press
Taylor & Francis Group
Boca Raton London New York

CRC Press is an imprint of the
Taylor & Francis Group, an **informa** business

AN AUERBACH BOOK

CRC Press
Taylor & Francis Group
6000 Broken Sound Parkway NW, Suite 300
Boca Raton, FL 33487-2742

First issued in hardback 2017

© 2010 by Taylor & Francis Group, LLC
CRC Press is an imprint of Taylor & Francis Group, an Informa business

No claim to original U.S. Government works

ISBN 13: 978-1-4200-7637-0 (pbk)
ISBN 13: 978-1-1384-6849-8 (hbk)

**Visit the Taylor & Francis Web site at
http://www.taylorandfrancis.com**

**and the CRC Press Web site at
http://www.crcpress.com**

Library of Congress Cataloging-in-Publication Data

Garmus, David.
   Certified function point specialist examination guide / David Garmus, Janet Russac, and Royce Edwards.
      p. cm.
   Includes bibliographical references and index.
   ISBN 978-1-4200-7637-0 (alk. paper)
   1. Electronic data processing personnel--Certification. 2. Computer software--Development--Examinations--Study guides. 3. Function point analysis--Examinations--Study guides. 4. Software measurement--Examinations--Study guides. I. Russac, Janet. II. Edwards, Royce. III. Title.

QA76.3.G394 2010
005.1'4--dc22
                                           2010014703

We dedicate this work to Caren Garmus,
who passed away on December 12, 2008,
after a 2-year battle with lung cancer.
She was an inspiration to us and many of you.

Contents

Foreword

The standard economic definition for *productivity* for more than 200 years has been "goods or services produced per unit of labor or expense." For software it was long difficult to perform valid economic studies because the "lines of code" metric is not a suitable economic unit for the "goods or services" that software provides.

As of 2010, there are more than 2500 programming languages in existence. Many of these languages have no standard rules for even counting lines of code. The software literature that does attempt to count lines of code is divided between counts of physical lines and counts of logical statements. There can be as much as a 500% difference in apparent size between physical and logical code counts for many common programming languages. Some applications have as many as 15 different programming languages in use at the same time, and a majority of software applications have at least two programming languages in use at the same time. There are no standard rules for counting applications using multiple programming languages concurrently.

More than half of the total effort devoted to software development is not concerned with coding itself, but rather with gathering requirements, with architecture, with design, with creation of user documents, with testing, with management, and with scores of other noncoding activities. None of these can be measured using "lines of code" metrics, but all can be measured using function point metrics.

Even worse, the "lines of code" metric tends to penalize modern high-level programming languages such as Java, C++, Ruby, and the like. This is because noncode development activities are a higher percentage of total effort with modern languages than they are with low-level languages such as Assembler or C. The bottom line is that "lines of code" metrics are essentially worthless for software economic studies. In fact, "lines of code" metrics are actually harmful because they violate the assumptions of standard economics.

In the 1970s, A.J. Albrecht and his colleagues at IBM developed the function point metric. This metric has since been used successfully for economic analysis of individual projects and for large-scale economic studies of industry segments and even national software studies. The function point metric has become the *de facto* standard for software economic analysis, for benchmarks of software productivity and quality, for studies of software portfolios, and for all serious measurement purposes.

In 1978, IBM put the function point metric into the public domain. A nonprofit organization of function point users was quickly created to share data and maintain the rules for counting function point metrics. This organization is the International Function Point Users Group, commonly identified as IFPUG. As of 2010, IFPUG has grown to become the largest software metric association in the world, with thousands of individual members and hundreds of corporations as members. As of 2010, there are IFPUG affiliates in about 25 countries, and the number is increasing each year.

To ensure accuracy and consistency in counting function points, the IFPUG organization has created formal counting rules. In addition, the IFPUG organization has created a certification examination that is administered several times a year. Successful completion of the IFPUG certification examination has long been a criterion for consultants who count function point metrics.

Over time, as new kinds of software emerged, it has been necessary to update the function point counting rules to ensure that the rules encompass all known forms of software. The current IFPUG counting rules as of 2010 are version 4.3. The function point counting rules have also grown in size and sophistication. In 1978, the IBM counting rules consisted of about 15 pages of general guidance. Today, the IFPUG counting rules top 100 pages and include a number of detailed counting practices that need to be understood for accurate counts.

David Garmus, Janet Russac, and Royce Edwards have long been involved with function point analysis and with establishing the IFPUG counting rules. All have been members of IFPUG for more than 20 years and have served as officers and committee members. Their new book, *Certified*

Function Point Specialist Examination Guide, is intended as a study guide for function point specialists who plan to take the IFPUG certification examination. Although a number of solid books on counting function points are available, this new book fills a gap in the function point literature by providing useful information on the specifics of becoming a certified function point counter. The authors are all qualified for the work at hand and indeed have contributed to the function point counting methodology.

It is interesting that after more than 60 years of usage there has never been any kind of certification or examination for counting lines of code. Not only does the "lines of code" metric have serious economic flaws, but it also remains one of the most ambiguous metrics ever utilized by any engineering field. Code counting variations can cause apparent size differences of more than 10 to 1, which is an astonishing range of uncertainty.

By contrast, results of studies involving certified function point counters using standard test cases usually come within about 5% of achieving identical counts. This precision is about as high as any form of analysis based on learned skills. In fact, the accuracy of function point counting is higher than the accuracy levels noted for other analytical tasks such as preparing income taxes or preparing financial reports.

Function point metrics have become the *de facto* standard for software economic studies in part because function points are valid for economic analysis and in part because function point metrics are based on formal counting rules and are supported by formal examinations and certification procedures. This new book by David Garmus, Janet Russac, and Royce Edwards fills an important niche in the function point literature.

Capers Jones
President, Capers Jones & Associates LLC

Preface

As consultants in function point analysis, each of us has been involved with information technology (IT) for at least 25 years. Although our experiences have been different, we each came to the conclusion early in our careers that measurement was a key to success. You have heard many times that you cannot manage what you cannot measure. It is our opinion that functional sizing is the most effective measurement in software development and maintenance. We have chosen the International Function Point Users Group (IFPUG) method as the most consistent functional size measurement method. IFPUG function point analysis measures software by quantifying functionality provided to users.

The rules and definitions of the IFPUG method have continued to be enhanced since function point analysis was introduced during the mid-1970s by Allan Albrecht of IBM as a form of sizing software development. Since its formation in 1986, the IFPUG has maintained and updated a *Function Point Counting Practices Manual* (CPM) that provides the rules, as well as guidance in applying the rules, for determining types of counts, establishing application boundaries, and measuring data and transactional functions. Release 4.3 of the CPM conforms to the ISO/IEC 14143-1:2007 standard for functional measurement. The rules by themselves in CPM 4.3 are essentially unchanged, but the terminology has changed to comply with the ISO Functional Size Measurement (FSM) standard. As members of the IFPUG Counting Practices Committee (CPC), we have been immersed in the process of releasing this latest version of the CPM. It was our intent in writing this book to guide readers in preparing for the IFPUG Certified Function Point Specialist (CFPS) exam, but the guidelines contained herein should also serve as a useful reference book for anyone applying the rules of function point analysis.

While writing this book, we were blessed to receive comments and constructive criticism from three book reviewers who are leaders in the software measurement community and well known in IFPUG circles. We particularly wish to express our appreciation to Bonnie Brown, Vice Chair of the IFPUG CPC; Joe Schofield, Vice President of IFPUG; and Mary Bradley, Past President of IFPUG and Past Chair of the CPC. Their contribution to this effort was significant.

We hope you find this book to be useful in any sizing effort as well as in preparation for the CFPS exam.

Acknowledgments

It is impossible to remember all of those individuals who have contributed to the content and substance of this book. Without the opportunity to practice the International Function Point Users Group (IFPUG) functional sizing method and the related software metrics, we would not have even begun. We have been blessed over the years by our relationships with a large number of great clients as well as IFPUG members and those who have served on the IFPUG board and committees, especially the Counting Practices Committee (CPC). Our special thanks to each of those individuals.

Our efforts on this book have presented a wonderful opportunity for continued learning. We had the good fortune to receive thoughtful comments and constructive criticisms from three reviewers who are industry experts and strong representatives of the software measurement and management industry, particularly in function point analysis. We are especially appreciative of the review efforts by Bonnie Brown, Vice Chair of the IFPUG CPC; Joe Schofield, Vice President of IFPUG; and Mary Bradley, Past President of IFPUG and Past Chair of the CPC.

We are very thankful for the IFPUG organization, which is directly responsible for function point analysis. This document contains material that has been extracted from Release 4.3 of the IFPUG *Function Point Counting Practices Manual*. It is reproduced in this document with the permission of IFPUG. You may contact IFPUG through their website at http://www.ifpug.org, by e-mail to ifpug@ifpug.org, or by phone at 609-799-4900 and fax at 609-799-7032.

Finally, we must acknowledge the love and support that we have received from our families. They have endured the many trials and tribulations that come with professionals who are constantly on the road and all too often experience delays in travel and demands of clients that keep them away from important events. Our families have given us space as we sat at the dining room table with papers spread about and pounded away on our laptops. We say a special thanks to David's late wife, Caren Garmus; his children, Kim Garmus and Danelle Hughes; and his grandson, Jeffrey Hughes. Also, to Janet's mom, Ann Harris; her children, Brooke Winn and Austin Towery; and her grandchildren, Ricky and Halee Klusmeier and Haley, Megan, Kathryn, and Ryleigh Winn. Special thanks are also extended to Royce's brother, Raymond Boehm, who introduced Royce to function point analysis.

We continue to be amazed by how blessed we have been by our God. We pray that His blessings be upon each of you as well.

Introduction

This book provides comprehensive guidance on the International Function Point Users Group (IFPUG) Functional Size Measurement method and is intended to prepare practitioners to take the IFPUG Certified Function Point Specialist (CFPS) exam. Toward that end, we have included and further expanded upon the rules and guidelines prescribed by IFPUG with the latest release (4.3) of the *Function Point Counting Practices Manual* (CPM). Together with the counting rules and guidelines included in the IFPUG Function Point CPM 4.3, we have presented detailed examples and questions throughout the book to aid the reader in understanding how to apply the IFPUG method. The book culminates with two CFPS practice exams.

Although this book is intended to be used primarily as a learning and preparation guide for the CFPS exam, just as important is our intent to raise the level of awareness and understanding of function point analysis. The business of developing software is relatively low on the industry maturity scale when compared to other professions such as accounting, medicine, and manufacturing; these fields have standard sets of metrics that are incorporated into their business models. We expect that this will eventually occur in information technology (IT). Consequently, we hope that you will retain and frequently use this book as a reference manual on the functional sizing of user requirements.

The health and well-being of function points are directly related to the ongoing effectiveness of IFPUG. Since 1986, IFPUG has increased in membership and its importance to the software measurement community. Today, IFPUG enjoys a worldwide membership of thousands of individual, corporate, educational, and institutional members. IFPUG is a volunteer organization, whose mission is to be a recognized leader in promoting and encouraging the effective management of application software development and maintenance activities through the use of function point analysis and other software measurement techniques. IFPUG serves to facilitate the exchange of knowledge and ideas among its members and seeks to provide a composite environment that stimulates their personal and professional development. Its challenge is to continue to enhance the counting methodology and to raise the level of awareness among organizations that are not function point literate.

Committee work is the core of IFPUG. The two most visible committees are the Counting Practices Committee and the Certification Committee. The Counting Practices Committee is responsible for maintaining the current counting guidelines, the CPM. The Certification Committee is responsible for establishing and enforcing the certification guidelines and administering the certification process, including the CFPS exam. Other committees that generate guidelines for either counting or using function points include New Environments, IT Performance, and Management Reporting.

The use of functional size metrics provides the software project manager, the IT organization, and the business user with a key piece of information that can be used to improve the effectiveness of how they design, develop, and deploy software. Understandably, this book is not for everyone involved in software, but it is intended for anyone who wants to improve his or her software development environment through the effective utilization of functional size metrics.

Authors

David Garmus' previous two books were coauthored with his business partner, David Herron, on functional measurement. Mr. Garmus is an acknowledged authority in the sizing, measurement, and estimation of software application development and maintenance. As a cofounder of the David Consulting Group, he supports software development organizations in achieving software excellence with a metric-centered approach. Mr. Garmus is a Past President of IFPUG and a member of the IFPUG Counting Practices Committee. He has a BS from the University of California at Los Angeles and an MBA from Harvard University Graduate School of Business Administration. He has spoken at numerous conferences and written many articles and books on various measurement-related topics. Mr. Garmus is a Certified Function Point Specialist, having fulfilled all IFPUG requirements for this title under all releases of the IFPUG *Counting Practices Manual*, and is a Certified Software Measurement Specialist.

Janet Russac has over 25 years of experience as a programmer, analyst, and measurement specialist in software application development and maintenance. She is the founder of Software Measurement Expertise and leads a team of experienced consultants that offer expertise in function point analysis, software measurement, estimation, auditing, training, and mentoring. She is a published author who presents workshops at companies, professional organizations, and conferences and is often a featured speaker at conferences. Ms. Russac served as the Chair of the IFPUG Management Reporting Committee from 2002 to 2004 and led the creation of an international industry certification process for individuals in the field of software measurement as Certified Software Measurement Specialists. She currently serves on the IFPUG Counting Practices Committee and the IFPUG Communications and Marketing Committee. Ms. Russac is a Certified Function Point Specialist and a Certified Software Measurement Specialist.

Royce Edwards is a senior consultant for Software Composition Technologies, where he applies function point analysis and software estimation techniques to resolve business challenges in software development organizations. He is a software management professional with over 25 years of experience in development, reverse engineering, systems administration, architecture, and software analysis. Mr. Edwards brings an accomplished and unique skill set to software measurement and estimation. He has advised a diverse list of clients in the telecommunications, manufacturing, scientific, government, and information technology areas, and he has mastered the adaptation of solutions to meet the needs of varied organizational environments. Mr. Edwards frequently teaches workshops related specifically to Web application measurement. He has presented research papers at conferences and has written articles and white papers for various publications. Mr. Edwards is a Certified Function Point Specialist and a member of the IFPUG Counting Practices Committee.

Chapter 1

Function Point Analysis Overview

Frederick Brooks was among the first to draw attention to information technology (IT) productivity in his book *The Mythical Man-Month* (Addison-Wesley, 1975). Unfortunately, although Brooks raised awareness of serious problems, significant solutions have not been achieved.

In the mid-1970s, Allan Albrecht of IBM introduced function point analysis[1] as a form of sizing software development. As opposed to other methods such as counting lines of source code, function point analysis measured the functionality requested and received by the user independent of the technical details involved.[1] Using this method, the measurement of an application remains consistent whether that application is coded in assembly language or Java.

Since its formation in 1986, the International Function Point Users Group (IFPUG) has continued to enhance the method Albrecht pioneered for functionally sizing software. The IFPUG Functional Size Measurement Method is known as *function point analysis*, and its units of functional size are called *function points*.[1] Function point analysis conforms to the ISO/IEC 14143-1:2007 standard for functional measurement.

Access to the size of the application is a starting point to answering important business questions. When used in conjunction with other measurements such as hours of effort, cost, and delivery time, function points can provide valuable information to the key decision makers with accurate projections for resourcing, productivity and quality.[1]

Other techniques exist to size software. Counting lines of source code is a popular method because the counting can be automated. Although it is easy to count lines of code, the results achieved are notoriously unreliable. First, there is no clear way to compare two applications written in different computer languages; for example, how many lines of COBOL are equal to a line of C++? Many organizations have tried to answer questions like these by providing conversion tables, but the results have been less than optimal. Second, comparing results is difficult using lines of code; two developers can vary widely in how they code a specific function based on their individual style of coding. A study conducted at Sandia National Laboratories (Albuquerque, NM) compared the same small program written by students in a Personal Software Process (PSP) course using the same programming language and found a variation of not less than 200% and as much as 2200%.[2]

Balanced scorecards and return on investment (ROI) calculations have been used to portray IT performance. Both of these methodologies offer a moderate degree of success; however, without a size measurement, they are unable to provide the fundamental metric of cost per unit of work. Function point analysis provides the size measurement that enables specific and accurate metrics.

Studies have found that two certified function point analysts measuring the same application will achieve the same result within a margin of error of ±10%. This margin of error approaches zero when the application is fully documented or there is access to a subject matter expert (SME) who is very familiar with the application.

What Are Function Points?

A function point is a unit of measure for functional size as defined within the IFPUG Functional Size Measurement Method.[3] Imagine that you are a tourist in a new land, lost

---

[1] Refer to IFPUG, *Function Point Counting Practices Manual* (CPM), Release 4.3, Part 1, page iii.

[2] Refer to Joe Schofield, The statistically unreliable nature of lines of code, *CrossTalk*, April, pp. 29–33, 2005.

[3] Refer to IFPUG, *Function Point Counting Practices Manual* (CPM), Release 4.3, Part 1, page 6; Part 5, page G-4.

and hoping to find directions. You pull up to the curb and ask for assistance. Would you rather hear, "You travel down the road a piece, make a left at Joe Franklin's store, drive until you see the big oak tree that fell during the storm of 1972 and make a sharp right" or "You drive 1.2 miles, make a left, drive 4.3 miles, and make a sharp right turn—your destination will be 400 feet on your right"?

Function points are a precise measurement of software size designed to remove the ambiguity from consideration of the software being examined. Instead of the abstract notion of "This will be a big project unless Joe can work on it," we have a solid estimate of a project's size. Statements become: "This enhancement is estimated at 1200 function points," with a follow-up that possibly includes: "Most of our developers produce 30 function points per month, but Joe has produced 45 function points per month on a consistent basis. He would be a real asset to the team if we need this done as quickly as possible."

How can function point analysis deliver these results? The function point method is designed around the concept of measuring a unit of work. Functional size enables the estimate of cost and resources required for software development and maintenance regardless of any nonfunctional constraints.

How Function Points Are Used

Function point analysis permits us to estimate the size of a planned application and measure the size of an existing application. It can also be used to measure the size of changes to an existing application, whether those changes are in the detailed design phase or have already been completed. Knowing the functional size allows many other useful metrics to be determined.

Productivity

1. *Hours per function point* is calculated by dividing the total number of project hours by the total number of function points delivered. This industry-accepted metric of productivity allows an organization to compare their productivity against other organizational projects or industry standards within their own industry.
2. *Overall productivity* is calculated by dividing the total number of function points by the total work effort. The overall productivity metric is useful for administrating outsourcing contracts because it can be used effectively by senior management to monitor overall productivity.
3. *Rate of delivery* is calculated by dividing the number of function points by the elapsed calendar time, usually expressed in months. This metric can enable

management to plan time to market for a new project or to analyze the time-to-market result once an existing project has been delivered.

Quality

1. *Functional requirement size* measures the total number of functions requested by the end user or customer expressed in terms of function points. This measure allows the developer to develop a high-level plan to deliver the requested project.
2. *Completeness* is a metric of the delivered functionality vs. the originally requested functionality. Obviously, if changes to the specifications have not occurred during development, the functionality delivered should be exactly equal to the functionality requested.
3. *Rate of change (volatility)* is a metric that takes into account "scope creep" that occurred during the time between the original design and when the completed application was delivered. As the scope of the project increases, the project manager can use this information to justify increases in budget and extensions to the delivery date.
4. *Defect density* is calculated by dividing the number of defects by the total number of function points. This metric can be calculated by project phase to determine whether defects are removed before the rollout of an application or after application delivery to compare against other developments, either in-house or industrywide.

Financial

1. *Cost per function point* can be calculated by dividing the total cost by the total number of function points. This metric not only can clarify the cost of development but is also useful for deciding the benefits of developing an application in-house vs. purchasing a commercial off-the-shelf solution.
2. *Repair cost ratio* is used to calculate the costs of repairing a newly deployed application for a fixed period of time, such as the first 6 months. This metric is calculated by multiplying the total hours required to repair the application by the cost per hour for these repairs and dividing the total by the released number of function points.
3. *Portfolio asset value* is an important metric to set a value for an organization's entire portfolio of software. It is calculated by multiplying the total cost per function point by the total number of function points. This metric provides the basis for informed decisions regarding the replacement cost of legacy

systems. When combined with maintenance metrics and measures of commercial off-the-shelf applications it can also highlight in-house applications that can be replaced with commercial applications that will be less expensive to maintain over their useful life.

Maintenance

1. *Maintainability* is a metric of the effort, expressed in cost, required to maintain an application. This metric is used to monitor both core business applications and applications that historically have a high cost of maintenance. It is calculated by dividing the maintenance cost by the application's function point size.
2. *Reliability* is a metric of the number of failures of an application relative to its functional size. Often this is thought of as mean time to failure (MTTF). Reliability is calculated by dividing the number of failures by the total functional size.
3. *Assignment scope* is a metric of the number of resources required to support the maintenance of an application. It is calculated by dividing the number of function points by the number of full-time equivalent resources required to support the application.
4. *Rate of growth* determines the growth of an application over a specified period of time and is calculated by dividing the current size by the original size in function points.
5. *Stability ratio* is used to monitor the degree to which an application or enhancement has satisfied the needs of the user. This metric is based on the number of changes required during a fixed period of time, usually 60 to 90 days. It is calculated by dividing the number of changes by the number of function points.

Supporting Activities

1. *Volume of documentation* can be used to calculate or estimate the amount of documentation of all types required to support an application. It is calculated by dividing the number of pages of documentation by the total number of function points. This number can be broken down to specify select classes of documentation such as detailed design, user manuals, etc.
2. *Test case coverage* calculates the number of test cases that are required to adequately support testing. Like volume of documentation, this can be used either as an estimate of the required number of test cases or as a measurement of currently existing test cases. The calculation is the number of test cases divided by the total number of function points.

Functional size enables normalizing metrics such as those above. Without an accurate sizing measure, there can be no practical point of comparison. An organization should pick and choose those metrics that are most important to determine how well it is achieving business objectives.

Measuring Value Delivered

Whether the task at hand is new development or a change to an existing application, businesses have a variety of questions. Some of the common ones are:

1. How much will the project cost?
2. How long will it take to complete the project?
3. If a different development team is used, will it either cut cost or shorten delivery time?

The basis for making an informed decision on any of these questions is knowing the size of the task at hand. By combining the measurement delivered using function point analysis with other cost and effort drivers, an accurate answer can be delivered for all of these business questions. Let's look at an example:

Company Drain-X has developed a revolutionary foaming pipe cleaner. In addition to enzyme cleaning the entire pipe in the record time of 10 minutes, this product coats the pipe with a nonstick coating that prevents future buildup. The marketing director for Drain-X has stated that two of the organization's competitors are on the verge of releasing equivalent products and that the first organization to get its product to market will likely have market share for the life of the product. In order to release the product, an application must be developed to track sales and profit. This application has been sized by a Certified Function Point Specialist (CFPS) at 1000 function points.

Table 1.1 illustrates the fact that Development Team 4 would complete the project in the shortest time (4 weeks) but would also have the greatest cost ($160,000). Development Team 3 would take an additional week but would cost $60,000 less.

As another example, let's say that time to market is still important, but this time the marketing director has stated that the product development will not be completed for 3 months. Development Team 2 can easily complete the task in the time frame required and at the least cost.

Ultimately, the key decision makers will need to decide the correct balance between development time and cost.

Table 1.1 Development Rates and Costs

Team	Development Rate per Week (FP)	Cost per Week	Weeks to Complete	Cost to Complete
1	100	$10K	10	$100K
2	100	$8K	10	$80K
3	200	$25K	5	$125K
4	250	$40K	4	$160K

Additional criteria are often worth considering. If data about the defect rates for each delivery team is available, it would be important to consider quality together with delivery time and cost.

The simple fact is that everything starts with an accurate measurement of the functional size of the software to be delivered. Without an accurate measurement of the size of an application, the additional measurements of delivery time, cost, quality, etc. are incomplete.

Benefits and Objectives

Technology is useful when it provides information. The ultimate decision must be made not by machine but by the key stakeholders after developing an appropriate business case. Still, without reliable information, developing a business case that meets the business' needs can be nearly impossible. It is possible that assumptions will be based on vague information, or, worse yet, information believed to be complete contains serious flaws.

Having an accurate measurement at the beginning of the analysis overcomes the ambiguity of statements such as, "This is a big application." Having a specific and reproducible measurement based on a consistent set of rules also assures the customer (and management) that every reasonable precaution has been taken to eliminate any flaws from the equation.

Function point analysis measures software by quantifying the tasks and services (i.e., functionality) that the software provides to the user based primarily on logical design. The objectives of function point analysis are to measure:[4]

■ Functionality implemented in software that the user requests and receives
■ Functionality impacted by software development, enhancement, and maintenance independently of technology used for implementation

The process of function point analysis is:[5]

■ Simple enough to minimize the overhead of the measurement process
■ A consistent measure among various projects and organizations

Further Reading

The information included in this chapter has been extracted from Part 1 of the IFPUG *Function Point Counting Practices Manual*, Release 4.3. A review of this chapter is recommended before taking the CFPS exam.

Exam Guidance

■ Read and study this chapter.
■ Memorize the various definitions:
   – Function point
   – Function point analysis
■ Make sure you know the objectives of function point analysis and the process of function point analysis.
■ Complete the practice questions in this chapter, and go back to determine why you answered any question incorrectly.

Sample Exam Questions

1. Organizations can apply the international standard of the IFPUG Functional Size Measurement Method known as function point analysis to measure the size of a software product to:
   A. Support quality and productivity analysis
   B. Provide a normalization factor for software comparison
   C. Estimate cost and resources required for software development, enhancement, and maintenance
   D. All of the above

2. The objectives of function point analysis are to measure:
   A. Functionality implemented in software that the user requests and receives
   B. Nonfunctional, technical requirements
   C. Functionality impacted by software development, enhancement, and maintenance independently of technology used for implementation
   D. A and C

---

[4] Refer to IFPUG, *Function Point Counting Practices Manual* (CPM), Release 4.3, Part 1, page iii.

[5] Refer to IFPUG, *Function Point Counting Practices Manual* (CPM), Release 4.3, Part 1, page iii.

3. The process of function point analysis is:
   A. Assisting users in determining the benefit of an application package to their organization by functionally sizing functions that specifically match their requirements
   B. A consistent measure among various projects and organizations
   C. Simple enough to minimize the overhead of the measurement process
   D. B and C

4. A function point is:
   A. The smallest unit of activity that is meaningful to the user
   B. A unit of measure for functional size as defined within the international standard of the IFPUG Functional Size Measurement Method known as function point analysis
   C. A unique, user-recognizable, nonrepeated attribute
   D. None of the above

5. Which of the following is true of the IFPUG Functional Size Measurement Method?
   A. It is known as function point analysis
   B. Its units of functional size are called function points
   C. It cannot provide a normalization factor for software comparison
   D. A and B

Chapter 2

Identifying User Requirements

In this chapter, we will discuss:

- Functional User Requirements
- Function point counting procedures
- Gathering documentation
- Sizing during the life cycle
- User
- User view

Functional User Requirements

The International Function Point Users Group (IFPUG) method for function point analysis is an ISO standard and conforms to ISO/IEC 14143-1:2007. The IFPUG methodology discussed in this book measures functional size only.

Functional size is a size of the software derived by quantifying the Functional User Requirements.[1] Functional User Requirements (FURs) are a subset of the user requirements specifying what the software should do in terms of tasks and services.

Functional User Requirements include but are not limited to:

- *Data transfer*—for example, adding a new order, sending an invoice, forwarding location coordinates
- *Data transformation*—for example, calculating the cost of that order to send an invoice, determining the location coordinates

- *Data storage*—for example, storing the new order, saving location information
- *Data retrieval*—for example, search and display order information, search and display location information

Functional size can be measured using the IFPUG Functional Size Measurement (FSM) Method discussed in this book based on the Functional User Requirements. The IFPUG IT Performance Committee has established a subgroup, Software Non-Functional Assessment Process (SNAP), which is leading an effort to determine other sizing measures that can be used to size nonfunctional requirements. User requirements that are considered to be nonfunctional include but are not limited to technical and quality aspects and constraints.

Function Point Counting Procedure[2]

The following are the steps in the function point counting procedure (see Figure 2.1):

- Gather the available documentation.
- Determine counting scope and boundary, and identify Functional User Requirements.
- Measure data functions.
- Measure transactional functions.
- Calculate the functional size.
- Document and report.

---

[1] Refer to IFPUG, *Function Point Counting Practices Manual* (CPM), Release 4.3, Part 2, pages 1–3.

[2] Refer to IFPUG, *Function Point Counting Practices Manual* (CPM), Release 4.3, Part 2, page 2-2.

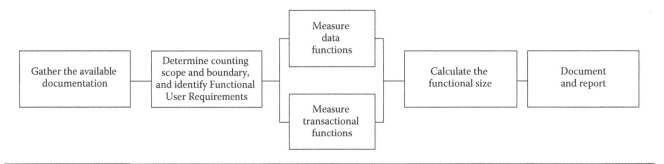

Figure 2.1 Procedure diagram.

Gathering Documentation[3]

To commence the function point counting procedure, documentation that describes the functionality delivered by the software or the functionality that is impacted by the software project being measured must be gathered. To properly determine all of the Functional User Requirements, sufficient documentation must be obtained as well as access to subject matter experts who are able to provide additional information to address any gaps in the documentation.

The following list of documentation is not exhaustive but is useful when conducting any Functional Size Measurement:[4]

- Project proposals
- Requirement documents
- Procedural descriptions
- High-level system diagrams (showing relationships to other interacting applications)
- Logical data models
- Data flow diagrams
- Entity relationship diagrams
- Data/object models
- Database layouts
- Class diagrams
- Process models
- Prototypes
- Functional specifications
- Use/feature cases
- System specifications
- Detailed design specifications
- Physical design models
- Operational models
- Program and module specifications
- File layouts
- Screens and screen prints
- Copies of reports or report layouts

- Test cases (features)
- User manuals and technical documentation
- Training materials
- System help
- Other software development artifacts

Sizing During the Life Cycle

The timing of Functional Size Measurement varies depending on the particular status of an application in its life cycle. Significantly more information is available as an application moves through its life cycle. Early in the life cycle, the only information available might be verbal.

Initial User Requirements Phase[5]

- The Initial User Requirements phase represents user requirements prior to the sessions between the users and the software developers.
- This phase may have one or more of the following characteristics:
  - It may be incomplete; for example, Initial User Requirements may lack specifications necessary for referential integrity.
  - It may lack "utility" functionality; for example, essential validation reports or inquiries may be missing.
  - It may be impossible to implement or very difficult to use; for example, a user may ask for an on-line inquiry that requires an hour of CPU processing.
  - It may be too general; for example, requirements may not include the specific list of user-recognizable fields.
  - It does not address the needs of all users of the application; for example, the requirements of a specific project may vary from one user to another if they do not have the same functional needs.

---

[3] Refer to IFPUG, *Function Point Counting Practices Manual* (CPM), Release 4.3, Part 2, page 2-4.

[4] Refer to IFPUG, *Function Point Counting Practices Manual* (CPM), Release 4.3, Part 2, page 3-9.

[5] Refer to IFPUG, *Function Point Counting Practices Manual* (CPM), Release 4.3, Part 2, page 3-4.

– Requirements are stated without regard for application boundaries; for example, current or future application boundaries may not have been considered.
– Requirements may be expressed in a different context or a terminology incompatible with function point analysis; for example, Initial User Requirements may refer to the physical or manual aspects of the system.

Example

In the purchasing department of an organization, a user states his requirements as:

> When I am processing purchase orders in the purchase order application, I would like to be able to view a purchase order using the purchase order number and the vendor identification number from the vendor application.

This requirement implies the development of an inquiry and the purchase order data group and the ability to use the vendor data group from the vendor application in this transaction.

Functions

The functions identified from the Initial User Requirements phase might be identified as:

- EQ (external inquiry)—inquiry on a specific purchase order
- ILF (Internal Logical File)—purchase order data group
- EIF (External Interface File)—vendor data group

Technical Requirements Phase[6]

- The Technical Requirements phase represents the software developers' view of requirements created from the feasibility study.
- These requirements may include elements necessary for the implementation but which are not considered in Functional Size Measurement (e.g., temporary files, index).
- This phase may have one or more of the following characteristics:
  – It is dependent on technology; for example, physical files vary based on the database environment.

– Terminology unfamiliar to the users may be used; for example, software developers may refer to physical files rather than to logical groups of data.
– Functionality may be determined by placing too much emphasis on technical constraints; for example, some developers tend to limit the scope of the requirements by focusing on the computing capacity currently available in the organization.
– Boundaries may be determined according to the technical architecture rather than by business processes; for example, there may be separate technical requirements for the client and server, but they would be contained in the same application boundary when measuring the functional size.

Example

Developer: "I understand the need for a purchase order inquiry using the vendor application data. To make the retrieval more efficient, we need to build a join table of purchase order numbers and vendor key data to get the vendor identification numbers."

Functions

The functions identified from the Technical Requirements phase might be identified as:

- EQ—inquiry on a specific purchase order
- ILF—purchase order data group
- EIF—vendor data group
- ILF join table of purchase order and vendor key data[7]

Final Functional User Requirements Phase[8]

- The Final Functional User Requirements phase results from the joint sessions between users and software developers that are necessary to achieve consistent and complete Functional User Requirements for the application.
- This phase provides the final version of the Functional User Requirements before the development phase begins.
- The Final Functional User Requirements phase has the following characteristics:
  – Terminology can be understood by both users and software developers.

---

[6] Refer to IFPUG, *Function Point Counting Practices Manual* (CPM), Release 4.3, Part 2, page 3-5.

[7] Join tables are not counted as part of Functional Size Measurement. In this example, the join table was incorrectly identified as an ILF to illustrate a potential counting error by software developers.
[8] Refer to IFPUG, *Function Point Counting Practices Manual* (CPM), Release 4.3, Part 2, page 3-6.

– Integrated descriptions of all user requirements are provided, including requirements from all groups of users.
– All business processes are fully defined, including all user actions, fields coming into and leaving the application boundary, sources of data for each business process, and validations that occur as part of each business process.
– Each process and group of data is agreed upon by the user and developer.
– The feasibility and usability are approved by the software developers.

Example

User: "When I am processing purchase orders in the purchase order application, I would like to be able to view a purchase order using purchase order number and the vendor identification number from the vendor application."

Developer: "I recognize the need for a purchase order inquiry using the vendor application data. In order to speed up the retrieval process, may I suggest a list of purchase orders (containing purchase order and vendor identification number) from which to make a selection? We will have to join purchase order numbers with the appropriate vendor keys in order to get the vendor identification numbers."

User: "I agree that the list is an excellent way to implement this retrieval. We will also find this useful in other parts of the application."

Results of the Discussion Between User and Developer

■ Add the selection list containing the purchase order and vendor identification numbers.
■ Exclude the join table from the functional size, as it is a technical solution.

Functions

The functions identified from the Final Functional User Requirements phase might be identified as:

■ EQ—inquiry on a specific purchase order
■ EQ—selection list of purchase orders with vendor identification numbers
■ ILF—purchase order data group
■ EIF—vendor data group

The Final Functional Requirements document is the final version of the requirements before beginning the development phase. At this time, there should be agreement that

the documented requirements are complete, formal, and approved. The Functional Size Measurement, assuming no additional changes of scope, should be consistent with the measurement at the completion of development.[9]

User[10]

The following definition of a user is critical to the understanding of Functional User Requirements:

> A *user* is any person or thing that communicates or interacts with the software at any time.

User View[10]

A user view is the Functional User Requirements *as perceived* by the user. It represents a formal description of the user's business needs in the user's language. Developers translate the user information into information technology language to provide a solution. A user view:

■ Is a description of the business functions
■ Can be verbal statements made by the user as to what their view is
■ Is approved by the user
■ Can be used to measure the functional size
■ Can vary in physical form (e.g., project proposals, requirements document, logical data model, functional specifications, detailed specifications, user handbook)

Further Reading

The rules included in this chapter have been extracted from Part 2, Chapters 1 through 3, of the IFPUG *Function Point Counting Practices Manual* (CPM), Release 4.3. A review of these chapters is recommended before taking the CFPS exam.

Exam Guidance

■ Read and study this chapter, including all related examples.
■ Memorize the various definitions:
 – User
 – User view
 – Functional User Requirements

---

[9] Refer to IFPUG, *Function Point Counting Practices Manual* (CPM), Release 4.3, Part 2, page 3-7.
[10] Refer to IFPUG, *Function Point Counting Practices Manual* (CPM), Release 4.3, Part 2, page 3-2.

■ Memorize the steps in the function point counting procedure and where they belong on the procedure diagram.

■ Become familiar with the terminology changes between CPM 4.2.1 and CPM 4.3 regarding Functional User Requirements (FURs).

■ Know the phases of sizing during the life cycle as well as what each phase represents and its characteristics.

■ Familiarize yourself with the related examples in this chapter as well as CPM 4.3, Part 2, Chapter 1 (Relationship between IFPUG and ISO); CPM 4.3, Part 2, Chapter 2 (IFPUG FSM Method Overview); and CPM 4.3, Part 2, Chapter 3 (Gather Available Documentation), because it is unlikely that you will have time to look up everything during the exam.

■ Complete the practice questions in this chapter, and go back to determine why you answered any question incorrectly.

Sample Exam Questions

1. A user view:
   A. Can be used to measure the functional size
   B. Can be used to measure the technical size
   C. Can be verbal statements made by the user as to what his or her view is
   D. A and C

2. Steps in the function point counting procedure include:
   A. Measure the data functions
   B. Measure the transactional functions
   C. A and B
   D. None of the above

3. The size of the software derived by quantifying the Functional User Requirements is the:
   A. Technical size
   B. Functional size
   C. A and B
   D. None of the above

4. Functional User Requirements are:
   A. A subset of the user requirements
   B. Requirements that describe what the software should do, in terms of tasks and services
   C. A and B
   D. None of the above

5. Functional User Requirements may include:
   A. Data storage
   B. Data transformation
   C. Data retrieval
   D. All of the above

6. A user is:
   A. Any person who communicates or interacts with the software at any time
   B. Any thing that communicates or interacts with the software at any time
   C. A and B
   D. None of the above

7. Technical Requirements may have one or more of the following characteristics:
   A. Lack of "utility" functionality
   B. Terminology that can be understood by both users and software developers
   C. Technology dependence
   D. All of the above

8. Initial User Requirements
   A. Represent user requirements prior to the sessions between the users and the software developers
   B. Do not address the needs of all users of the application
   C. Lack "utility" functionality
   D. All of the above

9. A user view:
   A. Can vary in physical form
   B. Is approved by the user
   C. Is the Functional User Requirements *as perceived* by the user
   D. All of the above

10. Which of the following documentation is useful when conducting any Functional Size Measurement?
    A. Class diagrams
    B. Data/object models
    C. Requirements
    D. All of the above

Chapter 3

The Process of Counting

As presented in Chapter 2, the following are steps in the function point counting procedure:

- Gather the available documentation.
- Determine counting scope and boundary, and identify Functional User Requirements.
- Measure data functions.
- Measure transactional functions.
- Calculate the functional size.
- Document and report.

In this chapter, we will discuss determination of the counting scope and boundary. The counting scope is determined by the purpose of the count.

Purpose of the Count[1]

Functional Size Measurement is conducted to provide an answer to a business question, and it is the business question that determines the purpose. The purpose is to:

- Determine the type of function point count and the scope of the required count to obtain the answer to the business problem under investigation.
- Influence the positioning of the boundary between the software under review and the surrounding software.

The purpose identifies what will be sized, such as the systems, applications, or subsets of an application. Examples of a purpose include:

- Identifying those functions that will be satisfied by one or more packages
- Identifying applications that will be outsourced
- Identifying those functions within an application that perform a specific purpose
- Identifying the functions to be included in a development project
- Identifying changes (enhancements) necessary for an existing application

Types of Counts[2]

Function point counts can be determined, based on the purpose, for either projects or applications, as one of the following:

- Development project function point count
- Enhancement project function point count
- Application function point count

The functional size can be measured for either projects or applications. A brief description of each of the three types of counts follows.

A *development project function point count* is the activity of applying the International Function Point Users Group (IFPUG) Functional Size Measurement (FSM) Method to measure the functional size of a development project. It includes all functions impacted (built or customized) by the project activities. It also includes functions developed as part of the development project. A development project function point count must often

---

[1] Refer to IFPUG, *Function Point Counting Practices Manual* (CPM), Release 4.3, Part 2, page 5-2.

[2] Refer to IFPUG, *Function Point Counting Practices Manual* (CPM), Release 4.3, Part 2, page 4-2.

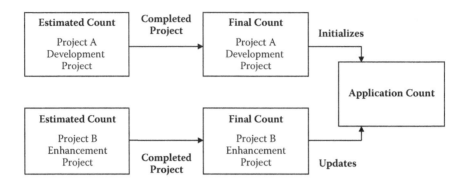

Figure 3.1 Relationships between types of counts.

be updated as development proceeds. These subsequent counts would not start from scratch, but they would validate previously identified functionality and attempt to capture added functionality, commonly called "scope creep." Counts often occur throughout the development process.[3]

- A development project is a project to develop and deliver the first release of a software application.
- The development project functional size is a measure of the functionality provided to the users with the first release of the software, as measured by the development project function point count by the activity of applying the IFPUG FSM Method.

An *enhancement project function point count* is the activity of applying the IFPUG Functional Size Measurement (FSM) Method to measure the functional size of an enhancement project. It includes all the functions being added, changed, and deleted. It also includes conversion functions developed as part of the enhancement project.[4]

- An enhancement project is a project to develop and deliver adaptive maintenance.[5]
- The enhancement project functional size is a measure of the functionality added, changed, or deleted at the completion of an enhancement project, as measured by the enhancement project function point count by the activity of applying the IFPUG FSM Method.

An *application function point count* is the activity of applying the IFPUG Functional Size Measurement (FSM) Method to measure an application's functional size.[6]

- An application is a cohesive collection of automated procedures and data supporting a business objective; it consists of one or more components, modules, or subsystems.
- An application's functional size is a measure of the functionality that an application provides to the user, determined by the application function point count by the activity of applying the IFPUG FSM Method.
- It is also referred to as the *baseline* or *installed functional size*.
- This size provides a measure of the current functions the application provides the user.
- This number is initialized when the development project function point count is completed.
- It is updated every time a completed enhancement project alters the functions of the application.

Example

A development project is often estimated a number of times before its completion (see Figure 3.1). At the time of completion, a final development project count is measured, and an application count is determined. Later, enhancements to that application can be estimated until their completion. Upon completion of each enhancement project, a final enhancement project count is measured, and the application count is modified to reflect the changes.

---

[3] Refer to IFPUG, *Function Point Counting Practices Manual* (CPM), Release 4.3, Part 1, page 4; Part 2, page 4-2; part 5, page G-3.

[4] Refer to IFPUG, *Function Point Counting Practices Manual* (CPM), Release 4.3, Part 1, page 4, definition 3.24; Part 2, page 4-2; Part 5, page G-3.

[5] Refer to IFPUG, *Function Point Counting Practices Manual* (CPM), Release 4.3, Part 2, page 4-20.

---

[6] Refer to IFPUG, *Function Point Counting Practices Manual* (CPM), Release 4.3, Part 1, page 4, definition 3.4; Part 2, page 4-3; Part 5, page G-1.

Determine Counting Scope[7]

The counting scope defines the set of Functional User Requirements to be included in the function point count. As stated earlier in this chapter, the counting scope is determined by the purpose of the count. The scope:

- Defines a (sub)set of the software being sized
- Is determined by the purpose for performing the function point count
- Identifies which functions will be included in the Functional Size Measurement so as to provide answers relevant to the purpose for counting
- Could include more than one application

The scope of:

- A development project function point count includes all functions impacted (built or customized) by the project activities. It also includes conversion functions developed as part of the development project.
- An enhancement project function point count includes all of the functions being added, changed, and deleted. It also includes conversion functions developed as part of the enhancement project. The boundary of the application impacted remains the same. The functionality of the application reflects the impact of the functions being added, changed, or deleted.
- An application function point count may include, depending on the purpose (e.g., provide a package as the software solution), either of the following:
  - Only the functions being used by the user
  - All of the functions delivered

Determine Boundary[8]

The application boundary is the border between the application being measured and either external applications or the user domain. IFPUG has defined specific rules for identifying boundaries: The boundary is a conceptual interface between the software under study and its users, and the boundary (also referred to as *application boundary*):

- Defines what is external to the application
- Indicates the border between the software being measured and the user

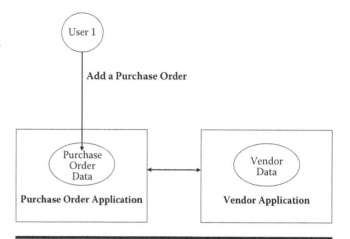

Figure 3.2   Application boundary diagram.

- Acts as a membrane through which data processed by transactions (external inputs [EIs], external outputs [EOs], and external inquiries [EQs]) passes into and out from the application
- Encloses the logical data maintained by the application (Internal Logical Files, or ILFs)
- Assists in identifying the logical data referenced by but not maintained within this application (External Interface Files, or EIFs)
- Is dependent on the user's external business view of the application; it is independent of technical and/or implementation considerations

Example

(See Figure 3.2.) Vendor data is used by the Purchase Order Application to complete its transactions (e.g., add a new purchase order). Both applications are considered to be independent with their own boundaries. Purchase order data is maintained by the Purchase Order Application; vendor data is maintained by the Vendor Application and referenced by the Purchase Order Application.

The following rules apply for boundaries:[9]

- The boundary is determined based on the user's view. The focus is on what the user can understand and describe.
- The boundary between related applications is based on separate functional areas as seen by the user, not on technical considerations.
- The initial boundary already established for the application or applications being modified is not influenced by the counting scope.

---

[7] Refer to IFPUG, *Function Point Counting Practices Manual* (CPM), Release 4.3, Part 2, page 5-3.
[8] Refer to IFPUG, *Function Point Counting Practices Manual* (CPM), Release 4.3, Part 2, page 5-4.

[9] Refer to IFPUG, *Function Point Counting Practices Manual* (CPM), Release 4.3, Part 2, page 5-5.

The Microsoft® Office® Standard Suite currently consists of Word®, Excel®, PowerPoint®, and Access®; to the user, each is a separate application within the Microsoft Office Standard Suite. Our Purchase Order Application might consist of an on-line data entry process that is followed by a nightly batch file update process; the Purchase Order Application is a single application that includes both on-line and the batch processes.

Further Reading

The rules included in this chapter have been extracted from Part 2, Chapters 4 and 5, of the IFPUG *Function Point Counting Practices Manual* (CPM), Release 4.3. A review of these chapters is recommended before taking the CFPS exam.

Exam Guidance

- Read and study this chapter, including all related examples.
- Memorize the various definitions:
  - Purpose of the count
  - Types of counts: development project function point count, enhancement project function point count, application function point count
- Know the definition of counting scope and how it relates to the types of counts.
- Understand (application) boundary and applicable rules.
- Familiarize yourself with the related examples in this chapter as well as CPM 4.3, Part 2, Chapter 4 (Determine Type of Count), and Chapter 5 (Determine the Counting Scope and Boundary and Identify Functional User Requirements), because it is unlikely that you will have time to look up everything during the exam.
- Complete the practice questions in this chapter, and go back to determine why you answered any question incorrectly.

Sample Exam Questions

1. Which of the following is not true of a boundary:
   A. Is dependent on technical and/or implementation considerations
   B. Is dependent on the user's external business view of the application
   C. Encloses the logical data maintained by the application (ILFs)
   D. Assists in identifying the logical data referenced by but not maintained within this application (EIFs)

2. The scope of an enhancement project function point count includes:
   A. All the functions being added, changed, and deleted, as well as conversion functions developed as part of the enhancement project
   B. Only the functions being added
   C. Only the functions being added and deleted
   D. Only the functions being changed

3. Which of the following is not true of counting scope:
   A. It is determined by the purpose for performing the function point count
   B. It defines the functionality that will be included in a particular function point count
   C. It defines a (sub)set of the software being sized
   D. It can include only one application

4. The boundary:
   A. Defines what is external to the application
   B. Encloses the logical data maintained by the application (ILFs)
   C. Is dependent on the user's external business view of the application
   D. All of the above

5. The boundary:
   A. Indicates the border between the software being measured and the user
   B. Defines what is external to the application
   C. Acts as a membrane through which data processed by transactions (EIs, EOs, and EQs) passes into and out from the application
   D. All of the above

6. The purpose of a function point count is to:
   A. Determine the type of function point count and the scope of the required count to obtain the answer to the business problem under investigation
   B. Influence the positioning of the boundary between the software under review and the surrounding software
   C. None of the above
   D. A and B

7. What are the types of function point counts?
   A. Development project function point count and enhancement project function point count
   B. Enhancement project function point count and application function point count
   C. Application function point count, development project function point count, and enhancement project function point count
   D. Application function point count and development project function point count

8. A development project's functional size:
   A. Is a measure of the functionality added, changed, or deleted at the completion of an enhancement project, as measured by the enhancement project function point count by the activity of applying the IFPUG Functional Size Measurement (FSM) Method
   B. Is a measure of the functionality provided to the users with the first release of the software, as measured by the development project function point count by the activity of applying the IFPUG Functional Size Measurement (FSM) Method
   C. Is a measure of the functionality that an application provides to the user, as measured by the application project function point count by the activity of applying the IFPUG Functional Size Measurement (FSM) Method
   D. Is associated with an installed application

9. An enhancement project's functional size:
   A. Is a measure of the functionality added, changed, or deleted at the completion of an enhancement project, as measured by the enhancement project function point count by the activity of applying the IFPUG Functional Size Measurement (FSM) Method
   B. Is a measure of the functionality provided to the users with the first release of the software, as measured by the development project function point count by the activity of applying the IFPUG Functional Size Measurement (FSM) Method
   C. Is a measure of the functionality that an application provides to the user, as measured by the application project function point count by the activity of applying the IFPUG Functional Size Measurement (FSM) Method
   D. Is associated with an installed application

10. An application's functional size:
    A. Is a measure of the functionality added, changed, or deleted at the completion of an enhancement project, as measured by the enhancement project function point count by the activity of applying the IFPUG Functional Size Measurement (FSM) Method
    B. Is a measure of the functionality provided to the users with the first release of the software, as measured by the development project function point count by the activity of applying the IFPUG Functional Size Measurement (FSM) Method
    C. Is a measure of the functionality that an application provides to the user, as measured by the application project function point count by the activity of applying the IFPUG Functional Size Measurement (FSM) Method
    D. Includes conversion functionality

11. A baseline or installed functional size is synonymous with:
    A. An application functional size
    B. A development project function point count
    C. An enhancement project function point count
    D. A and B

12. Which is not true of an application's functional size:
    A. This size provides a measure of the current functions the application provides the user
    B. It includes conversion functionality
    C. This number is initialized when the development project function point count is completed
    D. It is updated every time completion of an enhancement project alters the application's functions

Chapter 4

Data Functions

Introduction

Data functions relate to logical data that is stored and made available for update and retrieval. Data functions may be identified as Internal Logical Files (ILFs) or External Interface Files (EIFs). ILFs and EIFs are user-identifiable groups of logically related data or control information. As such, they are logical groupings and not physical representations of those groupings of data. It is possible, but very unlikely, that the logical will match the physical. Consequently, ILFs and EIFs should be counted in an identical manner regardless of the physical database structure in an application, even if the delivery and maintenance requirements and the productivity rates are different because of the nonfunctional characteristics outside of function points. ILFs are maintained within the boundary of the application being measured, and EIFs are read or referenced only within the boundary of the application being measured but are maintained within a different application boundary. When function point counters size an application in function points, they typically experience the greatest degree of counting difficulty in identifying the data functions.

This chapter describes the International Function Point Users Group (IFPUG) definitions, rules, and guidelines for identifying both ILFs and EIFs. More detailed guidance and examples are contained within the IFPUG *Function Point Counting Practices Manual*. The previous chapter discussed determination of the counting scope and boundary. Chapter 6 will describe transactional functions.

The total process used to size function points was presented previously, but it is repeated here. As presented in Chapter 2, the following are steps in the function point counting procedure:

- Gather the available documentation.
- Determine counting scope and boundary and identify Functional User Requirements.
- Measure data functions.
- Measure transactional functions.
- Calculate the functional size.
- Document and report.

Remember that the application boundary separates the application being measured from the user domain and/or other independent applications. The data functions relate to the logical data that is stored and is available for update and retrieval. The transactional functions—external inputs (EIs), external outputs (EOs), and external inquiries (EQs)—perform the processes of updates, retrieval, outputs, etc. (transactions you would expect to see in a process model). Experienced function point practitioners typically attempt to count data functions first for two reasons.

First, we must know which ILFs and EIFs are maintained and/or referenced by each transactional function in order to assign each its own complexity rating. Complexity ratings will be discussed later for all functions, but each data and transactional function is assigned a weight of low, average, or high based on standard matrices. Second, by identifying the files first, their designations as ILFs or EIFs can be validated when the transactional functions are identified. Remember from the previous chapter (Figure 3.2) that vendor data was used by the Purchase Order Application to complete its transactions (e.g., add a new purchase order). Both applications were considered to be independent with their own boundaries. The purchase order data was maintained by the Purchase Order Application, and the vendor data was maintained by the Vendor Application and only referenced by the Purchase Order Application. The purchase order data (an ILF) was maintained within the boundary of the Purchase Order Application. The vendor data was considered to be an EIF to the Purchase Order Application because the data was used by the Purchase Order Application solely for reference.

What They Are: Internal Logical Files and External Interface Files

Data Functions[1]

■ A data function represents functionality provided to the user to meet internal and external data storage requirements.

■ A data function is either an Internal Logical File or an External Interface File.

Internal Logical File[2]

■ An ILF is a user-recognizable group of logically related data or control information maintained within the boundary of the application being measured.

■ The primary intent of an ILF is to hold data maintained through one or more elementary processes of the application being measured.

External Interface File[2]

■ An EIF is a user-recognizable group of logically related data or control information that is referenced by the application being measured but which is maintained within the boundary of another application.

■ The primary intent of an EIF is to hold data referenced through one or more elementary processes within the boundary of the application measured. This means an EIF counted for an application must be in an ILF in another application.

Difference Between ILFs and EIFs

The primary difference between an Internal Logical File and an External Interface File is that an EIF is not maintained by the application being measured, while an ILF is.

Definitions for Embedded Terms[3]

Control Information

Control information is data that influences an elementary process by specifying what, when, or how data is to be processed; for example, control information could include rules or parameters that are stored and maintained within the application. Control data is maintained in the print manager, and edit data is maintained to reject improper or inappropriate input data. Dates and times are maintained by the users to establish the sequence or timing of events, or certain thresholds are established to control an event such as setting the temperature on a thermostat to control the timing of heating or air conditioning.

User-Recognizable

The term *user-recognizable* refers to requirements for processes and/or data that are agreed upon, and understood by, both the users and software developers; for example, a record of accounts receivable and/or accounts payable might be required in a financial application.

Maintain

The term *maintain* refers to the ability to add, change, or delete data through an elementary process; for example, the data or control data could be maintained through such transactions as add, bill, change, delete, delegate, evaluate, fail, grant, hold, populate, revise, or update.

Elementary Process

An *elementary process* is the smallest unit of activity that is meaningful to the user. An elementary process is identified by composing or decomposing the Functional User Requirements into the smallest unit of activity that satisfies *all* of the following:

■ Is meaningful to the user
■ Constitutes a complete transaction
■ Is self-contained
■ Leaves the business of the application being counted in a consistent state

For example, the sale of an item in a store might be decomposed into various subprocesses such as Create, Read, Update, and Delete (CRUD) so the sale creates an amount

---

[1] Refer to IFPUG, *Function Point Counting Practices Manual* (CPM), Release 4.3, Part 2, page 6-1.
[2] Refer to IFPUG, *Function Point Counting Practices Manual* (CPM), Release 4.3, Part 2, page 6-2.

[3] Refer to IFPUG, *Function Point Counting Practices Manual* (CPM), Release 4.3, Part 2, page 6-2.

due, reads a file to validate whether the individual has credit, and updates the quantity of stock on hand. The sale is the elementary process, and it may update more than one ILF through the same transaction. Much more information will be provided in the next chapter.

Rules for Counting[4]

Data Function Identification Rules

To identify data functions:

- Identify all logically related and user-recognizable data or control information within the counting scope.
- Exclude entities that are not maintained by any application.
- Group related entities that are entity dependent; entities that are entity independent are separate logical groups of data.
- Exclude those entities referred to as *Code Data*:
  - Substitution Data entity that contains a code and an explanatory name or description
  - Single occurrence entity that contains one or more attributes that rarely change, if at all
  - Entity that contains data that is basically static or may change very rarely
  - Default values entity that contains values for populating attributes
  - Valid values entity that contains available values for selection or validation
  - Entity that contains a range of values for validation
- Exclude entities that do not contain attributes required by the user.
- Remove associative entities that contain additional attributes not required by the user and associative entities that contain only foreign keys; group foreign key attributes with the primary entities. Foreign key attributes are data required by the user to establish a relationship with another data function.

Data Function Classification Rules

Classify data as an ILF if the data is maintained by the application being measured. For example, when a group of data has been identified as an ILF within an application, it cannot also be counted as an EIF within the same application even if used for reference by other transactions, nor can it be counted as an EIF during an enhancement project for that application. Some additional examples of ILFs follow. These are examples only; any group of data or control information must conform to the above definition and rules in order to be counted as ILFs:

- Application transaction data such as inventory issue records, employee training records, payroll records, credit card transactions, product sales, customer calls, or accounts payable
- Application security or password data maintained within the application
- Help data maintained within the application
- Edit rules maintained within the application
- Parameter data maintained within the application
- Error files and their descriptions maintained within the application

Following are examples of files that have frequently been erroneously identified as ILFs; be sure that they are not counted as ILFs:

- Temporary files or various iterations of the same file (these are not counted within function point analysis)
- Work files (these are not counted within function point analysis)
- Sort files (these are not counted within function point analysis)
- Extract files, or view files, that contain data extracted from other ILFs or EIFs prior to display or print (these are not counted within function point analysis but are recognized as part of the processing necessary to produce the external output or external inquiry)
- Files introduced because of technology (these are not counted within function point analysis)
- Copies of the same file (a file arranged or sorted differently or maintained in additional locations is not counted separately)
- Alternative indices, joins, relationships, or connections, unless they contain separately maintained non-key attributes
- Audit or historical data (these should be counted together with the application transaction data)
- Files maintained by other applications and read or referenced only (these should be counted as External Interface Files)
- Back-up data such as that used for corporate back-up and recovery
- Suspense files containing incomplete transactions, unless they are separately maintained

---

[4] Refer to IFPUG, *Function Point Counting Practices Manual* (CPM), Release 4.3, Part 2, page 6-4.

Classify data as an EIF if the data is:

- Referenced but not maintained by the application being measured
- Identified in an ILF in one or more other applications

Once a group of data has been identified as an EIF within an application, the EIF cannot be counted twice within the same application even if it is used for reference by other transactions or contains different data from the same logical file.

In our earlier example of the sale of an item in a store where the sale reads a file to validate whether the individual has credit, that credit information is identified as an EIF if it is maintained in a different application than what might be called the sales application. If three additional transactions in the sales application read credit information from that same EIF and each of the four transactions read (or reference) some common data and possibly some additional data from that same EIF, then that EIF would still be counted as only one EIF within the sales application.

Some common examples of EIFs follow. These are examples only; any group of data or control information must meet the above definition and rules in order to be counted as EIFs:

- Application data extracted and read from other applications
- Application security or password data maintained outside of the application
- Help data maintained outside of the application
- Edit rules maintained outside of the application
- Parameter data maintained outside of the application
- Error files and their descriptions maintained outside of the application

Following are examples of files that have frequently been erroneously identified as EIFs; be sure that they are not counted as EIFs:

- Data received from another application that maintains one or more ILFs within the application being measured (this is considered transactional data and should be counted as one or more external inputs)
- Data maintained by the application being measured
- Data formatted and sent by the application being measured to other applications (should be counted as external outputs or external inquiries)
- Temporary files or various iterations of the same file (these are not counted within function point analysis)
- Work files (these are not counted within function point analysis)
- Sort files (these are not counted within function point analysis)

- Extract files, or view files, that contain data extracted from previously counted EIFs prior to display or print (these are not counted within function point analysis but are recognized as part of the processing necessary to produce the external output or external inquiry)
- Files introduced because of technology (these are not counted within function point analysis)
- Alternative indices, joins, relationships, or connections, unless they contain separately maintained non-key attributes
- Audit or historical data, which should be counted together with the application transaction data

Complexity and Contribution Definitions and Rules[5]

The number of ILFs, EIFs, and their relative functional complexity determine the contribution of the data functions to the functional size. Assign each identified ILF and EIF a functional complexity based on the number of Data Element Types (DETs) and Record Element Types (RETs) associated with the ILF or EIF.

DET Definition[5]

A *Data Element Type* is a unique, user-recognizable, nonrepeated attribute.

DET Rules[5]

To count Data Element Types for a data function, the following rules shall be performed:

- Count one DET for each unique user-recognizable, nonrepeated attribute maintained in or retrieved from the data function through the execution of an elementary process within the counting scope. For example, the check number, amount, date, payee, memo entry, and account number, which are maintained in a checking account record, would each count as one DET regardless of the number of checks written with unique data for each and regardless of how the data is physically stored. Consequently, in this case, we would count six DETs.
- Count only those DETs being used by the application being measured when two or more applications maintain and/or reference the same data function. Attributes that are not referenced by the application being measured are not counted. For example, an ILF that is updated

---

[5] Refer to IFPUG, *Function Point Counting Practices Manual* (CPM), Release 4.3, Part 2, page 6-5.

by two applications (A and B) and referenced by a third (C) would count the DETs uniquely as follows:

Part number	Primary key to A, B, C	DET to A, B, C
Part name	Maintained by A	DET to A
	Referenced by B and C	DET to B and C
Weekly usage	Maintained by B	DET to B
Department using	Maintained by B	DET to B
Purchase price	Maintained by A	DET to A
	Referenced by B	DET to B
Supplier name	Maintained by A	DET to A
	Referenced by B	DET to B
Supplier street address	Maintained by A	DET to A
Supplier city	Maintained by A	DET to A
Supplier state	Maintained by A	DET to A
Supplier postal code	Maintained by A	DET to A
Supplier total address (read as one block of data)	Referenced by B	One DET to B

Consequently, A would be counted with eight DETs, B would be counted with seven DETs, and C would be counted with two DETs.

■ Count one DET for each attribute required by the user to establish a relationship with another data function. For example, a relationship exists to another ILF/EIF that requires a key with the part number and manufacturer code; these would be counted as two DETs unless, of course, either or both had previously been counted.

■ Review related attributes to determine if they are grouped and counted as a single DET or whether they are counted as multiple DETs; grouping will depend on how the elementary processes use the attributes within the application. For example, the supplier total address referenced in the example above is counted as one DET to B because it is read as one block of data.

RET Definition[6]

A *Record Element Type* (RET) is a user-recognizable subgroup of Data Element Types within a data function.

RET Rules[6]

To count the Record Element Types for a data function, the following activities shall be performed:

■ Count one RET for each data function (by default, each data function has one subgroup of DETs to be counted as one RET).

■ Count one additional RET for each of the following additional logical subgroups of DETs (within the data function) that contains more than one DET:

  – Associative entity with non-key attributes
  – Subtype (other than the first subtype)
  – Attributive entity, in a relationship other than mandatory 1-1

There are two types of subgroups:

■ *Optional subgroups*—Subgroups for which the user has the option of using one or none of during an elementary process that adds or creates an instance of the data
■ *Mandatory subgroups*—Subgroups where the user must use at least one during an elementary process that adds or creates an instance of the data (e.g., salaried or hourly employees as used in the CPM)

Do not count RETs for any data that exists because of technology or methodology (e.g., headers, trailers, separate text files). RETs can also be identified by the existence of secondary keys used for data storage and to create relationships between the data. When counting the DETs above for the check number, amount, date, payee, memo entry, and account number, which are maintained in a checking account record, this checking account record would be considered as one RET, with all DETs being maintained under the primary key of check number. For the ILF that was updated by two applications (A and B) and referenced by a third (C), each would count one RET with a primary key of part number. Note that the same field may serve as the primary key in different applications.

Determination of Complexity and Contribution[7]

The functional complexity of each data function is determined using the steps below:

1. Use the complexity and contribution counting rules to identify and count the number of RETs and DETs.
2. Rate the functional complexity using the complexity matrix provided in Table 4.1. For example, our checking account file has six DETs and one RET, so it would be assigned a functional complexity of low. The part number file updated by application A has eight DETs and one RET and would be assigned a functional complexity of low. Within both applications A and B, the EIF referenced from application C would be counted as having two DETs and one RET and would be assigned a functional complexity of low.

---

[6] Refer to IFPUG, *Function Point Counting Practices Manual* (CPM), Release 4.3, Part 2, page 6-7.

[7] Refer to IFPUG, *Function Point Counting Practices Manual* (CPM), Release 4.3, Part 2, page 6-8.

Table 4.1   ILF and EIF Complexity Matrix

	1 to 19 DETs	20 to 50 DETs	51 or more DETS
1 RET	Low	Low	Average
2 to 5 RETS	Low	Average	High
6 or more RETs	Average	High	High

Table 4.2   ILF Translation Table

Functional Complexity Rating	Function Points
Low	7
Average	10
High	15

Table 4.3   EIF Translation Table

Functional Complexity Rating	Function Points
Low	5
Average	7
High	10

Table 4.4   ILF and EIF Functional Complexity Matrix

Function Type	Functional Complexity		Complexity Totals	Function Type Totals
ILF	1	Low	× 7 =	1	7
	0	Average	× 10 =	0	—
	0	High	× 15 =	0	—
EIF	1	Low	× 5 =	1	5
	0	Average	× 7 =	0	—
	0	High	× 10 =	0	—

3. Translate the ILFs and EIFs to function points using the appropriate translation table for either ILFs or EIFs:

 A. ILF translation table—Use Table 4.2 to translate the ILFs to function points.

 B. EIF translation table—Use Table 4.3 to translate the EIFs to function points.

 For example, application A, above, has an ILF with a functional complexity of low which would be valued at seven function points. Application A also has an EIF with a functional complexity of low which would be valued at five function points.

4. Calculate each ILF and EIF contribution to the functional size (Table 4.4).

Data Entities: Business Data, Reference Data, and Code Data

Business Data[8]

Business Data may also be referred to as *Core User Data* or *Business Objects*. This type of data reflects the information needed to be stored and retrieved by the functional area

addressed by the application. Such data usually represents a significant percentage of the entities identified and has most of the following logical and physical characteristics.

Logical Characteristics

■ The data is mandatory for operation of the users' functional area.

■ The data is user identifiable (usually by a business user).

■ The data is user maintainable (usually by a business user).

■ The data stores the users' Core User Data to support business transactions.

■ The data is very dynamic in that normal business operations cause it to be regularly referenced and routinely added to, changed, or deleted.

■ The data is reported on.

Physical Characteristics

■ The data has key fields and usually many attributes.

■ The data may have zero to infinity records.

Examples

Examples of Business Data include the customer file, invoice file, employee file, and job file. The job file, within the Job Management System, would include such items as job number, job name, division name, job initiation date, etc.

Reference Data[9]

This type of data is stored to support the business rules for the maintenance of the Business Data and usually represents

---

[8] Refer to IFPUG, *Function Point Counting Practices Manual* (CPM), Release 4.3, Part 3, page 1-4.

[9] Refer to IFPUG, *Function Point Counting Practices Manual* (CPM), Release 4.3, Part 3, page 1-5.

a small percentage of entities identified. Reference Data has most of the following logical and physical characteristics.

Logical Characteristics

- The data is mandatory for operation of the users' functional area.
- The data is user identifiable (usually by a business user).
- The data is usually user maintainable (usually by an administrative user).
- The data is usually established when the application is first installed and maintained intermittently.
- The data supports core user activities.
- The data is less dynamic (occasionally changes in response to changes in the environment, external functional processes, and/or business rules of the functional area).
- Transactions processing Business Data often need to access Reference Data.

Physical Characteristics

- The data has key fields and few attributes.
- The data contains usually at least one record or a limited number of records.

Examples

Examples of Reference Data include Jobs Rates, Discount Rates, Tax Rates, and Threshold Settings. Another example is the job rates file, which stores information about the rates paid for each type of job and the skill required to do that type of job. Such information would include job type, state, charge rate, effective date (1:n), and job skill description (1:n).

Code Data[10]

Code Data, sometimes referred to as *List Data* or *Translation Data*, provides a list of valid values that a descriptive attribute may have. In order to satisfy nonfunctional requirements, developers often create one or more tables containing the Code Data to have a means of translating the code into something more recognizable to the user. Logically, the code and its related description have the same meaning. Typically, the attributes of the Code Data are code, description, or other standard attributes describing the code (e.g., standard abbreviation, effective date, termination date, audit trail data). Code Data has most of the following logical and physical characteristics.

---

[10] Refer to IFPUG, *Function Point Counting Practices Manual* (CPM), Release 4.3, Part 3, page 1-6.

Logical Characteristics

- The data is mandatory to the functional area but optionally stored as a data file.
- The data is not usually identified as part of the functional requirements but are usually identified as part of the design to meet nonfunctional requirements.
- The data is sometimes user maintainable (usually by a user support person).
- The data is used to standardize and facilitate business activities and business transactions.
- The data is essentially static and only changes in response to changes in the way that the business operates.
- Business transactions access Code Data to improve ease of data entry, improve data consistency, ensure data integrity, etc.
- If recognized by the user, the data is sometimes considered as a group of the same type of data and could be maintained using the same processing logic.

Physical Characteristics

- The data consists of key fields and usually one or two attributes only.
- The data typically has a stable number of records.
- The data can represent 50% of all entities in the third normal form.
- The data is sometimes denormalized and placed in one physical table with other Code Data.
- The data may be implemented in different ways (e.g., via separate application, data dictionary, hard-coded within the software).

Key Differences Between Code Data and Reference Data

- With Code Data, you can substitute one for the other without changing the meaning of the Business Data (e.g., Airport-Code vs. Airport-Name, Color-Id vs. Color-Description)
- With Reference Data, you cannot substitute (e.g., Tax-Code with Tax-Rate)

Examples of Code Data

- State
  - State Code
  - State Name
- Payment Type
  - Payment Type Code
  - Description of Payment Type

Counting Code Data

Code Data is not considered part of the functional size, so:

- Do not count Code Data as a logical file.
- Do not count Code Data as RETs or DETs.
- Do not count Code Data as a File Type Referenced (FTR).
- Do not count functions to maintain or view Code Data.

Types of Code Data

The three general areas of Code Data are Substitution Data, Static or Constant Data, and Valid Values.[11]

Substitution Data

- Substitution Data provides a code and an explanatory name or description for an attribute of a business object.
- Substitution Data may serve as a quick means of data entry for experienced users; the explanatory name/description are useful for less experienced users or for listings in reports.
- Substitution Data may also be implemented to save storage space or may be a result of normalization.

Examples include states (e.g., State Code, State Name) and colors (e.g., Color Code, Color Description).

Static or Constant Data

Static or Constant Data rarely changes. The three types of Static or Constant Data are One Occurrence, Static Data, and Default Values (template). The One Occurrence type of data contains one and only one occurrence, regardless of the number of attributes, and has only one row of data. The attributes are relatively constant; the data may change, but very rarely. Examples include an entity with data about a particular organization (e.g., name and address) and commercial, off-the shelf software (COTS) with airline name customized by user organizations. The static type of data, as the name implies, contains data that is essentially static. The number of instances of Static Data may change, but very rarely, and the contents of an instance rarely change. Examples include an entity of chemical elements (e.g., mnemonic, atomic number, description) and function point tables for valuing function types and complexity levels. Default Values (template) contain the default values for some attributes in new instances of a business object.

Valid Values Data

Valid Values Data provides a list of available values for an attribute of one or more business object types. This type of data is implemented to satisfy requirements such as reducing

errors and increasing user friendliness; it is typically used to list available values for user selection or validation of input provided by the user. Valid Values Data is basically static; if not, it may be Reference Data or Business Data. Examples include State Name (contains all valid values for the attribute state name), State Code (contains all valid values for the attribute state code), and Color (contains all valid values for the attribute color for a business object).

Range of Valid Values

The range of Valid Values Data contains data that is basically static; if the data is not static, it may be Reference Data. Examples include a range of allowable telephone number (e.g., lowest telephone number, highest telephone number) and a heating temperature range.

Logical Files and Data Modeling
Data Modeling Concepts
Definitions
Entity (Type)[12]

An entity is:

- Any distinguishable person, place, thing, event, or concept about which information is kept[13]
- A thing that can be distinctly identified[14]
- Any distinguishable object that is to be represented in the database[15]
- A data entity that represents some "thing" that is to be stored for later reference (the term *entity* refers to the logical representation of the data)[16]
- Anything about which we store information (e.g., a customer, supplier, machine tool, employee, utility pole, airline seat); for each entity, certain attributes are stored[17]

An entity may also:

- Represent the relationship between two or more entities, called *associative entities*[18]

---

[11] Refer to IFPUG, *Function Point Counting Practices Manual* (CPM), Release 4.3, Part 3, page 1-10.

[12] Refer to IFPUG, *Function Point Counting Practices Manual* (CPM), Release 4.3, Part 3, page 2-3.

[13] Thomas Bruce, *Designing Quality Databases with IDEF1X Information Models*, Dorset House, New York, 1992.

[14] Peter Chen, *The Entity-Relationship Approach to Logical Database Design*, John Wiley & Sons, New York, 1977.

[15] C. J. Date, *Relational Database: Selected Writings*, Addison-Wesley, Boston, 1986.

[16] Clive Finkelstein, *An Introduction to Information Engineering*, Addison-Wesley, Sydney, Australia, 1989.

[17] James Martin, *Information Engineering*, Prentice-Hall, Upper Saddle River, NJ, 1989.

[18] Michael C. Reingruber and William W. Gregory, *The Data Modeling Handbook: A Best-Practice Approach to Building Quality Data Models*, Wiley, New York, 1994.

Table 4.5 Mapping Data Concepts to Function Point Terminology

Data Modeling Concept	Data Modeling Term	Relational Database Term	Function Point Analysis Term	Function Point Analysis Concept
Smallest named unit of data that has meaning to the real world	Data item	Attribute or column	Data Element Type (DET)	A Data Element Type (DET) is a unique, user-recognizable nonrepeated field
Groups of related items that are treated as a unit	Record	Row or tuple	Record Element Type (RET)	A Record Element Type (RET) is a user-recognizable subgroup of data elements within an ILF or EIF
Collection of records of a single type	File	Table	Logical file—Internal Logical File (ILF) or External Interface File (EIF)	File refers to a logically related group of data and not the physical implementation of those groups of data

■ Represent a subset of information relevant to an instance of an entity, called *subtype entity* (also known as a *secondary* or *category entity*)[19]

To summarize, an entity:

■ Is a principal data object about which information is collected
■ Is a person, place, thing, or event of information
■ Can have an instance (an occurrence)
■ Is a fundamental thing of relevance to the user, about which a collection of facts is kept (an association between entities that contains attributes is itself an entity)
■ Involves information that is representative of similar things that share characteristics or properties
■ Is often depicted in a data model by a rectangle with the entity name written inside the rectangle

Data Element[20]

In the world of data modeling, the base element is called the *data element* or *data item*. It is:

■ The fundamental component
■ The fundamental atomic particle in the information system universe[21]

■ The smallest named unit of data that has meaning in the real/user world[22]

Data Modeling Activities[23]

Data modeling addresses data items, logical records, and files. A file system is composed of records and data items:

■ *Data items* are defined as the smallest named unit of data that has meaning to the real world; a data item is also referred to as an "attribute" or "column" in the physical implementation of data through relational databases.
■ A group of related items that is treated as a unit is known as a *record*; a record is also called a "row" or "tuple" in the physical implementation of data through relational databases.
■ A *file* is a collection of records of a single type; a file is also called a "table" in the physical implementation of data through relational databases.

Mapping Data Concepts to Function Point Terminology[24]

We can map these terms to function point analysis as shown in Table 4.5.

---

[19] Michael C. Reingruber and William W. Gregory, *The Data Modeling Handbook: A Best-Practice Approach to Building Quality Data Models*, Wiley, New York, 1994.

[20] Refer to IFPUG, *Function Point Counting Practices Manual* (CPM), Release 4.3, Part 3, page 2-4.

[21] Gary Schuldt, *Information Modeling for Information Systems Analysts*, paper presented at an AT&T Bell Laboratories workshop, Holmdel, NJ, May 1992.

[22] Graeme C. Simsion and Graham C. Witt, *Data Modeling Essentials: Analysis, Design, and Innovation*, 2nd ed., Coriolis, Scottsdale, AZ, 2001.

[23] Refer to IFPUG, *Function Point Counting Practices Manual* (CPM), Release 4.3, Part 3, page 2-4.

[24] Refer to IFPUG, *Function Point Counting Practices Manual* (CPM), Release 4.3, Part 3, page 2-5.

Data Modeling Terms[25]

Entity (or Entity Type)

- Principal data objects about which information is collected
- Person, place, thing, or event of information
- Entity instance (an occurrence)
- Depicted through a rectangle with the entity name written inside the rectangle
- A fundamental thing of relevance to the user, about which a collection of facts is kept (an association between entities that contains attributes is itself an entity)

Associative Entity Type

An associative entity type contains attributes that further describe a many-to-many relationship between two other entity types.

Attributive Entity Type

An attributive entity type further describes one or more characteristics of another entity type.

Entity Subtype

A subdivision of entity type, an entity subtype inherits all of the attributes and relationships of its parent entity type and may have additional, unique attributes and relationships.

Relationships

Relationships represent real-world associations among one or more entities:

- One-to-one
- One-to-many
- Many-to-many

They are represented by a line that connects the entities. The relationship name is written beside the line. Relationships are defined by the way the entities are connected:

- Optional, shown in text with parentheses—1:(N), (1):(N)
- Mandatory, shown in text without parentheses—1:1, 1:N

Attributes

Attributes are the characteristics of an entity. Attributes are generally analogous to Data Element Types (DETs).

Normalization

Data is normalized by applying the following five rules:

1. Eliminate repeating groups (first normal form).
2. Eliminate redundant data (second normal form).
3. Eliminate columns not dependent on the key (third normal form).
4. Isolate independent multiple relationships; no table may contain two or more 1:N or N:M relationships (fourth normal form).
5. Isolate semantically related multiple relationships; practical constraints may justify separating logically related many-to-many relationships (fifth normal form).

When performing function point analysis, it is preferable to analyze the logical data model in the third normal form. Ignore multiple entities placed for technology (often fifth normal form).

Entity Relationship Concepts[26]

Table 4.6 can be applied to further understand the concept of Record Element Types.

Methodology for Identifying Logical Files[27]

A stepwise process for establishing the set of logical files (Internal Logical Files and External Interface Files) is used where each step looks at the data at a finer level of detail. An overview of these steps is shown in Table 4.7, and details of each step are explained in the subsequent sections. Use the stepwise process to establish the set of logical files. The first step, identify logical files, is the most significant step in determining functional size because identification of the correct number of logical files is crucial in achieving intercounter consistency. The remaining steps influence the functional size to a considerably lesser degree because they do not affect the number of logical files, only their type and complexity rating.

Step 1. Identify Logical Files[27]

The process to group the candidate data entities identified into one or many logical files consists of the following substeps that are explained in detail in the following paragraphs of this section:

---

[25]Refer to IFPUG, *Function Point Counting Practices Manual* (CPM), Release 4.3, Part 3, page 2-5.

[26]Refer to IFPUG, *Function Point Counting Practices Manual* (CPM), Release 4.3, Part 3, page 2-7.

[27]Refer to IFPUG, *Function Point Counting Practices Manual* (CPM), Release 4.3, Part 3, page 2-8.

Table 4.6 Entity Relationships and Record Element Types

Entity Relationship Concept	Entity Relationship Term	Function Point Analysis Term	IFPUG Definition
Principal data objects about which information is collected (person, place, thing, or event); a fundamental item of relevance to the user about which a collection of facts is kept	Entity or Entity Type	Internal Logical File (ILF) or External Interface File (EIF)	File refers to a logically related group of data and not the physical implementation of those groups of data
An entity type that contains attributes that further describe relationships between other entities	Associative Entity Type	Record Element Type (RET)	User-recognizable (optional or mandatory) subgroup of data elements within an ILF or EIF
An entity type that further describes one or more characteristics of another entity type	Attributive Entity Type	Record Element Type (RET)	User-recognizable (optional or mandatory) subgroup of data elements within an ILF or EIF
A division of an entity type that inherits all of the attributes and relationships of its parent entity type; may have additional, unique attributes and relationships	Entity Subtype	Record Element Type (RET)	User-recognizable (optional or mandatory) subgroup of data elements within an ILF or EIF

1. Identify all logically related and user-recognizable data or control information within the counting scope.
2. Exclude entities that are not maintained by any application.
3. Group related entities that are entity dependent into logical files.
4. Exclude those entities referred to as Code Data.
5. Exclude entities that do not contain attributes required by the user.
6. Remove associative entities that contain additional attributes not required by the user and associative entities that contain only foreign keys; group foreign key attributes with the primary entities.

Substep 1.1. Identify All Logically Related and User-Recognizable Data or Control Information within the Counting Scope

Before deciding which entities should be grouped together into logical files, determine which candidate entities should be taken into consideration for the logical grouping of the entities (see Substep 1.3) and which should be excluded. Consider only entities that are significant to and required by the user. When identifying logical files from a (normalized) data model:

■ Do not assume that all entities are logical files (e.g., index files, entities on a physical data model).

Table 4.7 Stepwise Process for Establishing the Set of Logical Files

Step	Action
1	*Identify logical files.* For each logical data entity, identify how related entities are to be grouped into logical files that reflect the user view; for example, determine whether data entities are themselves an independent logical file or whether related entities should be grouped into a single logical file.
2	*Classify logical files.* Each identified logical file is classified as ILF or EIF.
3	*Identify Data Element Types.* For each logical file, identify the data elements used by the application being measured.
4	*Identify Record Element Types.* For each logical file, identify how related data are to be grouped into Record Element Types that reflect the user view.

■ Logical files may exist from a user perspective but may not be identified in the (normalized) data model in some cases (e.g., historical files containing aggregated data); remember to include these logical files in the rest of the process.

Substep 1.2. Exclude Entities That Are Not Maintained by Any Application

Determine which entities are not maintained by an elementary process in this or another application. Exclude these entities from further consideration because they are not counted.

Substep 1.3. Group Related Entities That Are Entity Dependent into Logical Files

Substep 1.3a. Identify Logical Files Using Elementary Process Method

Review how the elementary processes within the boundary maintain the entities. If several entities are always created together and deleted together, then this is a strong indication that they should be grouped into a single logical file. Also review the elementary processes used to extract the data to determine if the extraction processes access the same group of entities. *Note:* Transactions that modify data will often just target one entity in the group, so the modify transactions are not as effective for grouping data as the create and delete transactions. For example, a purchase order file probably would have entities for items being ordered on that purchase order, shipping information for that purchase order, payment information for that purchase order, and possibly header information for that purchase order, but all of those entities would typically be part of the same purchase order and would not be meaningful on their own.

Substep 1.3b. Identify Logical Files Using Entity (In)Dependency Method

The Entity (In)Dependency method groups entities by assessing the relationships and interdependencies of the entities against the business rules. The guiding principles are entity independence and entity dependence. Note that the term "entity" in this section refers to an entity in a data model in a normalized form (usually third normal form).

Entity independence means that an entity is meaningful or significant to the business, in and of itself without the presence of other entities. *Entity dependence* means that an entity is not meaningful or is not significant to the business, in and of itself without the presence of other entities such that:

■ An occurrence of entity X must be linked to an occurrence of entity Y.
■ The deletion of an occurrence of entity Y results in the deletion of all related occurrences of entity X.

To determine whether entity B is dependent on or independent of A, one needs to answer the question: "Is B significant to the business apart from the occurrence of A linked to it?" An easy test to determine the entity dependence or independence situation follows.

Even if there is no user requirement for deletion, still ask yourself the question: "Suppose we would want to delete an occurrence "a" of entity A, what would happen to an occurrence "b" of entity B linked to "a"?" Depending on the business rules, two essentially different situations can be identified:

1. If an occurrence of B according to the business rules does not have independent meaning or significance to the user and might be deleted as well, then apparently the occurrence of B does not have meaning to the user apart from the linked occurrence of A. Entity B is considered to be an entity dependent on A. The entities A and B should be grouped together into one logical file.
2. If the occurrence of B does have meaning to the business, even apart from the linked occurrence of A, the business rules will not allow deleting the occurrence of B. The entities A and B are considered to be separate logical files.

Assessing the data model of an information system by assessing all pairs of linked entities results in the identification of the logical files.

Types of Relationships[28]

Before making the Entity (In)Dependence principle conclusive for all types of relationships, one should clearly understand the different types/natures of relationships. This section explains the types of relationships as well as the concepts of *optional* and *mandatory*.

Consider two entities, Job and Employee, that can be connected to each other via a relationship. The nature of the relationship determines how many employees can work on a job according to the data model (zero, one, or more) and how many jobs a single employee can work on (zero, one, or more):

---

[28]Refer to IFPUG, *Function Point Counting Practices Manual* (CPM), Release 4.3, Part 3, page 2-14.

1:N Relationship

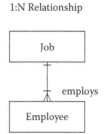

Figure 4.1   1:N relationship.

(1):N Relationship

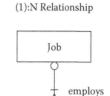

Figure 4.3   (1):N relationship.

1:(N) Relationship

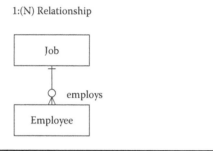

Figure 4.2   1:(N) relationship.

(1):(N) Relationship

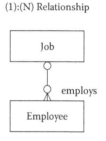

Figure 4.4   (1):(N) relationship.

- 1:N—Several employees are assigned to a job (but at least one), and each employee must be assigned to one (and only one) job. The relationship between Job and Employee is mandatory and is described as 1:N. (See Figure 4.1.)
- 1:(N)—A job *can* have a vacancy with no employees assigned to that job. In this case, the relationship between Job and Employee is described as 1:(N). (See Figure 4.2.)
- (1):N—An employee need not be assigned to any job, but each job must have at least one employee assigned to it. The relationship between Job and Employee in this case is described as (1):N. (See Figure 4.3.)
- (1):(N)—A job *can* have a vacancy with no employees assigned to that job, and an employee need not be assigned to any job. In this case, the relationship between Job and Employee is optional and is described as (1):(N). (See Figure 4.4.)

The following list summarizes entity (in)dependence for all types of relationships:[29]

- *Entity (in)dependence in a (1):(N) relationship*—If a relationship between two entities, A and B, is bilaterally optional, the entities can exist independently, and all occurrences of A and B are significant to the business

apart from the linked occurrence(s) of the other entity. Therefore, A and B are considered to be entity independent of each other. Function point analysis counts the entities A and B as two separate logical files, as indicated in Table 4.8.

- *Entity (in)dependence in a 1:(N) relationship*—In this relationship between two entities, A and B, an occurrence of entity A may exist to which none, one, or many occurrences of entity B are linked. On the other hand, each occurrence of B must be assigned to an occurrence of A. Even if there is no user requirement for deletion, ask yourself the question: "When you delete an occurrence of entity A, what happens to the linked occurrences of entity B, which has a mandatory link to an occurrence of A?" If the deletion of A is allowed, then all Bs linked to it must be deleted as well, because the business is no longer interested in the occurrences of B. Consequently, B is entity dependent on A, and A and B together are identified as one logical file. If the deletion of A is not allowed as long as Bs are still linked to it because the business is still interested in the Bs, then B is entity independent of A, and both A and B are identified as separate logical files.
- *Entity (in)dependence in a (1):N relationship*—This relationship between two entities, A and B, can be treated in a similar way. Each A must be assigned one or many Bs, but a B may (but need not) be assigned to one occurrence of A. You must ask the reverse of the question above. If the deletion of B is allowed, then

---

[29]Refer to IFPUG, *Function Point Counting Practices Manual* (CPM), Release 4.3, Part 3, page 2-15.

all As linked to it must be deleted as well, because the business is no longer interested in the occurrences of A. Consequently, A is entity dependent on B, and A and B together are identified as one logical file. If the deletion of B is not allowed as long as As are still linked to it, because the business is still interested in the As, then A is entity independent of B, and both A and B are identified as separate logical files.

■ *Entity (in)dependence in a 1:N relationship*—In this relationship between two entities, A and B, each B must be assigned to one and only one A, and each A must be assigned to at least one B. The same guidelines regarding entity dependence and independence apply. If B is not significant to the business apart from the A linked to it, then B is considered to be entity dependent on A, and A and B together are identified as one logical file. If B is significant to the business apart from the A linked to it, then it is considered to be entity independent of A, and both A and B are identified as separate logical files.

Summary: From Entities to Logical Files via Entity (In)Dependence

As shown in Table 4.8, A and B are two entities from a normalized data model that should be counted according to this section and that are interconnected via a relationship. The table summarizes how occurring situations are counted.

Substep 1.4. Exclude Those Entities Referred to as Code Data

Filter out Code Data. Code Data is included as a response to nonfunctional user requirements from the user (quality requirements, physical implementation, and/or technical reasons).

Substep 1.5. Exclude Entities That Do Not Contain Attributes Required by the User

Determine which entities do not contain user-recognizable attributes required by the user but contain nonfunctional attributes only.

Substep 1.6. Remove Associative Entities That Contain Additional Attributes Not Required by the User and Associative Entities That Contain Only Foreign Keys; Group Foreign Key Attributes with the Primary Entities

Determine which entities are associative entities. An associative entity contains the foreign keys of the connected entities in addition to other attributes. Note that two situations can arise as a result:

Table 4.8 Summary: from Entities to Logical Files via Entity (In)Dependence

Type of Relationship Between Two Entities, A and B	When This Condition Exists	Then Count
(1):(N)	(A and B are independent)	2 LFs
1:N	If B is entity dependent on A	1 LF
	If B is entity independent of A	2 LFs
1:(N)	If B is entity dependent on A	1 LF
	If B is entity independent of A	2 LFs
(1):N	If A is entity dependent on B	1 LF
	If A is entity independent of B	2 LFs
(1):(1)	(A and B are independent)	2 LFs
1:1	(A and B are dependent)	1 LF
1:(1)	If B is entity dependent on A	1 LF
	If B is entity independent of A	2 LFs
(N):(M)	(A and B are independent)	2 LFs
N:M	If B is entity dependent on A	1 LF
	If B is entity independent of A	2 LFs
N:(M)	If B is entity dependent on A	1 LF
	If B is entity independent of A	2 LFs

Note: (1) When in doubt, choose entity independent; (2) In some situations, more than two entities can also form a logical file.

Legend: LF, logical file (ILF or EIF); (..), optional side of relationship.

1. The additional non-key attributes are the result of a design or implementation consideration or satisfy a nonfunctional user requirement. These nonfunctional attributes are not counted as data elements. Treat these entities as key-to-key entities.
2. The additional non-key attributes are necessary to satisfy the Functional User Requirements and are required by the user. (See Substeps 1.3a and 1.3b, above.)

Determine which entities are key-to-key (intersection) entities; that is, they only have keys as their data elements and do not have any other non-key attributes. These entities typically represent the implementation of a many-to-many (N:M) relationship in a normalized data model. They exist for data modeling and database design purposes only and not as the result of a user requirement.

Step 2. Classify Logical Files[30]

Check the identified logical files against the ILF and EIF rules:

- Classify a logical file as an ILF if elementary processes within the boundary of the application being measured maintain (create, update, or delete) data elements within the file.
- Classify a logical file as an EIF if elementary processes within the boundary of the application being measured only reference data elements within the file, and the logical file is maintained by an elementary of another application.
- If an identified logical file is not maintained by an elementary process (either within the application or in another), then the logical file is not counted at all.

Step 3. Identify Data Element Types[31]

The data element is the smallest unit that has meaning to the user and represents a specific fact about a business. Refer to the definitions and rules for DETs earlier in this chapter.

Data Element Terms and Definitions

An attribute represents a specific fact about an entity or a relationship. In Table 4.9 the entities are shown in UPPERCASE and the attributes in lowercase. Data elements/attributes can be found in:

- User views (reports, screens)
- Data dictionaries (business models, data models)
- Current files (record structures in programs, file layouts)

When reviewing the data, the data analyst follows this basic premise: Every data element known to the user must be treated as an attribute and thus must be shown in relation to a specific entity. The attribute may have the following properties:

- Attribute name (alias)
- Characteristic
- Purpose (usage)
- Value source
- Value range

Table 4.9 Data Entities and Attributes

Representation	Example
ENTITY_attribute	COURSE_fee
ENTITY.attribute	CLIENTCOMPANY.name

- Value (structure)
- Unit of expression
- Dependencies

Refer to the IFPUG *Function Point CPM*, Release 4.3, Part 3, pages 2-22 through 2-23, for definitions and examples of these attributes.

Mapping Data Elements to Function Point Analysis DETs

The basic concepts of data elements and attributes from a data modeling perspective can be related to the IFPUG function point definitions and rules (Table 4.10). Following are some examples of counting DETs in special situations.

Attributes[32]

Attributes that are composed of several related data elements are stored separately. Review the transactions within the application to determine whether the attribute is treated as one item or more than one. Consider the following items when making a decision:

- If the attribute is always used in its entirety, then it is counted as a single DET. There should be no situations when an individual component of the attribute is used without the others. Based on that usage, the attribute is counted as a single data element.
- If in some situations, only one part of the attribute (e.g., last name) is used, then more than one data element would be counted. Look at the usage of the components within the application to determine how many recognizable pieces exist. It need not be a one-or-all option. Based on the usage, it might be appropriate to count just two DETs, even though there are actually five physical pieces.
- Look for the existence of sort or edit requirements and selection criteria. If lists or reports are sorted or filtered by a single component of the attribute, this suggests independence of the components in the user view.

---

[30]Refer to IFPUG, *Function Point Counting Practices Manual* (CPM), Release 4.3, Part 3, page 2-21.

[31]Refer to IFPUG, *Function Point Counting Practices Manual* (CPM), Release 4.3, Part 2, page 6-5; Part 3, page 2-21.

[32]Refer to IFPUG, *Function Point Counting Practices Manual* (CPM), Release 4.3, Part 3, page 2-25.

Table 4.10 Mapping Data Elements to FPA Data Element Types

Data Modeling Concept	Data Modeling Term	Relational Database Term	FPA Term	Function Point Analysis Concept
Smallest named unit of data that has meaning to the real world	Data item	Attribute or Column	Data Element Type (DET)	A Data Element Type (DET) is a unique, user-recognizable, nonrepeated field.
Groups of related items that are treated as a unit	Record	Row or Tuple	Record Element Type (RET)	A Record Element Type (RET) is a user-recognizable subgroup of data elements within an ILF or EIF.
Collection of records of a single type	File	Table	Logical file—Internal Logical File (ILF) or External Interface File (EIF)	File refers to a logically related group of data and not the physical implementation of those groups of data.

Counting Names (First Name, Middle Initial, and Last Name)

- Many applications are required to keep track of people's names.
- Should the name be counted as multiple data elements or a single data element?
- Review the transactions within the application to determine whether the name is treated as one item or more than one. Does it always use the entire name, or does it sometimes just use one piece?

Counting Addresses (Street Address, City, State, and Zip Code)

- Many applications are required to keep track of addresses.
- Should the address be counted as multiple data elements or a single data element?
- Review the transactions within the application to determine whether the address is treated as one item or more than one.

Counting Repeating Fields

- Often, applications maintain multiple occurrences of a data element. According to the DET rules, count a repeating field only once.
- After the repeating fields are reduced to a single DET, verify that the business requirements are still being met.

Counting Status Fields

- Applications frequently keep track of the current status of data (e.g., active, inactive, pending, approved).
- This status is typically updated through various transactions within the application.

- These status fields may or may not actually be physically visible to the user through the application's transactions.

Counting System Dates

- Applications frequently retain system dates associated with their data to reflect the currency of the data.
- System dates may have many different names (e.g., last updated, last approved) and are often accompanied by a user ID (last updated by, last approved by).
- System dates are typically updated through various transactions within the application.
- In many cases, the system date is being kept for business purposes. The user needs to know when the data was changed or approved.
- There are also cases where the system date is being kept for technical reasons only.

Counting Foreign Keys

- Applications frequently maintain relationships from one entity to another.
- In some cases, they exist to satisfy data validation requirements, but in other cases they indicate some business interaction between the two entities.
- The data modeling concept of Attribution is best illustrated by the assignment of foreign keys.

Step 4. Identify Record Element Types[33]

The Record Element Type (RET) represents the user's view of coherent subgroups of data within an identified logical file. RETs typically correspond to the entities that were

---

[33] Refer to IFPUG, *Function Point Counting Practices Manual* (CPM), Release 4.3, Part 3, page 2-31.

Table 4.11 Understanding the Concept of Record Element Types

Entity Relationship Concept	Entity Relationship Term	Function Point Analysis Term	Function Point Analysis Concept
Principal data objects about which information is collected (person, place, thing, or event); a fundamental item of relevance to the user about which a collection of facts is kept	Entity or Entity Type	Logical file	File refers to a logically related group of data, not the physical implementation of those groups of data; if there are no other subgroups, the logical file is counted with a single Record Element Type (RET)
An entity type that contains attributes that further describe relationships between other entities	Associative Entity Type	Could be a logical file or a possible Record Element Type (RET); see the "Analyzing Associative Entities to Determine RETs" section for further consideration	User-recognizable subgroup of data elements within an ILF or EIF; can be optional or mandatory
An entity type that further describes one or more characteristics of another entity type	Attributive Entity Type	Possible Record Element Type (RET); see the "Analyzing Attributive Entities to Determine RETs" section for further consideration	User-recognizable subgroup of data elements within an ILF or EIF; can be optional or mandatory
A division of entity type that inherits all the attributes and relationships of its parent entity type and may have additional, unique attributes and relationships	Entity Subtype	Possible Record Element Type (RET); see the "Analyzing Attributive Entities to Determine RETs" section for further consideration	User-recognizable subgroup of data elements within an ILF or EIF; can be optional or mandatory

grouped into the logical files as discussed earlier under "Step 1. Identify Logical Files." They need to be reviewed closely to ensure that the user would identify them as a logical subgroup and thus would count as a RET. Refer to the definitions and rules for RETs earlier in this chapter and to the IFPUG *Function Point CPM*, Release 4.3, Part 2, page 6-9.

Refer back to Table 4.5 for a review of data modeling terms that can be mapped to function point analysis. Table 4.11 can be applied to further understand the concept of RETs.

Function point analysis looks at associative and attributive entity types and subtypes as subgroups of data. The following discusses these in relation to counting RETs.

Analyzing Associative Entities to Determine RETs[34]

An associative entity is used to associate two or more entities as a way of defining the many-to-many relationship. This type of entity is often created by the data modeler to resolve some of the business rules required to relate two separate

entities. There are three possibilities to consider when looking at associative entities:

1. An associative entity is not counted as a RET when the associative entity contains only the keys of each entity.
2. An associative entity is counted as a RET when the associative entity contains the keys of each entity as well as other user-required noncommon attributes.
3. An associative entity is counted as a logical file with a single RET when the associative entity is more than a key-to-key mapping between two entities, and it is more than a RET associated with either logical file that the user requires be retained independently.

Analyzing Attributive Entities to Determine RETs[35]

An attributive entity is an entity type that further describes one or more characteristics of another entity type. By definition, it is a logical extension of another entity. In function

---

[34]Refer to IFPUG, *Function Point Counting Practices Manual* (CPM), Release 4.3, Part 3, page 2-34.

[35]Refer to IFPUG, *Function Point Counting Practices Manual* (CPM), Release 4.3, Part 3, page 2-37.

point analysis, an attributive entity represents a RET of that entity. An attributive entity is counted as either a RET of the logical file it is further defining (situation 1) or as an extension of the logical file (situation 2).

Analyzing Subtypes to Determine RETs[36]

An entity subtype is a subdivision of entity type. A subtype inherits all of the attributes and relationships of its parent entity type and may have additional, unique attributes and relationships. Data modeling rules state that an entity may have any number of sets of independent subtypes associated with it which can be optional or mandatory. Each subtype can have only one generic parent. In data modeling, although the parent and subtype are represented as different entities, they are logically part of the same entity. When analyzing subtypes in a data model, look at the required relationship to the parent entity to determine whether it is a subgroup and should be counted as a RET.

If the subtype is not a subgroup, it should not be counted as a RET. If there are unique attributes among entity subtypes, evaluate whether a separate subgroup really exists that would constitute a RET. A single optional, unique attribute would not result in a different RET from a user perspective, even if depicted as an entity subtype in a logical data model.

It depends on the user view and business rules as to whether these entity subtypes are relevant to the user and should be considered as RETs. If there are separate add/update transactions with unique attributes for these entity subtypes, this would be an indication that we may have separate RETs for these entity subtypes.

If in doubt, do not count a subgroup of information as a RET. Identifying the correct number of RETs does not influence the number of logical files identified; rather, it influences only the complexity of the logical file. Although this step does influence the functional size, it does so to a lesser degree than identifying logical files in Step 1 (Identify Logical Files).

Considering Data Element Types and Record Element Types in Conjunction with Logical Files via Entity (In)Dependence

Table 4.8 is expanded in Table 4.12 to include DETs and RETs.

---

[36]Refer to IFPUG, *Function Point Counting Practices Manual* (CPM), Release 4.3, Part 3, page 2-38.

Further Reading

The rules included in this chapter have been extracted from Part 2, Chapter 6, and Part 3, Chapters 1 and 2, of the *Function Point Counting Practices Manual* (CPM), Release 4.3. A review of these chapters is recommended before taking the CFPS exam.

Exam Guidance

- Read and study this chapter, including all related examples.
- Memorize the various definitions (e.g., ILF, EIF, DET, RET).
- Memorize the various embedded terms.
- Be able to differentiate among the types of data entities: Business Data, Reference Data, and Code Data.
- Fully understand the concept of data entities, subgroups, and relationships
- Memorize the data modeling terms.
- Memorize the data function rules (e.g., ILF, EIF, DET, RET), including the additional detail found in the *Function Point CPM*, Release 4.3, Part 2, Chapter 6.
- Memorize or at least be extremely familiar with the complexity and contribution matrices.
- Familiarize yourself with the related examples in this chapter as well as CPM 4.3, Part 2, Chapter 6 (Measure Data Function), and Part 4, Chapter 1 (Data Function Counting Examples), because it is unlikely that you will have time to look up everything during the exam.
- Complete the practice questions in this chapter, and go back to determine why you answered any question incorrectly.

Sample Exam Questions

1. An Internal Logical File (ILF) is a:
   A. User-recognizable group of logically related data or control information that is referenced by the application being measured but which is maintained within the boundary of another application
   B. Unique user-recognizable, nonrepeated attribute
   C. User-recognizable group of logically related data or control information maintained within the boundary of the application being measured
   D. User-recognizable subgroup of data elements

Table 4.12 Considering Data Element Types and Record Element Types in Conjunction with Logical Files via Entity (In)Dependence

Relationship between Two Entities A and B	When this Condition Exists	Then Count as LFs with RETs and DETs as Follows
(1):(N)	(A and B are independent)	2 LFs, 1 RET and DET to each
1:N	If B is entity dependent on A	1 LF, 2 RETs, sum DETs
	If B is entity independent of A	2 LFs, 1 RET and DETs to each
1:(N)	If B is entity dependent on A	1 LF, 2 RETs, sum DETs
	If B is entity independent of A	2 LFs, 1 RET and DETs to each
(1):N	If A is entity dependent on B	1 LF, 2 RETs, sum DETs
	If A is entity independent of B	2 LFs, 1 RET and DETs to each
(1):(1)	(A and B are independent)	2 LFs, 1 RET and DETs to each
1:1	(A and B are dependent)	1 LF, 1 RET, sum DETs
1:(1)	If B entity dependent on A	1 LF, 1 or 2 RETs, sum DETs
	If B entity independent of A	2 LFs, 1 RET and DETs to each
(N):(M)	(A and B are independent)	2 LFs, 1 RET and DETs to each
N:M	If B is entity dependent on A	1 LF, 2 RETs, sum DETs
	IF B is entity independent of A	2 LFs, 1 RETs, sum DETs
N:(M)	If B is entity dependent on A	1 LF, 2 RETs, sum DETs
	If B is entity independent of A	2 LFs, 1 RET and DETs to each

Note: (1) 1 RET and DETs to each means that it is necessary to assess both entities on their own. (2) Sum DETs means that it is necessary to count all unique, nonrepeated attributes of the linked entities together. (3) Count the foreign key on the many side of the relationships. (4) In some situations, more than two entities can also form a logical file; in such cases, more than two RETs should be counted.

Legend: L, logical file (ILF or EIF); (..), optional side of relationship; RET, Record Element Type; DET, Data Element Type.

2. An External Interface File (EIF) is a:
   A. User-recognizable group of logically related data or control information that is referenced by the application being measured but which is maintained within the boundary of another application
   B. Unique user-recognizable, nonrepeated attribute
   C. User-recognizable group of logically related data or control information maintained within the boundary of the application being measured
   D. User-recognizable subgroup of data elements

3. A Data Element Type (DET) is a:
   A. User-recognizable group of logically related data or control information that is referenced by the application being measured but which is maintained within the boundary of another application
   B. Unique user-recognizable, nonrepeated attribute
   C. User-recognizable group of logically related data or control information maintained within the boundary of the application being measured
   D. User-recognizable subgroup of data elements

4. A Record Element Type (RET) is a:
   A. User-recognizable group of logically related data or control information that is referenced by the application being measured but which is maintained within the boundary of another application
   B. Unique user-recognizable, nonrepeated attribute
   C. User-recognizable group of logically related data or control information that is maintained within the boundary of the application being measured
   D. User-recognizable subgroup of Data Element Types within a data function

5. Mandatory subgroups are:
   A. Those that the user has the option of using one or none of during an elementary process that adds or creates an instance of the data
   B. Subgroups where the user must use at least one during an elementary process that adds or creates an instance of the data
   C. Represent the functionality provided to the user to meet internal and external data requirements
   D. Unique user-recognizable, nonrepeated attributes

6. Data function types include:
   A. Internal Logical Files (ILFs)
   B. External Inputs (EIs)
   C. External Interface Files (EIFs)
   D. A and C

7. The primary intent of an ILF is:
   A. To hold data maintained through one or more elementary processes of the application being measured
   B. To hold data referenced through one or more elementary processes within the boundary of the application being measured
   C. A and B
   D. None of the above

8. The primary intent of an EIF is:
   A. To hold data maintained through one or more elementary processes of the application being measured
   B. To hold data referenced through one or more elementary processes within the boundary of the application measured
   C. A and B
   D. None of the above

9. Which of the following counting rules must *not* apply for the information to be counted as an EIF?
   A. The group of data or control information is logical and user recognizable
   B. The group of data is referenced by, but not maintained by, the application being measured
   C. The group of data is identified by the application being measured
   D. The group of data is maintained in an ILF of one or more other applications

10. The functional complexity of an ILF is based on:
    A. The number of DETs and FTRs
    B. The number of DETs and RETs
    C. The number of FTRs and RETs
    D. The number of DETs, RETs, and FTRs

11. Which of the following rule(s) apply when counting RETs:
    A. Count one RET for each data function
    B. Count one additional RET for each additional logical subgroup of DETs (within the data function) that contains more than one DET
    C. A and B
    D. None of the above

12. How many function points is a low complexity ILF?
    A. 5
    B. 7
    C. 10
    D. 15

13. How many function points is a low complexity EIF?
    A. 5
    B. 7
    C. 10
    D. 15

14. How many function points is a high complexity EIF?
    A. 5
    B. 7
    C. 10
    D. 15

15. Which of the following combinations would result in an average ILF?
    A. 1 RET and 5 DETs
    B. 2 RETs and 19 DETs
    C. 6 RETs and 20 DETs
    D. 5 RETs and 50 DETs

16. Which of the following combinations would result in an average EIF?
    A. 1 RET and 5 DETs
    B. 2 RETs and 19 DETs
    C. 6 RETs and 20 DETs
    D. 5 RETs and 50 DETs

17. What are the total function points for 2 low ILFs, 3 high ILFs, and 1 low EIF?
    A. 46
    B. 64
    C. 60
    D. 49

18. Data functions:
    A. Represent the functionality provided to the user to meet internal and external data storage requirements
    B. Consist of one or more components, modules, or subsystems

C. Are the functionality provided to the user to process data by an application

D. Are unique user-recognizable, nonrepeated attributes

19. The primary difference between an Internal Logical File and an External Interface File is that:
    A. An EIF is maintained by the application being measured, but an ILF is not
    B. An EIF is not maintained by the application being measured, but an ILF is
    C. An ILF can contain control information but an EIF cannot
    D. An EIF can contain control information but an ILF cannot

20. What is the total function points value for 2 average ILFs, 3 low EIFs, and 4 low ILFs?
    A. 55
    B. 69
    C. 63
    D. 73

21. Control information:
    A. Is the ability to modify data through an elementary process
    B. Is data that influences an elementary process
    C. Specifies what, when, or how data are to be processed
    D. B and C

22. An elementary process:
    A. Is the smallest unit of activity that is meaningful to the user
    B. Is a cohesive collection of automated procedures and data supporting a business objective
    C. Must be self-contained and leave the business of the application being counted in a consistent state
    D. A and C

23. Which categories of data entities are usually identified to satisfy the Functional User Requirements?
    A. Code Data
    B. Business Data
    C. Reference Data
    D. B and C

24. Which categories of data entities are usually identified to satisfy the nonfunctional user requirements?
    A. Code Data
    B. Business Data
    C. Reference Data
    D. B and C

25. Providing a code and an explanatory name or description for an attribute of a business object is an example of:
    A. Valid Values Data
    B. Substitution Data
    C. Static Data
    D. Constant Data

26. Which of the following may also be referred to as Core User Data or Business Objects?
    A. Code Data
    B. Business Data
    C. Reference Data
    D. B and C

27. Data that rarely changes is an example of:
    A. Valid Values Data
    B. Substitution Data
    C. Static or Constant Data
    D. None of the above

28. Providing a list of available values for an attribute of one or more business object types is an example of:
    A. Valid Values Data
    B. Substitution Data
    C. Static Data
    D. Constant Data

29. Data stored to support the business rules for the maintenance of the Business Data is an example of:
    A. Code Data
    B. Business Data
    C. Reference Data
    D. None of the above

30. Data that reflects the information that must be stored and retrieved by the functional area addressed by the application is an example of:
    A. Code Data
    B. Business Data
    C. Reference Data
    D. All of the above

31. Business Data characteristics include which of the following logical characteristics?
    A. Very dynamic—normal business operations cause it to be regularly referenced and routinely added to, changed, or deleted
    B. Essentially static—only changes in response to changes in the way that the business operates
    C. Less dynamic—occasionally changes in response to changes in the functional area's environment, external functional processes, or business rules
    D. None of the above

32. Reference Data characteristics include which of the following logical characteristics?
    A. Mandatory for the operation of the users' functional area
    B. User identifiable (usually by a business user)
    C. Usually user maintainable (usually by an administrative user)
    D. All of the above

33. Code Data characteristics include which of the following logical characteristics?
    A. Provide business transactions access to improve ease of data entry, improve data consistency, ensure data integrity, etc.
    B. Store the data to support core user activities
    C. Store data to standardize and facilitate business activities and business transactions
    D. A and C

34. Valid Values Data:
    A. Provides a code and an explanatory name or description for an attribute of a business object
    B. Contains data that is basically static
    C. Is implemented to satisfy requirements such as reducing errors and increasing user friendliness
    D. Contains one and only one occurrence regardless of the number of attributes

35. States (e.g., State Code, State Name) are an example of:
    A. Static or Constant Data
    B. Substitution Data
    C. Valid Values Data
    D. None of the above

36. Color (e.g., all valid values for the attribute color of a business object) is an example of:
    A. Static or Constant Data
    B. Substitution Data
    C. Valid Values Data
    D. All of the above

37. Examples of Business or Reference Data that should not be considered Code Data include:
    A. Tax Rate Ranges for a Progressive Tax System
    B. Currency Exchange Rate Table
    C. Entity Types with Financial Amounts, Exchange Rates, and Tax Rates, if they are not constants
    D. All of the above

38. "User-recognizable" refers to:
    A. A logical group of permanent data seen from the perspective of the user
    B. The border between the software being measured and the user
    C. The functionality that will be included in a particular function point count
    D. Requirements for processes and/or data that are agreed upon, and understood by, both the users and software developers

39. Reference Data:
    A. Reflects the information that must be stored and retrieved by the functional area addressed by the application
    B. Is stored to support the business rules for the maintenance of the Business Data
    C. May also be referred to as Core User Data or Business Objects
    D. Is sometimes referred to as List Data or Translation Data

40. Code Data:
    A. Reflects the information that must be stored and retrieved by the functional area addressed by the application
    B. Is stored to support the business rules for the maintenance of the Business Data
    C. May also be referred to as Core User Data or Business Objects
    D. Is sometimes referred to as List Data or Translation Data

41. Business Data:
    A. Reflects the information that must be stored and retrieved by the functional area addressed by the application
    B. Is stored to support the business rules for the maintenance of the Business Data
    C. May also be referred to as Core User Data or Business Objects
    D. Is sometimes referred to as List Data or Translation Data

42. The definition of entity independence is:
    A. An association between entities that contains attributes
    B. An entity that is meaningful or significant to the business, in and of itself without the presence of other entities

    C. An entity that is not meaningful or is not significant to the business, in and of itself without the presence of other entities

    D. An entity containing attributes that further describe a many-to-many relationship between two other entity types

43. An attribute is:
    A. A fundamental thing of relevance to the user about which a collection of facts is kept
    B. Included in the count as a RET
    C. Generally analogous to a Data Element Type
    D. A and C

44. An entity is:
    A. A fundamental thing of relevance to the user about which a collection of facts is kept
    B. The smallest unit of activity that is meaningful to the user
    C. Data that influence an elementary process of the application being measured
    D. Is composed of records and data items

45. Entity dependence is:
    A. A logically related group of data
    B. An entity that is meaningful or is significant to the business, in and of itself without the presence of other entities
    C. An entity that is not meaningful or is not significant to the business, in and of itself without the presence of other entities
    D. An entity that is not meaningful or significant in and of itself without the presence of another entity linked to it via a relationship

46. A file system is composed of:
    A. Technical attributes
    B. A cohesive collection of automated procedures and data supporting a business objective
    C. Records and data items
    D. None of the above

Chapter 5

Elementary Process

Introduction

An elementary process is the smallest unit of activity that is meaningful to the user, constitutes a complete transaction, is self-contained, and leaves the business of the application being counted in a consistent state. Elementary processes relate to transactions (i.e., external inputs, external outputs, and external inquiries). The total process used to measure function points was presented previously, but it is repeated here.

As presented in Chapter 2, the following are steps in the function point counting procedure:

- Gather the available documentation.
- Determine counting scope and boundary and identify Functional User Requirements.
- Measure data functions.
- Measure transactional functions.
- Calculate the functional size.
- Document and report.

Remember that the application boundary separates the application being measured from the user domain and/or other independent applications. The data functions relate to the logical data stored and available for update and retrieval. The transactional functions—external inputs (EIs), external outputs (EOs), and external inquiries (EQs)—perform the processes of updates, retrieval, outputs, etc. (transactions you would expect to see in a process model). The specific rules and guidelines for EIs, EOs, and EQs are included in the following chapter, but first, in this chapter, we will discuss the concept of an elementary process as it applies to transactions.

Definition of an Elementary Process[1]

An elementary process (EP) is the smallest unit of activity that is meaningful to the user. For example, an input form for a purchase order could consist of three screens; however, if the form is incomplete until all three screens are completed, then the elementary process would require the completion of all three screens. One screen might identify the items ordered, the second screen might identify the payment information, and the third screen might identify the shipping information. All screens would have to be completed prior to sending the purchase order to a vendor. We would not question this decision if the form is to be completed manually; we would just complete the entire purchase order. In this example, completing some of the fields, even those on one screen, would neither be self-contained nor leave the business in a consistent state. If all information, recognizing that some of the fields may not be mandatory and could be left blank, is completed, then this transaction would be complete. Error and/or confirmation messages might also be returned; these messages are also part of the elementary process.

Identifying Each Elementary Process[2]

Identify an elementary process by composing and/or decomposing the functional requirements into the smallest unit of activity that satisfies all of the following:

---

[1] Refer to IFPUG, *Function Point Counting Practices Manual* (CPM), Release 4.3, Part 2, page 7-5.

[2] Refer to IFPUG, *Function Point Counting Practices Manual* (CPM), Release 4.3, Part 2, page 7-10.

- *Is meaningful to the user* (i.e., is user recognizable and satisfies a Functional User Requirement [FUR])
- *Constitutes a complete transaction*
- *Is self-contained* (i.e., no prior or subsequent processing steps are needed to initiate or complete the Functional User Requirements)
- *Leaves the business of the application being counted in a consistent state* (i.e., the point at which processing has been fully executed; the Functional User Requirement has been satisfied and there is nothing more to be done)

Example 1

- *Is meaningful to the user* (i.e., is user recognizable and satisfies a Functional User Requirement [FUR]). The FUR requires the ability to enter a purchase order.
- *Constitutes a complete transaction.* The purchase order discussed above required three screens to identify the items, the payment information, and the shipping information.
- *Is self-contained* (i.e., no prior or subsequent processing steps are needed to initiate or complete the Functional User Requirements). The process is not self-contained unless all mandatory information for the purchase order is entered and all of the processing steps are included (e.g., validations, calculations, referencing EIFs, updating ILFs).
- *Leaves the business of the application being counted in a consistent state* (i.e., at the point where processing has been fully executed; the Functional User Requirement has been satisfied and there is nothing more to be done). If all of the purchase order information is not added, the purchase order has not yet been created. Adding some of the information alone leaves the business of entering a purchase order in an inconsistent state. Error and/or confirmation messages might also be returned; these messages are also part of the elementary process.

Example 2

- *Is meaningful to the user* (i.e., is user recognizable and satisfies a Functional User Requirement [FUR]). The FUR may also require the ability to separately update the items to be ordered, the payment information, and the shipping information for a purchase order.
- *Constitutes a complete transaction.* The three screens to identify the items, the payment information, and the shipping information in this case would each constitute a separate transaction. Consequently, although there is only one transaction for the create transaction, there would be three transactions for the update.
- *Is self-contained* (i.e., no prior or subsequent processing steps are needed to initiate or complete the Functional

User Requirements). The process is not self-contained unless all mandatory information for the separate identification of the items, the payment information, and the shipping information is entered and all of the processing steps for each are included (e.g., validations, calculations, referencing EIFs, updating ILFs).

- *Leaves the business of the application being counted in a consistent state* (i.e., at the point where processing has been fully executed; the Functional User Requirement has been satisfied and there is nothing more to be done). If all of the purchase order information is not added, the purchase order has not yet been created. Adding some of the information alone leaves the business of entering a purchase order in an inconsistent state. Error and/or confirmation messages might also be returned; these messages are also part of the elementary process.

Determine Unique Elementary Processes[3]

When compared to an elementary process (EP) already identified, count two similar EPs as the same elementary process if they satisfy all of the following:

- They require the same set of Data Element Types (DETs).
- They require the same set of File Types Referenced (FTRs).
- They require the same set of processing logic to complete the elementary process.

Note: One elementary process may include minor variations in DETs or FTRs, as well as multiple alternatives, variations, or occurrences of processing logic. For example, when an EP to enter a purchase order requires additional DETs to account for Canadian as well as U.S. shipping addresses (postal code/Zip Code and providence/state), the EP is not divided into two EPs to account for the minor differences in shipping addresses. The EP is still to enter a purchase order, and variations in the processing logic and DETs are used to account for address differences.

When compared to an elementary process already identified, count two similar EPs as different elementary processes if they satisfy any of the following:

- They require different and unique DETs.
- They require different FTRs.
- They require different and unique processing logic to complete the elementary process.

---

[3] Refer to IFPUG, *Function Point Counting Practices Manual* (CPM), Release 4.3, Part 2, page 7-11.

For example, if an elementary process to hire a contractor requires additional and unique DETs and FTRs to account for the separate personal information and distinct tax status of a contractor in comparison to an employee, separate EPs would be assigned to hire a contractor and to hire an employee, regardless of some similarity between the processes.

Classify Each Elementary Process[4]

Classify each elementary process as an external input (EI), external output (EO), or an external inquiry (EQ) based on its primary intent. The primary intent of the elementary process shall be identified as one of the following:

■ Altering the behavior of the application
■ Maintaining one or more Internal Logical Files (ILFs)
■ Presenting information to the user

Classify the process as an EI if it has a primary intent of either of the following:

■ It maintains one or more ILFs.
■ It alters the behavior of the application.

and

■ It includes processing logic to accept data or control information that enters the application boundary.

Classify the process as an EO if it has a primary intent of presenting information to the user, and it includes at least one of the following forms of processing logic:

■ Mathematical calculations are performed.
■ One or more ILFs are updated.
■ Derived data is created.[5]
■ The behavior of the application is altered.

Classify the process as an EQ if it has a primary intent of presenting information to the user, and

■ It references a data function.
■ It does not satisfy the criteria to be classified as an EO.

Processing Logic[6]

Processing logic is defined as any of the requirements specifically requested by the user to complete an elementary process such as validations, algorithms, or calculations and reading

or maintaining a data function. Those requirements may include the following actions:

1. *Validations are performed.* For example, when adding a new employee to an organization, the employee process validates the employee type DET.
2. *Mathematical formulas and calculations are performed.* For example, when reporting on all employees within an organization, the process includes calculating the total number of salaried employees, hourly employees, and all employees.
3. *Equivalent values are converted.* For example, employee age is converted to an age range group using a table.
4. *Data is filtered and selected by using specified criteria to compare multiple sets of data.* For example, to generate a list of employees by their assignment, an elementary process compares the job number of a job assignment to select and list the appropriate employees with that assignment.
5. *Conditions are analyzed to determine which are applicable.* For example, processing logic exercised by the elementary process when an employee is added will depend on whether an employee is paid based on salary or hours worked. The entry of DETs (and the resulting processing logic) based upon a different choice (salary or hourly) in this example is part of one elementary process.
6. *One or more ILFs are updated.* For example, when adding an employee, the elementary process updates the employee ILF to maintain the employee data.
7. *One or more ILFs or External Interface Files (EIFs) are referenced.* For example, when adding an employee, the currency EIF is referenced for the correct U.S. dollar conversion rate to determine an employee's hourly rate.
8. *Data or control information is retrieved.* For example, to view a list of employees, employee information is retrieved from a data function.
9. *Derived data is created by transforming existing data to create additional data.* For example, to determine (derive) a patient's registration number (e.g., SMIJO01), the following data is concatenated:
   ■ The first three letters of the patient's last name (e.g., SMI for Smith)
   ■ The first two letters of the patient's first name (e.g., JO for John)
   ■ A unique two-digit sequence number (starting with 01)
10. *Behavior of the application is altered.* For example, the behavior of the elementary process of paying employees is altered when a change is made to pay

[4] Refer to IFPUG, *Function Point Counting Practices Manual* (CPM), Release 4.3, Part 2, page 7-13.
[5] *Note*: Calculated fields are a form of derived data, although derived data can also be created without performing a calculation.
[6] Refer to IFPUG, *Function Point Counting Practices Manual* (CPM), Release 4.3, Part 2, page 7-5.

Table 5.1
Summary of Processing Logic Used by EIs, EOs, and EQs

Form of Processing Logic	Transactional Functional Type		
	EI	EO	EQ
Validations are performed.	c	c	c
Mathematical calculations are performed.	c	m*	n
Equivalent values are converted.	c	c	c
Data is filtered and selected by using specified criteria to compare multiple sets of data.	c	c	c
Conditions are analyzed to determine which are applicable.	c	c	c
At least one ILF is updated.	m*	m*	n
At least one ILF or EIF is referenced.	c	c	m
Data or control information is retrieved.	c	c	m
Derived data is created.	c	m*	n
Behavior of the application is altered.	m*	m*	n
Information is prepared and then presented outside the boundary.	c	m	m
Data or control information entering the boundary of the application is accepted.	m	c	c
A set of data is sorted or arranged.	c	c	c

Note: c, the function type *can* perform the form of processing logic, but it is not mandatory; m, it is *mandatory* that the function type perform the form of processing logic; m*, it is *mandatory* that the function type perform at least one of these (m*) forms of processing logic; n, the function type *cannot* perform the form of processing logic.

them every other Friday vs. on the 15th and the last day of the month, resulting in 26 pay periods per year vs. 24.

11. *Prepare and present information outside the boundary.* For example, a list of employees is formatted and displayed for the user.

12. *Capability exists to accept data or control information that enters the boundary of the application.* For example, a user enters information to add a customer order to the application.

13. *Sorting or arranging a set of data.* This form of processing logic does not impact the identification of the type or contribute to the uniqueness of an elementary process; that is, the orientation of the data does not constitute uniqueness. For example, a list of employees can be sorted in either alphabetical or location order, or, on an order entry screen, the order header information is arranged at the top of the screen and the order details are placed below.

One elementary process may include multiple alternatives or occurrences of the above actions (e.g., validations, filters, resorts).

Summary of Processing Logic Used by EIs, EOs, and EQs[7]

Table 5.1 summarizes which forms of processing logic may be performed by EIs, EOs, and EQs. For each transactional function type, certain types of processing logic must be performed to accomplish the primary intent of that type. The 13 actions do not by themselves identify unique elementary processes.

---

[7] Refer to IFPUG, *Function Point Counting Practices Manual* (CPM), Release 4.3, Part 2, page 7-8.

Further Reading

The rules included in this chapter have been extracted from Part 2, Chapter 7, of the IFPUG *Function Point Counting Practices Manual* (CPM), Release 4.3. A review of these chapters is recommended before taking the CFPS exam.

Exam Guidance

- Read and study this chapter, including all related examples.
- Know the definition of elementary process, how to identifying each elementary process, how to determine unique elementary processes, and how to classify each elementary process.
- Know the definition of processing logic and the requirements they may include, and be familiar with Table 5.1.
- Familiarize yourself with the related examples in this chapter as well as CPM 4.3, Part 2, Chapter 7 (Measure Transactional Functions), because it is unlikely that you will have time to look up everything during the exam.
- Complete the practice questions in this chapter, and go back to determine why you answered any question incorrectly.

Sample Exam Questions

1. When compared to an elementary process (EP) already identified, count two similar EPs as the same elementary process if they:
   A. Require the same set of DETs and require the same set of FTRs
   B. Require the same set of FTRs and require the same set of processing logic to complete the elementary process
   C. Require the same set of DETs, require the same set of FTRs, and require the same set of processing logic to complete the elementary process
   D. Require the same set of processing logic to complete the elementary process

2. Identify an elementary process by composing or decomposing the Functional User Requirements into the smallest unit of activity that satisfies which of the following?
   A. Constitutes a complete transaction
   B. Is meaningful to the user
   C. Is self-contained and leaves the business of the application being counted in a consistent state
   D. All of the above

3. Classify each elementary process as an external input (EI), external output (EO), or an external inquiry (EQ) based on:
   A. The smallest unit of activity that is meaningful to the user
   B. Its primary intent
   C. Its processing logic
   D. None of the above

4. Which of the following can be a primary intent of a transactional function?
   A. Altering the behavior of the application
   B. Maintaining one or more ILFs
   C. Presenting information to the user
   D. All of the above

5. The smallest unit of activity that is meaningful to the user is the definition of:
   A. Elementary process
   B. Primary intent
   C. Processing logic
   D. Derived data

6. Which of the following can have a primary intent of maintaining one or more ILFs?
   A. External input
   B. External output
   C. External inquiry
   D. A and B

7. Classify an elementary process as an EQ if it:
   A. Has a primary intent of presenting information to the user
   B. References a data function to retrieve data or control information
   C. Does not satisfy the criteria to be classified as an EO
   D. All of the above

8. Processing logic is defined as:
   A. The smallest unit of activity that is meaningful to the user
   B. The functionality that will be included in a particular function point count
   C. Requirements specifically requested by the user to complete an elementary process
   D. The ability to modify data through an elementary process

9. Converting equivalent values is a form of processing logic that can be done by which of the following transactions?
   A. External input
   B. External output

C. External inquiry
D. All of the above

10. Which of the following forms of processing logic cannot be performed by an external inquiry?
   A. Update an ILF
   B. Sort or arrange a set of data
   C. Analyze conditions to determine which are applicable
   D. Validations

11 Processing logic:
   A. Is any of the requirements specifically requested by the user to complete an elementary process
   B. Can include validations, algorithms, or calculations
   C. Can include reading or maintaining a file
   D. All of the above

12. Data created by transforming existing data to create additional data is considered to be:
   A. Processing logic
   B. Control information
   C. External input
   D. Derived data

13. Presenting information to a user can be done by which of the following transaction types:
   A. External input
   B. External output
   C. External inquiry
   D. All of the above

Chapter 6

Transactional Functions

Introduction

As presented in Chapter 2, the following are steps in the function point counting procedure:

- Gather the available documentation.
- Determine counting scope and boundary and identify Functional User Requirements.
- Measure data functions.
- Measure transactional functions.
- Calculate the functional size.
- Document and report.

The data functions relate to the logical data stored and available for update and retrieval. The transactional functions—external inputs (EIs), external outputs (EOs), and external inquiries (EQs)—perform the processes of storing, updating, retrieving, and displaying the logical data. The specific rules and guidelines for EIs, EOs, and EQs are discussed in this chapter, but remember the concept of an elementary process (EP) as presented in Chapter 5, because a transaction must be confirmed to be an EP before it can be classified as an EI, EO, or EQ.

What They Are: External Inputs, External Outputs, and External Inquiries

A transactional function is an elementary process that provides functionality to the user to process data. A transactional function is an external input, external output, or external inquiry.

Definitions and Primary Intent[1]

External Input

An external input (EI) is an elementary process that processes data or control information sent from outside the boundary. The primary intent of an EI is to maintain one or more Internal Logical Files (ILFs) and/or alter the behavior of the system.

External Output

An external output (EO) is an elementary process that sends data or control information outside the application's boundary and includes additional processing beyond that of an external inquiry. The primary intent of an external output is to present information to a user through processing logic other than or in addition to the retrieval of data or control information. The processing logic must contain at least one mathematical formula or calculation, create derived data, maintain one or more ILFs, and/or alter the behavior of the system.

External Inquiry

An external inquiry (EQ) is an elementary process that sends data or control information outside the boundary. The primary intent of an external inquiry is to present information to a user through the retrieval of data or control information. The processing logic contains no mathematical formula or calculation and creates no derived data. No ILF is maintained during the processing, nor is the behavior of the system altered.

---

[1] Refer to IFPUG, *Function Point Counting Practices Manual* (CPM), Release 4.3, Part 2, page 7-3.

Summary of the Functions Performed by EIs, EOs, and EQs[2]

The main difference between the transactional function types is their primary intent. Table 6.1 summarizes functions that may be performed by each transactional function type and specifies the primary intent of each.

Definitions for Embedded Terms[3]

The following includes definitions necessary to determine EIs, EOs, and EQs. Some definitions have been provided in earlier chapters but are repeated here for your reference.

Control Information

Control information influences an elementary process by specifying what, when, or how data is to be processed.

Elementary Process

An elementary process is the smallest unit of activity that is meaningful to the user.

Maintain

The term *maintain* refers to the ability to add, change, or delete data through an elementary process. Examples include, but are not limited to, add, change, delete, populate, revise, update, assign, and create.

Meaningful

The activity is user recognizable and satisfies a Functional User Requirement.

User

A user is any person or thing that communicates or interacts with the software at any time.

Processing Logic[3]

Processing logic is defined as any of the requirements specifically requested by the user to complete an elementary process such as validations, algorithms, or calculations, as well as reading or maintaining a data function.

Table 6.1 Summary of the Functions Performed by EIs, EOs, and EQs

Function	Transactional Function Type		
	EI	EO	EQ
Alter the behavior of the system	PI	F	N/A
Maintain one or more ILFs	PI	F	N/A
Present information to a user	F	PI	PI

Note: F, a function of the transactional function type but is not the primary intent and is sometimes present; N/A, the function is not allowed by the transactional function type; PI, the primary intent of the transactional function type. Only an EO, and not an EQ, may perform the functions of altering the behavior of the system or maintaining one or more ILFs when performing the primary intent of presenting information to the user.

Summary of Processing Logic Used by EIs, EOs, and EQs

Table 6.2 summarizes which forms of processing logic may be performed by EIs, EOs, and EQs. For each transactional function type, certain types of processing logic must be performed to accomplish the primary intent of that type, and certain types of processing can or cannot be performed. The 13 actions do not by themselves identify unique elementary processes; each of the 13 actions was described in depth and with examples in Chapter 5.

Rules for Counting Transactions

Transactional Function Counting Procedures

The transactional function counting procedures include the following steps (see Table 6.3):

1. Identify each elementary process.
2. Determine unique elementary processes.
3. Classify each elementary process.

These steps were described in detail in Chapter 5. Refer to Chapter 5 and the *Function Point CPM*[4] for the rules and definitions of elementary process. Step 3 is repeated here in this chapter for clarity purposes.

---

[2] Refer to IFPUG, *Function Point Counting Practices Manual* (CPM), Release 4.3, Part 2, page 7-4.

[3] Refer to IFPUG, *Function Point Counting Practices Manual* (CPM), Release 4.3, Part 2, page 7-5.

[4] Refer to IFPUG, *Function Point Counting Practices Manual* (CPM), Release 4.3, Part 2, page 7-10.

Table 6.2   Summary of Processing Logic Used by EIs, EOs, and EQs

Form of Processing Logic		Transactional Functional Type		
		EI	EO	EQ
1.	Validations are performed.	c	c	c
2.	Mathematical calculations are performed.	c	m*	n
3.	Equivalent values are converted.	c	c	c
4.	Data is filtered and selected by using specified criteria to compare multiple sets of data.	c	c	c
5.	Conditions are analyzed to determine which are applicable.	c	c	c
6.	At least one ILF is updated.	m*	m*	n
7.	At least one ILF or EIF is referenced.	c	c	m
8.	Data or control information is retrieved.	c	c	m
9.	Derived data is created.	c	m*	n
10.	Behavior of the application is altered.	m*	m*	n
11.	Information is prepared and then presented outside the boundary.	c	m	m
12.	Data or control information entering the boundary of the application is accepted.	m	c	c
13.	A set of data is sorted or arranged.	c	c	c

Note: c, the function type *can* perform the form of processing logic, but it is not mandatory; m, it is *mandatory* that the function type perform the form of processing logic; m*, it is *mandatory* that the function type perform at least one of these (m*) forms of processing logic; n, the function type *cannot* perform the form of processing logic.

Table 6.3   Transactional Function Counting Steps

Step	Action
1.	Identify each elementary process.
2.	Determine unique elementary processes.
3.	Classify each transactional function as an external input (EI), external output (EO), or an external inquiry (EQ).
4.	Determine the functional complexity for each transactional function and its contribution to functional size.

Step 3. Classify Each Elementary Process[5]

Classify each elementary process as an external input (EI), external output (EO), or an external inquiry (EQ) based on its primary intent. The primary intent of the elementary process shall be identified as one of the following:

- Altering the behavior of the application
- Maintaining one or more Internal Logical Files (ILFs)
- Presenting information to the user

Classify the process as an EI if it has a primary intent of either of the following:

- Maintaining one or more ILFs.
- Altering the behavior of the application.

and

- It includes processing logic to accept data or control information that enters the boundary of the application.

The following transactions could be counted as EIs:

- Transactional data that is used to maintain an ILF, such as reporting a sale, entering a lost item, establishing a scheduled appointment, transferring an employee, or entering an insurance form
- Input that provides control information, such as seismological sensors reporting earth movement
- Messages from other applications that require processing

[5] Refer to IFPUG, *Function Point Counting Practices Manual* (CPM), Release 4.3, Part 2, page 7-13.

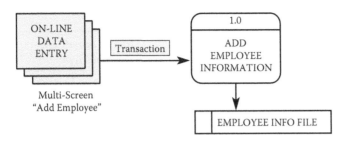

Figure 6.1 EI add employee.

■ Transaction files from other applications which may include multiple transactions of a different type that require separate and unique processing (e.g., cash sales and credit card transactions, in which case there would be multiple EIs)

■ Physical data that initiates processing, such as the temperature

■ Maintenance of any ILF, including user-maintained help, any message file, parameters, etc.

Be careful not to count the following as EIs:

■ Reference Data read by the application from data stored in another application but not used to maintain an ILF in the measured application (this is typically recognized as an EIF)

■ The input parameters of either an inquiry or an output

■ Menu screens used for navigation or selection and which do not maintain an ILF

■ Logon screens that facilitate user entry into an application

■ Multiple methods of invoking the same logic (e.g., two action keys that perform the same function or the same transaction on multiple screens should be counted only once)

■ Point and click of data on a screen in order to fill fields on the screen or to move data

■ Refresh or cancel screen data

■ Responses to messages that request a user to confirm a delete or any other transaction

■ Data passed between on-line and batch within the same application; it does not cross the application boundary

■ Data passed between the client and server within the same application; it does not cross the application boundary

Figure 6.1 provides an example of adding an employee, a process that would be recognized as an EI.

Classify the process as an EO if it has a primary intent of presenting information to the user, and it includes at least one of the following forms of processing logic:

■ Mathematical calculations are performed.
■ One or more ILFs are updated.
■ Derived data is created.[6]
■ The behavior of the application is altered.

The following transactions could be counted as EOs:

■ Reports that require the use of algorithms or calculations (e.g., monthly checking account statements or weekly sales reports)

■ Data transfers, files, and/or messages sent to other applications when data is calculated or derived or an update occurs as a part of the elementary process (e.g., a file of transactions sent from the accounts receivable application to the separately maintained general ledger application, when some totals are calculated or a database entry occurs within accounts receivable to indicate which transactions were sent—an EO to accounts receivable and one or more EIs to general ledger)

■ A check created that simultaneously updates the check record with the check number (this is one elementary process)

■ Derived or calculated information displayed on a screen or passed in a file to another application

■ Graphical displays, such as bar charts and pie charts, when they require calculations

■ A triangulated target location, returned to the user or sent to another application within the weapon system, for a weapon

■ Notification to a business manager that a credit card has been reported missing with the calculated totals of current charges

Be careful not to count the following as EOs:

■ Identical reports with different data values, such as a department report

■ Reports without formulas, calculations, or derived data and which do not maintain an ILF within the application sending the data (most likely counted as EQs)

■ Summary fields contained on a detail report (detail report is the EO)

■ Files sent to other applications that have no formulas, calculations, or derived data and do not maintain an ILF within the application sending the data (most likely counted as EQs)

■ Refresh or cancel screen data (not counted)

■ Reference Data read by another application from data stored in the application being measured (the data is not processed as an EO by the measured application)

---

[6] *Note*: Calculated fields are a form of derived data, although derived data can also be created without performing a calculation.

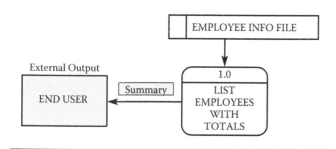

Figure 6.2   EO list employees with totals.

- Help (most likely counted as low EQs)
- Logoff
- Multiple methods of invoking the same output process
- Error messages that result from an edit or validation of an EI or the request side of an EO or EQ
- Confirmation messages that acknowledge that the data has been processed
- Messages that request a user to confirm a delete or any other transaction
- Identical data sent to more than one application
- *Ad hoc* reports that the user directs and controls through the use of a language such as SQL or FOCUS and consequently are nonfunctional or technical solutions
- Data passed between on-line and batch within the same application; it does not cross the application boundary
- Data passed between client and server within the same application; it does not cross the application boundary

Figure 6.2 provides the example of a list of employees with totals that would be recognized as an EO.

Classify the process as an EQ if it has a primary intent of presenting information to the user, and

- It references a data function.
- It does not satisfy the criteria to be classified as an EO.

The following transactions could be counted as EQs:

- Transactional data retrieved from one or more ILFs or EIFs and displayed (e.g., an appointment, an item description, employee data, payment data)
- User functions such as view, lookup, display, browse, print
- Implied inquiries (retrievals of data prior to a change or delete function), provided that the inquiry can be used as a stand-alone process and that it is not a duplication of another previously counted EQ

- Reports generated on a periodic basis that do not contain formulas, calculations, or derived data and do not maintain an ILF
- Return of maintained system data, parameters, and setup unless computed
- Logon screens that provide application-specific security, unless the application requires a tracking of who used the system and for how long, in which case it would be an EO
- Each level of help (e.g., system, field, or screen when retrieved from an ILF/EIF)
- Retrievals of maintained data via electronic data interface or phone (using tones)
- Files sent to other applications that do not have formulas, calculations, or derived data and do not maintain an ILF within the application sending the data (it may be an EI to the receiving application)
- Retrieval of mail from mailbox
- List boxes or point and click on a screen in order to return maintained data from an ILF/EIF

Be careful not to count the following as EQs:

- Multiple methods of invoking the same logic (e.g., two action keys that perform the same function or the same transaction on multiple screens—counted only once)
- Inquiries that can be accessed from multiple areas/screens of an application (counted only once)
- Menu screens used for navigation or selection and which do not retrieve maintained data (not counted)
- Logon screens that facilitate user entry into an application but do not invoke security (not counted)
- Derived or calculated data vs. retrieval of data (counted as an EO)
- Resorting or rearrangement of a set of data without other processing logic
- Responses to messages that request a user to confirm data
- Error and/or confirmation messages (counted as part of the transaction that generates the message)
- Data passed between on-line and batch processes within the same application; it does not cross the application boundary
- Data passed between the client and server within the same application; it does not cross the application boundary
- Data not retrieved from maintained data (e.g., hard-coded data, which is not counted)

Figure 6.3 provides an example of the display of employee information without calculations that would be recognized as an EQ.

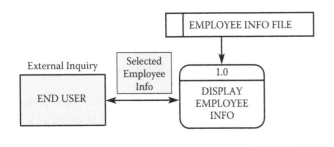

Figure 6.3 Display employee information without calculations.

Step 4. Determine the Functional Complexity for Each Transactional Function and Its Contribution to Functional Size[7]

The number of EIs, EOs, and EQs and their relative functional complexities determine the contribution of the transactional functions to the functional size. Assign each identified EI, EO, and EQ a functional complexity based on the number of File Types Referenced (FTRs) and Data Element Types (DETs).

FTR Definition

A File Type Referenced (FTR) is a data function read and/or maintained by a transactional function. A FTP includes:

- An Internal Logical File (ILF) read or maintained by a transactional function
- An External Interface File (EIF) read by a transactional function

FTR Rule

One FTR shall be counted for each unique data function that is accessed (read from and/or written to) by the transactional function.

DET Definition

A Data Element Type (DET) is a unique, user-recognizable, nonrepeated attribute.

DET Rules

Review everything that crosses (enters and/or exits) the boundary:

- Count one DET for each unique user-recognizable, nonrepeated attribute that crosses (enters or exits) the boundary during the processing of the transactional function.

- Count only one DET per transactional function for the ability to send an application response message even if there are multiple messages.
- Count only one DET per transactional function for the ability to initiate actions even if there are multiple means to do so.

Do not count the following items as DETs:

- Literals, such as report titles, screen or panel identifiers, column headings, and attribute titles
- Application-generated stamps such as date and time attributes
- Paging variables, page numbers, and positioning information (e.g., Rows 37 to 54 of 211)
- Navigation aids, such as the ability to navigate within a list using "previous," "next," "first," "last," and their graphical equivalents
- Attributes generated within the boundary by a transactional function and saved to an ILF without exiting the boundary
- Attributes retrieved or referenced from an ILF or EIF for participation in the processing without exiting the boundary

EI Complexity and Contribution Guidelines[8]

To determine the complexity and contribution of external inputs, use the following guidelines.

FTR Guidance for an EI

Recognizing that an EI must either update an ILF or control the behavior of the application, the following guidance applies when counting FTRs:

- Count an FTR for each ILF maintained.
- Count an FTR for each ILF or EIF read.
- Count only one FTR for each ILF that is both maintained and read.

DET Guidance for an EI

Recognizing that an EI must either update an ILF or control the behavior of the application, the following guidance applies when counting DETs.

Review everything that crosses (enters and/or exits) the boundary:

---

[7] Refer to IFPUG, *Function Point Counting Practices Manual* (CPM), Release 4.3, Part 2, page 7-14.

[8] Refer to IFPUG, *Function Point Counting Practices Manual* (CPM), Release 4.3, Part 2, page 7-15.

■ Count one DET for each unique user-recognizable, nonrepeated attribute that crosses (enters and/or exits) the boundary during the processing of the transactional function.

■ Count only one DET per transactional function for the ability to send an application response message even if there are multiple messages.

■ Count only one DET per transactional function for the ability to initiate actions even if there are multiple means to do so.

Do not count the following items as DETs:

■ Literals, such as report titles, screen or panel identifiers, column headings, and attribute titles

■ Application-generated stamps such as date and time attributes

■ Paging variables, page numbers, and positioning information (e.g., Rows 37 to 54 of 211)

■ Navigation aids, such as the ability to navigate within a list using "previous," "next," "first," "last," and their graphical equivalents

■ Attributes generated within the boundary by a transactional function and saved to an ILF without exiting the boundary

■ Attributes retrieved or referenced from an ILF or EIF for participation in the processing without exiting the boundary

Figure 6.4 provides an example of determining the complexity and contribution of the EI to add an employee previously recognized in Figure 6.1.

The add employee process requires completion of all three tabs. Once the third tab is completed, the SAVE button is enabled. Validity checks are done upon saving:

■ If there are no errors, Employee ID is generated, the data is saved on the Employee ILF, and a success message is returned.

■ If there are errors, no data is saved and error messages are returned.

The EI has an input side with a potential 23 DETs and an output side with a potential of two additional DETs (Employee ID is generated if add is successful plus a success or error message). One FTR is referenced.

Five drop-down boxes are present on the three screens. The dependent relationship drop-down box contains Static Data, thus it is not counted as an EQ. The other four boxes retrieve data from an ILF or EIF and thus are counted once per application as EQs. The fields themselves are DETs for the EI.

EO/EQ Complexity and Contribution Guidelines[9]

To determine the complexity and contribution of external outputs and external inquiries, use the following guidelines.

FTR Guidance for an EQ

Recognizing that an EQ cannot update an ILF, when counting FTRs for EQs:

■ Count an FTR for each ILF or EIF read.

FTR Guidance for an EO

Recognizing that an EO can update an ILF, the following additional guidance applies when counting FTRs for EOs:

■ Count an FTR for each ILF or EIF read.
■ Count one FTR for each ILF maintained.
■ Count only one FTR for each ILF that is both maintained and read.

Shared DET Guidance for EOs and EQs

The following guidance applies when counting DETs for both EOs and EQs.

Review everything that crosses (enters and/or exits) the boundary:

■ Count one DET for each unique user-recognizable, nonrepeated attribute that crosses (enters and/or exits) the boundary during the processing of the transactional function.

■ Count only one DET per transactional function for the ability to send an application response message even if there are multiple messages.

■ Count only one DET per transactional function for the ability to initiate actions even if there are multiple means to do so.

Do not count the following items as DETs:

■ Literals, such as report titles, screen or panel identifiers, column headings, and attribute titles

■ Application-generated stamps such as date and time attributes

■ Paging variables, page numbers, and positioning information (e.g., Rows 37 to 54 of 211)

■ Navigation aids, such as the ability to navigate within a list using "previous," "next," "first," "last," and their graphical equivalents

---

[9] Refer to IFPUG, *Function Point Counting Practices Manual* (CPM), Release 4.3, Part 2, page 7-17.

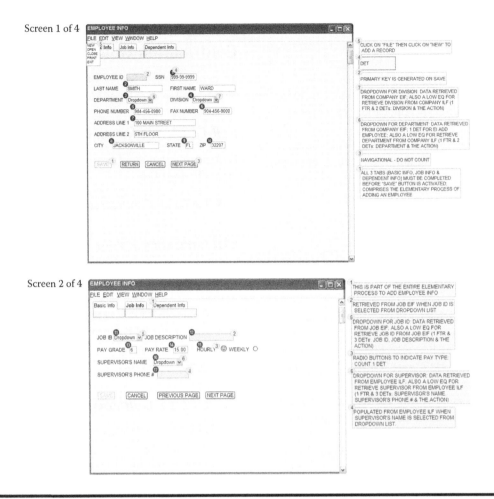

Figure 6.4   Determining complexity and contribution of EI.

■ Attributes generated within the boundary by a transactional function and saved to an ILF without exiting the boundary. *Note:* An EQ by rule cannot update an ILF, so this rule would not apply.

■ Attributes retrieved or referenced from an ILF or EIF for participation in the processing without exiting the boundary.

Figure 6.5 provides an example of determining the complexity and contribution of the EO that provides a list of employees with totals, as previously recognized in Figure 6.2. Find Employee returns a list with a total. The input side has two DETs (Employee Last Name, Find), and the output side has an additional four DETs. The Primary Key (PK) is ID. The transaction references two FTRs. Figure 6.6 provides an example of determining the complexity and contribution of the EQ to display employee information without totals, as previously recognized in Figure 6.3. To look at the details for an employee, select the correct name on the output side of the EO demonstrated in Figure 6.3 and hit enter. The Primary

Key "ID" on the output side becomes a DET on the input side of View Employee Details; consequently, there are two DETs on the input side of the EQ (Employee and Enter). The output side of View Employee Details is made up of three tabs and 21 additional DETs. The transaction references three FTRs.

Determination of Complexity and Contribution[10]

The functional complexity of each transactional function shall be determined using the steps shown in Table 6.4. In our three examples, we had one EI of average complexity and a contribution of four function points, one EO of average complexity and a contribution of five function points, and one EQ of high complexity and a contribution of six function points.

---

[10] Refer to IFPUG, *Function Point Counting Practices Manual* (CPM), Release 4.3, Part 2, pages 7-19 and 7-20.

Screen 3 of 4

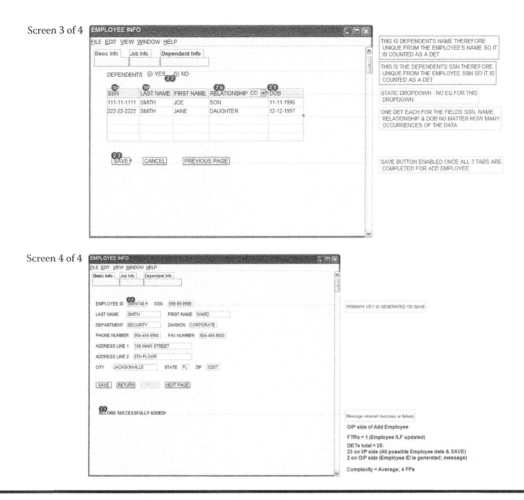

Figure 6.4 (cont.) Determining complexity and contribution of EI.

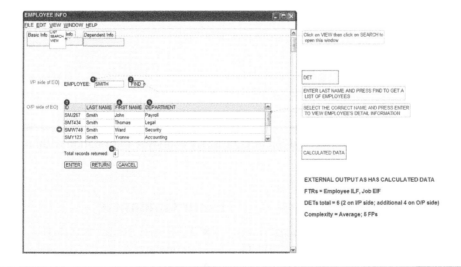

Figure 6.5 Determining complexity and contribution of EO.

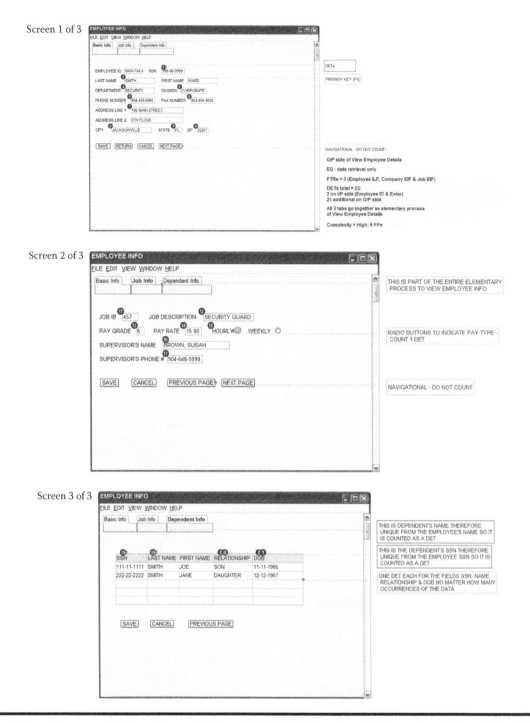

Figure 6.6   Determining complexity and contribution of EQ Display Employee Information without Calculations.

Further Reading

The rules included in this chapter have been extracted from Part 2, Chapter 7, and Part 4, Chapter 2, of the IFPUG *Function Point Counting Practices Manual* (CPM), Release 4.3. A review of these chapters is recommended before taking the CFPS exam.

Exam Guidance

- Read and study this chapter, including all related examples.
- Memorize the various definitions (e.g., EI, EO, EQ, DET, FTR).
- Memorize the primary intent for EI, EO, and EQ.

Table 6.4 Determination of Complexity and Contribution for EIs, EOs, and EQs

Step	Action
1.	To identify and count the FTRs and DETs, the complexity and contribution counting rules that begin on page 7-14 in Part 2 of the IFPUG *Function Point CPM*, Release 4.3, should be used.
2.	The functional complexity of each transactional function is determined using the number of FTRs and DETs in accordance with the following matrices:

External Inputs

	1 to 4 DETs	*5 to 15 DETs*	*16 or more DETs*
0 to 1 FTRs	Low	Low	Average
2 FTRs	Low	Average	High
3 or more FTRs	Average	High	High

External Outputs and External Inquiries

	1 to 5 DETs	*6 to 19 DETs*	*20 or more DETs*
0 to 1 FTRs	Low	Low	Average
2 to 3 FTRs	Low	Average	High
4 or more FTRs	Average	High	High

Step	Action
3.	The functional size of each transactional function is determined using the type and functional complexity in accordance with the tables below.

External Inputs and External Inquiries

Functional Complexity Rating	*Function Points*
Low	3
Average	4
High	6

External Outputs

Functional Complexity Rating	*Function Points*
Low	4
Average	5
High	7

- Memorize the DET and FTR guidance for EI, EO, and EQ.
- Memorize the various embedded terms.
- Memorize the transactional function counting procedures steps.
- Memorize or at least be extremely familiar with the complexity and contribution matrices.
- Familiarize yourself with the related examples in this chapter as well as CPM 4.3, Part 2, Chapter 7 (Measure Transactional Functions), and Part 4, Chapter 2 (Transactional Function Counting Examples), because it is unlikely that you will have time to look up everything during the exam.
- Complete the practice questions in this chapter, and go back to determine why you answered any question incorrectly.

Sample Exam Questions

1. To maintain one or more ILFs and/or alter the behavior of the system is the primary intent of an:
   A. External input
   B. External output
   C. External inquiry
   D. B and C

2. A File Type Referenced (FTR) can be:
   A. An Internal Logical File read by a transactional function
   B. An Internal Logical File maintained by a transactional function
   C. An External Interface File read by a transactional function
   D. All of the above

3. FTR guidance for an external input includes which of the following:
   A. Count an FTR for each ILF maintained
   B. Count an FTR for each ILF or EIF read during the processing of the external input
   C. Count only one FTR for each ILF that is both maintained and read
   D. All of the above

4. The primary intent of an external inquiry is:
   A. To maintain an ILF or alter the behavior of the system
   B. To present information to a user through the retrieval of data or control information
   C. To hold data referenced through one or more elementary processes within the boundary
   D. To hold data maintained through one or more elementary processes of the application being measured

5. Transactional functions include which of the following:
   A. Internal Logical Files
   B. External Interface Files
   C. External inquiries
   D. B and C

6. The primary intent of an external output is:
   A. To maintain an ILF or alter the behavior of the system
   B. To present information to a user through processing logic other than, or in addition to, the retrieval of data or control information
   C. To hold data referenced through one or more elementary processes within the boundary

   D. To hold data maintained through one or more elementary processes of the application being measured

7. DET guidance for an external input includes which of the following:
   A. Count one DET for each unique user-recognizable, nonrepeated attribute that crosses (enters and/or exits) the boundary during the processing of the transactional function
   B. Count only one DET per transactional function for the ability to send an application response message even if there are multiple messages
   C. Count only one DET per transactional function for the ability to initiate actions even if there are multiple means to do so
   D. All of the above

8. DET guidance for an external output includes which of the following:
   A. If a DET both enters and exits the boundary, count it twice for the elementary process
   B. Do not count literals such as report titles, screen or panel identifiers, column headings, and attribute titles as DETs
   C. Count paging variables or system-generated stamps as one DET
   D. All of the above

9. Count only one DET per transactional function for the ability to send an application response message even if there are multiple messages is a DET guidance for which type(s) of transaction(s):
   A. External output
   B. External input
   C. External inquiry
   D. All of the above

10. Count only one DET per transactional function for the ability to initiate actions even if there are multiple means to do so is a DET guidance for which type(s) of transaction(s):
    A. External output
    B. External input
    C. External inquiry
    D. All of the above

11. Which of the following is used to determine the complexity of a transaction:
    A. FTRs and RETs
    B. DETs and RETs
    C. FTRs and DETs
    D. FTRs, DETs, and RETs

12. Do not count attributes generated within the boundary by a transactional function and saved to an ILF without exiting the boundary is a DET guidance of which type(s) of transaction(s):
    A. External input
    B. External output
    C. External inquiry
    D. All of the above

13. Which of the following is true for an external inquiry:
    A. Count one DET for each unique user-recognizable, nonrepeated attribute that crosses (enters and/or exits) the boundary during the processing of the transactional function
    B. Count literals as DETs
    C. Count paging variables or system-generated stamps as DETs
    D. B and C

14. What is the total number of function points for 5 high EIs, 2 low EOs, 3 average EIs, and 2 average EQs:
    A. 48
    B. 63
    C. 61
    D. 58

15. A low EO is worth how many function points:
    A. 3
    B. 4
    C. 5
    D. 6

16. A low EQ is worth how many function points:
    A. 3
    B. 4
    C. 5
    D. 6

17. An average EI is worth how many function points:
    A. 3
    B. 4
    C. 5
    D. 6

18. What is the total number of function points for 2 average EIs, 1 low EIF, and 2 high ILFs:
    A. 44
    B. 43
    C. 23
    D. 41

19. The main difference between the transactional function types is:
    A. Their elementary process
    B. Their primary intent
    C. Their processing logic
    D. None of the above

20. An elementary process that sends data or control information outside the application's boundary and includes additional processing beyond that of an external inquiry is what type(s) of transactional function(s):
    A. External output
    B. External input
    C. External inquiry
    D. A and C

21. An elementary process that processes data or control information sent from outside the boundary is what type(s) of transactional function(s):
    A. External output
    B. External input
    C. External inquiry
    D. A and C

22. Which is true of transactional functions:
    A. They are defined as external inputs, external outputs, and external inquiries
    B. They are defined as Internal Logical Files and External Interface Files
    C. They are elementary processes that provide functionality to the user to process data
    D. A and C

23. Processing logic is defined as:
    A. The smallest unit of activity that is meaningful to the user
    B. The functionality that will be included in a particular function point count
    C. Requirements specifically requested by the user to complete an elementary process
    D. The ability to modify data through an elementary process

24. Preparing and presenting information outside of the boundary can be done by which of the following transactions:
    A. External input
    B. External output
    C. External inquiry
    D. All of the above

25. Converting equivalent values is a form of processing logic that can be done by which of the following transactions:
    A. External input
    B. External output
    C. External inquiry
    D. All of the above

26. Which of the following forms of processing logic cannot be performed by an external inquiry:
    A. Update an ILF
    B. Resort or rearrange a set of data
    C. Analyze conditions to determine which are applicable
    D. Validations

27. Which of the following is FTR guidance for both external outputs and external inquiries:
    A. Count one FTR for each ILF maintained
    B. Count an FTR for each ILF or EIF read
    C. Count only one FTR for each ILF that is both maintained and read
    D. None of the above

28. Which of the following is true about the function "altering the behavior of the system":
    A. It is the primary intent of an EI
    B. It is the primary intent of an EQ
    C. It is not allowed by an EO
    D. A and C

29. Processing logic:
    A. Includes any of the requirements specifically requested by the user to complete an elementary process
    B. Can include validations, algorithms, or calculations
    C. Can include reading or maintaining a data function
    D. All of the above

30. Data created by transforming existing data to create additional data is considered to be:
    A. Processing logic
    B. Control information
    C. External input
    D. Derived data

Chapter 7

Shared Data

Introduction

Internal Logical Files (ILFs) and External Interface Files (EIFs) are user-identifiable groups of logically related data or control information. ILFs are maintained within the boundary of the application being measured. EIFs are read and/or referenced only within the boundary of the application being measured, but they are maintained within a different application boundary.

An external input (EI) is an elementary process that processes data or control information sent from outside the boundary to maintain one or more ILFs and/or to alter the behavior of the system. An external output (EO) is an elementary process that sends data or control information outside the application's boundary to present information to a user through processing logic other than or in addition to the retrieval of data or control information. An external inquiry (EQ) is an elementary process that sends data or control information outside the boundary to present information to a user through the retrieval of data or control information.

This chapter provides guidelines and examples of shared data regarding what should be measured when we reference or utilize data from a logical file to complete a transaction being processed within the application receiving or accessing the data or when we maintain the Internal Logical Files within the application receiving or accessing the data.

Shared Data

Applications that share data with other applications:[1]

- Reference or utilize the data to complete a transaction being processed within the application receiving or accessing the data.
- Maintain the Internal Logical Files within the application receiving or accessing the data.

Methods of Sharing Data

Shared data, used by elementary processes within an application to maintain data on an Internal Logical File or to present data to the user, may be transferred via:

- On-line screens (e.g., screen scraping)
- Direct access of data files from other applications
- Transferred files
- On-line real-time information requests
- Web applications

Common Terms[2]

The following common terms are utilized in this chapter to describe physical implementation techniques:

Copy

The Institute of Electrical and Electronic Engineers (IEEE) definition:

---

[1] Refer to IFPUG, *Function Point Counting Practices Manual* (CPM), Release 4.3, Part 3, page 3-2.

[2] Refer to IFPUG, *Function Point Counting Practices Manual* (CPM), Release 4.3, Part 3, page 3-3.

1. To read data from a source, leaving the source data unchanged, and to write the same data elsewhere in a physical form that may differ from that of the source—for example, copying data from a magnetic disk onto a magnetic tape.
2. The result of a copy process as in above—for example, a copy of a data file.

File

The IEEE definition: "... a set of related records treated as a unit; for example, in stock control, a file could consist of a set of invoice records."

Image

An exact replication of another object, file, or table that is usually created through a utility.

Load

The IEEE definition: "... to copy computer instructions or data from external storage to internal storage."

Merge

Multiple files with the same data elements consolidated into a single file.

Refresh

The process of recreating a set of data to make it current with its source.

Scenarios

In each of the scenarios presented here, the application boundary separates the application being measured from the user domain and/or other independent applications. The data functions relate to the logical data stored and available for update and retrieval in an application. The transactional functions—EIs, EOs, and EQs—perform the processes of updates, retrieval, outputs, etc. With shared data, we might reference or utilize data to complete a transaction being processed within the application receiving or accessing the data, or we might maintain the Internal Logical Files within the application receiving or accessing the data.

Group 1[3]

The primary intent is for Application B to reference data maintained by Application A. Two areas are addressed: functional and nonfunctional.

Functional

For functional reasons (business requirements), applications share data in the following two scenarios:

1. *Read*—Application B physically accesses the data of Application A.
2. *Static image copy*—Application A generates an image copy of a data store that reflects the current state of the data at a certain time and remains within its boundary.

Nonfunctional

For nonfunctional reasons (e.g., performance, security), Application B must use Application A's data as shown in the following four scenarios:

3. *Image copy/load, no additional processing logic*—Application A generates an image copy with no additional processing logic and sends it to Application B; Application B loads the copy with no additional processing logic.
4. *Image copy/load one physical table, no additional processing logic*—Application A generates an image copy of a subset (e.g., Record Element Type, or RET) with no additional processing logic and sends it to Application B. Application B loads the RET with no additional processing logic.
5. *Copy/merge "refresh"*—Data stored in two applications is image copied and merged to form one file that is loaded into a third application.
6. *Screen scraping*—Application B accesses Application A's screen transactions to reference/obtain data to assist in processing a transaction.

Group 2[4]

The primary intent is for Application B to maintain its own data from data maintained by Application A.

7. *Maintain common data store*—The same data store is maintained by two different applications.
8. *Standard transaction data*—The transaction data is provided by the source application.

Analysis

These scenarios are provided to illustrate different occurrences of shared data along with guidelines on what should be measured. Each of the following sections provides a

---

[3] Refer to IFPUG, *Function Point Counting Practices Manual* (CPM), Release 4.3, Part 3, page 3-5.

[4] Refer to IFPUG, *Function Point Counting Practices Manual* (CPM), Release 4.3, Part 3, page 3-6.

description of the scenario, a diagram to aid in understanding it, a counting interpretation, a solution, and a counting summary:

- *Description*—A high-level statement of the example being discussed
- *Scenario*—An example presented that often describes a physical activity or transaction regarding files being transferred between two applications (e.g., sharing data)
- *Scenario diagram*—Graphic depiction of the scenario that serves as an aid to map a similar situation or scenario (arrows in the diagrams reflect the direction of flow of data, not the application initiating the interface)
- *Counting interpretation*—A counting interpretation for the scenario, which includes a discussion of the example and how the example should be counted, as well as any assumptions regarding primary intent
- *Solution diagram*—The solution is depicted graphically
- *Counting summary*—The data and transactional functions applicable to each application are summarized in a table

Symbols Used in Diagram Solution

- ☑ above a component type indicates that the component is counted for application.
- ☒ above a component type indicates that the component would not be counted for the scenario.
- ⇐ in the diagram depicts the direction of flow of data, not the application initiating the interface.

Scenario Naming Conventions

See Table 7.1.

Scenario 1. Read[5]

Description

Application B physically accesses Application A's data to execute a query.

Scenario

A transaction processed by Application B requires information from a data store maintained within Application A. Application B is responsible for accessing the data in Application A, and Application B maintains the software for that access.

---

[5] Refer to IFPUG, *Function Point Counting Practices Manual* (CPM), Release 4.3, Part 3, page 3-7.

Table 7.1   Scenario Naming Conventions

Term	Description
Application A	Application A is the source application for the reference/transaction data.
Application B	Application B is the receiving application for the reference/ transaction data.
File X	File X is an ILF counted in Application A.
File X′ (X Prime)	File X′ is an EIF counted in Application B which is a subset of the File X data.
File Y	File Y is an ILF counted in Application B.
File Z	File Z is a data transfer file generated by Application A and read (processed) by Application B.
Boundaries	Application A and Application B represent two *separate* applications and thus represent two separate boundaries

Diagram

See Figure 7.1.

Counting Interpretation

Application A

From Application A's perspective, there is no requirement to send data. The data is available in Application A. No credit is given to Application A for the transaction performed by Application B, although the data file is an ILF for Application A.

Application B

From Application B's perspective, both logically and physically, there is only one data store involved. Application B counts the data store that resides in Application A as an EIF. Application B also counts that data file as a File Type Referenced (FTR) in the transactional function (EI, EO, or EQ) that uses that data. It is important to note that this

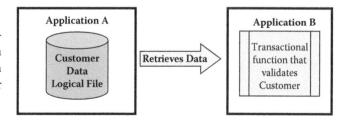

Figure 7.1   Scenario 1: Read diagram.

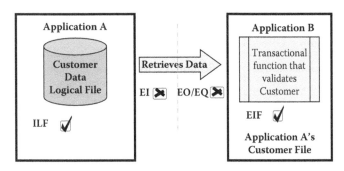

Figure 7.2   Scenario 1: Read solution diagram.

retrieval is not considered a separate transaction, nor are the fields retrieved counted as DETs because they are not considered to be crossing the boundary.

Solution Diagram

See Figure 7.2.

Counting Summary

See Table 7.2.

Scenario 2. Static Image Copy[6]

Description

Application A generates an image copy of an ILF, which reflects the current state of the data at a certain time and remains within its boundary.

Scenario

In the banking industry, financial transactions are settled daily between all financial institutions. Subsequent customer financial transactions are validated against the customer financial balance as of that settlement. To support that business requirement, Application A periodically makes an image copy of the data from the logical file Customer to Customer Prime (Customer′) so other applications can reference it. Customer′ remains within the boundary of Application A. Differences can occur between the current data in Customer and the data in Customer′. Application B makes use of Customer′.

Diagram

See Figure 7.3.

---

[6] Refer to IFPUG, *Function Point Counting Practices Manual* (CPM), Release 4.3, Part 3, page 3-9.

Table 7.2   Scenario 1: Read Summary

	ILF	EIF	EI	EO/EQ
Application A	☑	—	—	—
Application B[a]	—	☑	—	—

[a] Customer is also counted as FTR in transactional function.

Counting Interpretation

Application A

From Application A's perspective, Customer is an Internal Logical File for Application A. Customer′ is not counted as a separate ILF, nor is it counted as a RET of Customer. Customer′ is just a snapshot of Customer at a particular time.

Application B

From Application B's perspective, Customer is an External Interface File (EIF) for Application B and is also counted as an FTR for the transactional function (EI, EO, or EQ) in Application B. This retrieval is not considered a separate transaction, nor are the fields retrieved counted as DETs because they are not considered to be crossing the boundary.

Solution Diagram

See Figure 7.4.

Counting Summary

See Table 7.3.

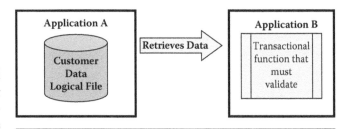

Figure 7.3   Scenario 2: Static image copy diagram.

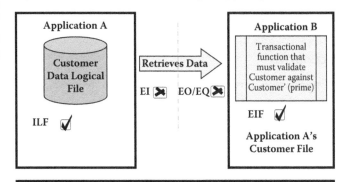

Figure 7.4   Scenario 2: Static image copy solution diagram.

Table 7.3 Scenario 2: Static Image Copy Counting Summary

	ILF	EIF	EI	EO/EQ
Application A	☑	—	—	—
Application B[a]	—	☑	—	—

[a] Customer is also counted as FTR in transactional function.

Scenario 3. Image Copy/Load, No Additional Processing Logic[7]

Description

Application A generates an image copy with no additional processing logic and sends it to Application B; Application B loads a copy with no additional processing logic.

Scenario

Application B requires the ability to access file X in Application A for validation and reference only. Application B requires (e.g., for performance) that Application A send a complete file to Application B. The existing data store in Application B is "refreshed" each time with the copy.

Diagram

See Figure 7.5.

Counting Interpretation

Application A

From Application A's perspective, this data transfer is a technical solution devised to satisfy the business requirement that Application B should have access, for data retrieval purposes, to the Application A File X. Logically, the data store remains in Application A. In this case, copying the data store from one application to another is the solution of a nonfunctional user requirement (e.g., the data in Application A is not available when it is required by Application B).

Application B

The primary intent for Application B is to reference the data that is logically in Application A. One additional indication would be that the file in Application B is "refreshed" each

---

[7] Refer to IFPUG, *Function Point Counting Practices Manual* (CPM), Release 4.3, Part 3, page 3-11.

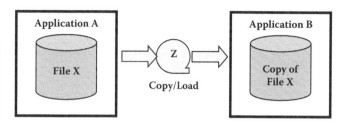

Figure 7.5 Scenario 3: Image copy/load, no additional processing logic diagram.

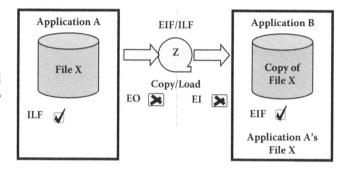

Figure 7.6 Scenario 3: Image copy/load, no additional processing logic solution diagram.

time with the copy. Also, no processing logic is performed in either Application A or Application B.

Data Transfer Transactions

Application A Download and Application B Load are part of the technical solution and are not counted in either application. In practice, when counting Application A in isolation, it may not be apparent to the function point analyst that this exists to satisfy a nonfunctional user requirement, and it may be incorrectly counted as an EO or EQ. Neither application counts File Z as a transactional function.

Files

Only one logical file is involved. Application A counts File X as an ILF. Application B counts its copied version of File X as an EIF. Neither application counts File Z as a data function.

Solution Diagram

See Figure 7.6.

Counting Summary

See Table 7.4.

Table 7.4   Scenario 3: Image Copy/Load, No Additional Processing Counting Summary

	ILF	EIF	EI	EO/EQ
Application A	☑	—	—	—
Application B	—	☑	—	—

Scenario 4. Image Copy/Load One Physical Table, No Additional Processing Logic[8]

Description

Application A generates an image copy of a physical table within a logical file of Application A with no additional processing logic and sends it to Application B. Application B loads the physical table without any additional processing logic.

Scenario

Application B requires (e.g., for performance) the ability to access a portion of File X in Application A for validation and reference only. Application A sends a physical table within a logical file to Application B. The existing view of that physical table in Application B is "refreshed" each time with the copy.

Diagram

See Figure 7.7.

Counting Interpretation

Because the data is an image copy of Application A's data, the File X' Table is part of the logical File X of Application A. Application B counts File X' (with only the data elements used from the File X' Table) as an EIF. Logically, the data store remains in Application A. In this case, copying the data store from one application to another is the solution of nonfunctional user requirements (e.g., the data in Application A is not available when Application B requires it). The primary intent is for Application B to reference the data that logically exist in Application A.

Transactions

Because there are no logical transactional functions in propagating or loading the copy, no transactions are counted for either application to support the copying and loading of the

---

[8] Refer to IFPUG, *Function Point Counting Practices Manual* (CPM), Release 4.3, Part 3, page 3-13.

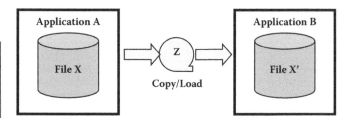

Figure 7.7   Scenario 4: Image copy/load one physical table, no additional processing logic diagram.

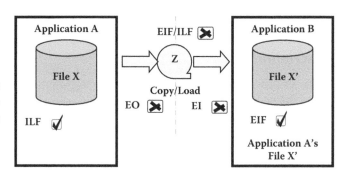

Figure 7.8   Scenario 4: Image copy/load one physical table, no additional processing logic solution diagram.

Table 7.5   Scenario 4: Image Copy/Load One Physical Table, No Additional Processing Counting Summary

	ILF	EIF	EI	EO/EQ
Application A	☑	—	—	—
Application B	—	☑	—	—

shared data. Therefore, Application A does not count the copy to Application B as an EO or EQ, and Application B does not count an EI. One additional indication would be that the file in Application B is "refreshed" each time with the copy.

Files

Only one logical file is involved. Application A counts File X as an ILF. Application B counts its copied table of File X' as an EIF.

Solution Diagram

See Figure 7.8.

Counting Summary

See Table 7.5.

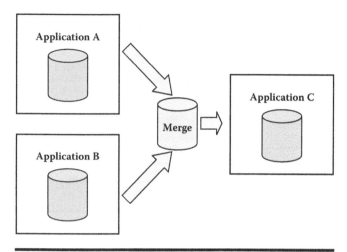

Figure 7.9   Scenario 5: Copy/merge diagram.

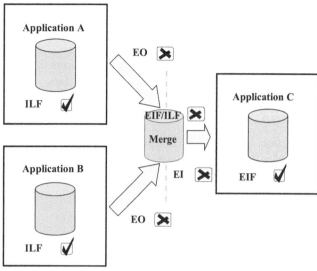

Figure 7.10   Scenario 5: Copy/merge solution diagram.

Scenario 5. Copy/Merge[9]

Description

Data stored in two applications is image copied and merged to form one file that is loaded into a third application. Multiple files with the same data elements are being consolidated into a single file.

Scenario

To avoid the overhead of Application C having to dynamically search the data from both Application A and Application B, the data is copied from Application A and Application B and then merged into a new data store in Application C. The user requires that the information from Application A and Application B be refreshed daily for validation or reference purposes only. Unload, Merge, and Load utilities are used. There is no business processing logic involved. This is typically a technical solution where two applications have different instances of the same logical data required by a third application.

Diagram

See Figure 7.9.

Counting Interpretation

Logically, the data stores remain in Applications A and B. Merging the data into one data store does not by itself create a new ILF for Application C. Again, the primary intent for

Table 7.6   Scenario 5: Copy/Merge Counting Summary

	ILF	*EIF*	*EI*	*EO/EQ*
Application A	☑	—	—	—
Application B	☑	—	—	—
Application C[a]	—	☑	—	—

[a] Also count as FTR in transactional function.

the usage of the data in Application C must be evaluated. Because the data is to be used only for reference or validation and it is a complete refresh, it is counted as an EIF. Because there is no additional processing logic, no transactions are counted for any application.

The data for application C must be evaluated in accordance with CPM 4.3, Part 2, Chapter 6 (Measure Data Functions), and Part 3, Chapter 2 (Logical Files). Even though the data comes from two different applications, the data elements are exactly the same (see the earlier definition for "merge"). Therefore, only a single logical file is identified for Application C as an EIF.

Solution Diagram

See Figure 7.10.

Counting Summary

See Table 7.6.

---

[9] Refer to IFPUG, *Function Point Counting Practices Manual* (CPM), Release 4.3, Part 3, page 3-15.

Scenario 6. Screen Scraping[10]

Description

Accessing another application's screen transactions to reference/obtain data or to update that application's data.

Scenario

Application B reads the content of an inquiry screen in Application A and uses that data in the processing of a transactional function.

Diagram

See Figure 7.11.

Counting Interpretation

Logically, Application B is reading Application A's data. Application A has already counted the data displayed as an EQ or EO (so not counted here), while Application B counts the data as an EIF. From a transaction perspective, Application A is passive and counts nothing extra. For Application B, the screen scraping is part of the elementary process of the transaction and is counted as an FTR (EIF), because the data was originally retrieved from Application A's ILF.

Solution Diagram

See Figure 7.12.

Counting Summary

See Table 7.7.

Scenario 7. Updating the Same Data Store[11]

Description

The same data store is maintained by two different applications.

Scenario

Both Application A and Application B maintain the same ILF. Each has its own unique view of the data. Some common data elements are common to both, and some are unique to each application.

---

[10] Refer to IFPUG, *Function Point Counting Practices Manual* (CPM), Release 4.3, Part 3, page 3-17.
[11] Refer to IFPUG, *Function Point Counting Practices Manual* (CPM), Release 4.3, Part 3, page 3-18.

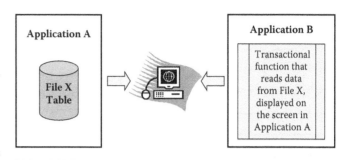

Figure 7.11   Scenario 6: Screen scraping diagram.

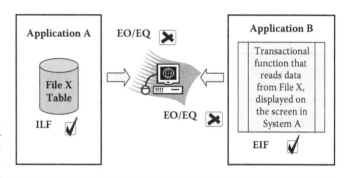

Figure 7.12   Scenario 6: Screen scraping solution diagram.

Table 7.7   Scenario 6: Screen Scraping Counting Summary

	ILF	EIF	EI	EO/EQ
Application A	☑	—	—	—
Application B	—	☑	—	—

Diagram

See Figure 7.13.

Counting Interpretation

An ILF is counted for both applications because each has transactions to maintain it. Applications A and B both maintain data in the same ILF. Each application counts only the RETs and DETs maintained, used, or referenced by that application.

Solution Diagram

See Figure 7.14.

Counting Summary

See Table 7.8.

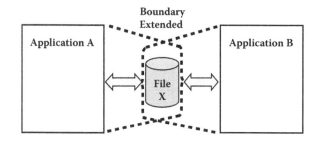

Figure 7.13 Scenario 7: Updating the same data store diagram.

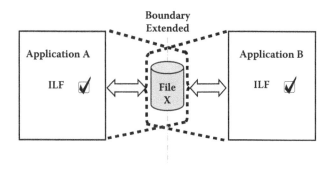

Figure 7.14 Scenario 7: Updating the same data store solution diagram.

Table 7.8 Scenario 7: Updating the Same Data Store Counting Summary

	ILF	EIF	EI	EO/EQ
Application A	☑	—	—	—
Application B	☑	—	—	—

Scenario 8. Standard Transaction Data[12]

Description

Transactional data is provided by the source application.

Scenario

Application A produces a transaction file of changes (File Z), which is loaded into Application B. The records are usually of more than one type. Application B processes the input transactions according to the transaction type on the File Z records, prior to updating the records on internal File Y. The DETs on Application A File X and Application B File Y are

---

[12]Refer to IFPUG, *Function Point Counting Practices Manual* (CPM), Release 4.3, Part 3, page 3-20.

different. For example, File X is a Master Material Catalog while File Y is a local Product List. Processing includes the following transaction types:

■ Add
■ Change
■ Delete

This data transfer is a user business requirement. Both Application A and Application B have a requirement to access a version of the File X; however, the DETs on the two files are different. Application A sends data related to changes only. Application B reads the records on File Z and based on the transaction type initiates different logical processing.

Diagram

See Figure 7.15.

Counting Interpretation

If every record written by Application A to the File Z is processed in the same way only one EO or EQ is counted. Only when there is different logical processing involved might you have multiple transactional functions (e.g., EO/EQ) within a single file. Application B counts EIs for each unique maintenance function on File Y. The number of transaction types on the transaction File Z usually determines the number of these functions, but this is not necessarily the case. Different logical processing must be demonstrated. Two files are involved. Application A counts File X as an ILF, and Application B counts File Y as an ILF. Neither application counts File Z as a logical file.

Solution Diagram

See Figure 7.16.

Counting Summary

See Table 7.9.

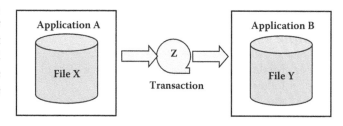

Figure 7.15 Scenario 8: Standard transaction data diagram.

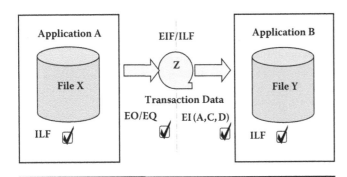

Figure 7.16 Scenario 8: Standard transaction data solution diagram.

Table 7.9 Scenario 8: Standard Transaction Data Counting Summary

	ILF	EIF	EI	EO/EQ
Application A	☑	—	—	☑
Application B	☑	—	☑	—

Further Reading

The rules included in this chapter have been extracted from Part 3, Chapter 3, of the IFPUG *Function Point Counting Practices Manual* (CPM), Release 4.3. A review of this chapter is recommended before taking the CFPS exam.

Exam Guidance

■ Read and study this chapter, including all related examples.
■ Memorize the various terminology:
 – Copy
 – File
 – Image
 – Load
 – Merge
 – Refresh
■ Have a thorough understanding of the various shared data scenarios and know how to count them.
■ Familiarize yourself with the related examples in this chapter as well as CPM 4.3 Part 3, Chapter 3 (Shared Data), because it is unlikely that you will have time to look up everything during the exam.
■ Complete the practice questions in this chapter, and go back to determine why you answered any question incorrectly.

Sample Exam Questions

1. Methods of sharing data include which of the following:
 A. Via online screens (e.g., screen scraping)
 B. Via Web applications
 C. Via on-line, real-time information requests
 D. All of the above

2. The term "copy" means:
 A. To copy computer instructions or data from external storage to internal storage
 B. To read data from a source, leaving the source data unchanged, and to write the same data elsewhere in a physical form that may differ from that of the source
 C. Multiple files with the same data elements are consolidated into a single file
 D. A and B

3. Accessing another application's screen transactions to reference/obtain data or to update that application's data is called:
 A. Image copy
 B. Screen scraping
 C. Image load
 D. Merging

4. Application B requires (for performance, etc.) the ability to access a portion of File X in Application A for validation and reference only. Application A sends a physical table within a logical file to Application B. The existing view of that physical table in Application B is "refreshed" each time with the copy. What is counted for Application A and Application B?
 A. Application A, an ILF; Application B, an EIF
 B. Application A, an ILF; Application B, an ILF
 C. Application A, an EIF; Application B, an EIF
 D. Application A, an EIF; Application B, an ILF

5. Application B requires the ability to access file X in Application A for validation and reference only. Application B requires (for performance, etc.) that Application A send a complete file to Application B. The existing data store in Application B is refreshed each time with the copy. What is counted for Application A and Application B?
 A. Application A, an ILF; Application B, an EIF
 B. Application A, an ILF; Application B, an ILF
 C. Application A, an EIF; Application B, an EIF
 D. Application A, an EIF; Application B, an ILF

6. A transaction processed by Application B, requires information from a data store maintained within Application A. Application B is responsible for accessing the data in Application A, and Application B maintains the software for that access. What is counted for Application A and Application B?
   A. Application A, an ILF; Application B, an ILF
   B. Application A, an ILF; Application B, an EIF and an FTR in the transactional function
   C. Application A, an EIF and an FTR in the transactional function; Application B, an EIF
   D. Application A, an EIF; Application B, an ILF

7. Both Application A and Application B maintain the same ILF. Each has its own unique view of the data. There are some common data elements, and some that are unique to each application. What is counted for Application A and Application B?
   A. Application A, an ILF; Application B, an EIF
   B. Application A, an ILF; Application B, an ILF
   C. Application A, an EIF; Application B, an EIF
   D. Application A, an EIF; Application B, an ILF

8. Application A produces a transaction file of changes (File Z) that is loaded into Application B. The records are usually of more than one type. Application B processes the input transactions according to the transaction type on the File Z records, prior to updating the records on internal File Y. The DETs on Application A File X and Application B File Y are different. Processing includes transaction types Add, Change, and Delete. What is counted for Application A and Application B?
   A. Application A, an ILF and EO/EQ; Application B, an EIF
   B. Application A, an ILF; Application B, an ILF and EI
   C. Application A, an ILF and EO/EQ; Application B, an ILF
   D. Application A, an ILF and EO/EQ; Application B, an ILF and three EIs

9. Application B "reads" the content of an inquiry screen in Application A and uses that data in the processing of a transactional function. For Application B, count:
   A. An EIF
   B. An EIF and EQ
   C. An EIF and EI
   D. An EIF and EO

10. Data stored in two applications (Application A and Application B) is image copied and merged to form one file that is loaded into a third application (Application C). Multiple files with the same data elements are being consolidated into a single file. What ILFs and EIFs are counted for the three applications?
    A. Application A, an ILF; Application B, an ILF; Application C, an ILF
    B. Application A, an EIF; Application B, an EIF; Application C, an EIF
    C. Application A, an ILF; Application B, an ILF; Application C, an EIF
    D. Application A, an EIF; Application B, an ILF; Application C, an EIF

11. The process of recreating a set of data to make it current with its source is the definition of:
    A. Copy
    B. Load
    C. Merge
    D. Refresh

12. To read data from a source, leaving the source data unchanged, and to write the same data elsewhere in a physical form that may differ from that of the source is what is meant by:
    A. Copy
    B. Load
    C. Merge
    D. Refresh

13. An exact replication of another object, file, or table usually created through a utility is the definition of:
    A. Image
    B. Copy
    C. Merge
    D. Refresh

Chapter 8

Enhancements

Introduction

Enhancements add, change, or delete functionality in an existing application. Of the three categories of maintenance (adaptive, corrective, and perfective), enhancements are considered adaptive maintenance. See the "Considerations and Hints" section of this chapter for a more detailed discussion of maintenance categories. As user requests are originated for application enhancement projects, organizations can use the function point method to determine the cost of the deliverable, manage expectations of the end user, and manage the delivery of the software product. An enhancement does not become its own application boundary; it is defined by the counting scope as discussed in Chapter 3 of this book.

The formula to calculate the enhancement project functional size considers the functionality added, changed, and deleted, as well as any conversion functionality to complete the enhancement. An enhancement project will most likely result in a change to the installed application functional size; however, the enhancement project functional size is not merely added to the previous application functional size. The formulas used to size enhancements and applications after enhancements are included in Chapter 10 of this book and in the IFPUG *Function Point Counting Practices Manual*, Release, 4.3, Part 3, Chapter 4 (Enhancement Projects and Maintenance Activities).

This chapter also presents other categories of maintenance (corrective maintenance and perfective maintenance) that are considered to be outside the scope of enhancement projects.

Measuring Enhancement Projects[1]

The *enhancement project functional size* measures the project's modifications to the existing installed application that add, change, or delete user functions. The changes in functionality might result from new or revised user requirements, statutory or regulatory changes, or new users.

Procedure[2]

Table 8.1 provides suggested steps for performing an enhancement project functional size; however, they may be performed in any order.

Scope and Boundary of an Enhancement Project[1]

The enhancement project functional size includes all functions being added, changed, and deleted. The boundary of the application(s) impacted remains the same. The functionality of the application(s) reflects the impact of the functions being added, changed, or deleted. More than one application may be included in the counting scope. If so,

---

[1] Refer to IFPUG, *Function Point Counting Practices Manual* (CPM), Release 4.3, Part 3, page 4-2.

[2] Refer to IFPUG, *Function Point Counting Practices Manual* (CPM), Release 4.3, Part 3, page 4-13.

Table 8.1 Steps for Performing an Enhancement Project Functional Size

Step	Action
1.	Gather and review available documentation.
2.	Meet with the subject matter expert to discuss changes planned/made.
3.	Identify and evaluate added functionality.
4.	Identify and evaluate changed functionality: Determine complexity of the function prior to change (from previous functional size measurement documentation or size as existing prior to change). Determine complexity of the function after change.
5.	Identify and evaluate deleted functionality.
6.	Identify and evaluate any conversion or one-time functionality required to implement this enhancement.

multiple boundaries would be identified, resulting in a separate enhancement project functional size for each affected application. If the total size of the enhancement project is required, it is calculated by summing the enhancement project functional size for all applications included in the counting scope.

Measuring Data Functions in Enhancement Projects[3]

The additions of new Internal Logical Files (ILFs) or External Interface Files (EIFs) by an enhancement project are generally easily identified and measured according to rules defined in Chapter 4 of this book. Consideration, however, should be given to the following:

- If the change involves only the addition of new records to a logical file or new values in an existing attribute within that logical file, there is no justification to count the data function as being changed.
- If a data function is changed because an attribute is added and that attribute is not used by the application being measured, then there is no change to that application.
- In order for a data function to be counted as a changed function, the general guideline is that it must be

structurally altered (e.g., adding or removing an attribute or changing the characteristics of the attribute).

- If an application is required to use (reference or maintain) an existing attribute that it did not previously use, the related data function is considered changed for that application. This can occur without any physical changes to the file.
- If new attributes are added to an ILF, look for new or modified transactional functions that maintain the attribute in that ILF to confirm that a change has occurred.
- If an attribute is added to an ILF that is maintained by two applications and if one application maintains the new attribute but the other only references it, then both applications take credit for the changed ILF. However, the second application will not have any new or changed transactional functions that maintain the attribute in that ILF.
- If an application neither maintains nor references a new or changed attribute, then it cannot take credit for a changed data function.
- If a physical file is added by an enhancement project, it does not necessarily result in a new logical file. First, a determination needs to be made as to whether the new physical file is a change to an existing logical file with additional Data Element Types (DETs) and possibly an additional Record Element Type (RET) or a new logical file.

Measuring Transactional Functions in Enhancement Projects[4]

The additions of new transactional functions by an enhancement project are generally easily identified and measured according to rules defined in Chapter 6 of this book. The identification of transactional functions that have been changed by adding or removing DETs is obvious. It is not as obvious when the user requirements are for changes in processing logic. When processing logic has been altered within an application to meet business requirements, the elementary process that embodies that logic should be identified and counted as being changed. A single change in processing logic does not always affect all related transactions.

For example, when an edit or validation change is made to input processing logic and Add, Delete, Update, and Implied Inquiry transactions exist, then only the Add and Update transactions are counted for the enhancement. Unless there is specific deletion logic change (e.g., referential integrity edit) or query logic change (e.g., selection or retrieval), the Delete and Implied Inquiry transactions will not change.

---

[3] Refer to IFPUG, *Function Point Counting Practices Manual* (CPM), Release 4.3, Part 3, page 4-2.

[4] Refer to IFPUG, *Function Point Counting Practices Manual* (CPM), Release 4.3, Part 3, page 4-3.

In some cases, a specific change may impact how multiple transactional functions are processed. Regardless of whether logic changes were physically made in a common routine used by multiple transactions, changed functions should be identified based on the elementary processes that embody that logic. If multiple elementary processes were affected, then count multiple transactional functions. If only a single elementary process was affected, then count one transaction as being changed. *In all cases, the user requirements and the business view should be the determining factor.* The challenge is to properly assess the appropriate level of functional change. The emphasis must be on the business requirements, with the enhancement project functional size reflecting the intent of the user request.

For example, the business requirements specified by the user for an enhancement project to an existing application could add three new low complexity external inputs (EIs), one low complexity external inquiry (EQ), and three average complexity external outputs (EOs). One average complexity EQ could be deleted. One of the existing low complexity Internal Logical Files (ILFs) could be revised to an average complexity ILF by adding attributes from the new EIs. One average complexity EI for conversion is included. Each of these would be accounted for by the formulas to size the enhancement as well as the revised application functional size; see Chapter 10 of this book for the calculation formulas and results.

Processing Logic[5]

As noted in Chapter 5 of this book, processing logic is defined as any of the requirements specifically requested by the user to complete an elementary process such as validations, algorithms, or calculations and reading or maintaining a data function. Those requirements may include the following actions, which are repeated here and further illustrated to explain how they relate to measuring transactional functions in enhancement projects:

1. *Validations are performed.* For example, when adding a new employee to an organization, the employee process validates the employee type DET.
   - If a requirement exists to perform a different validation or change the validation in an existing transactional function, then the transaction would be counted as changed in the enhancement project functional size.
2. *Mathematical formulas and calculations are performed.* For example, when reporting on all employees within

an organization the process includes calculating the total number of salaried employees, hourly employees, and all employees.
   - If a business requirement exists to modify an existing calculation (e.g., before, the formula was $A + B = C$ but now it is $C = A * B$), then the transaction that includes that calculation would be counted as changed in the enhancement project functional size.
   - Currently, there is a list of employees that is counted as an EQ. The enhancement project requirements state to display summary counts of those employees. The transaction would be identified as changed, and the function type would be changed from an EQ to an EO in the enhancement project functional size.
3. *Equivalent values are converted.* For example, employee age is converted to an age range group using a table.
   - If a business requirement exists to change the functionality to include the ability to convert employee salary into a pay range group, then the transaction would be counted as changed in the enhancement project functional size.
4. *Data is filtered and selected by using specified criteria to compare multiple sets of data.* For example, to generate a list of employees by their assignment, an elementary process compares the job number of a job assignment to select and list the appropriate employees with that assignment.
   - If a requirement exists to modify the selection criteria or add additional selection criteria, excluding changing or adding values, to an existing transaction (a list of employees now needs to display a list of employees who have been in their assignment less than a year), the transaction would be counted as changed in the enhancement project functional size.
   - If a requirement exists to modify only the values of existing criteria, such as selecting a different department or adding an additional department to a list of departments, then there is no count for changing the transaction.
   - If the requirement is to change the selection criteria from a single department to a list of departments, then this would be counted as a change.
   - If a requirement exists to modify the employee search screen to additionally filter on location, then this additional filter does not create a new elementary process. It is counted as a changed function in the enhancement project functional size.

---

[5] Refer to IFPUG, *Function Point Counting Practices Manual* (CPM), Release 4.3, Part 3, page 4-5.

5. *Conditions are analyzed to determine which are applicable.* For example, processing logic exercised by the elementary process when an employee is added will depend on whether an employee is paid based on salary or hours worked. The entry of DETs (and the resulting processing logic) based on a different choice (salary or hourly) in this example is part of one elementary process.

   ■ If a requirement exists to modify the condition or add additional conditions to an existing transaction, then the transaction would be counted as changed in the enhancement project functional size.

6. *One or more ILFs are updated.* For example, when adding an employee, the elementary process updates the employee ILF to maintain the employee data.

   ■ If a business requirement results in updating an additional ILF or different DETs by an existing transaction, the transaction would be counted as changed in the enhancement project functional size.

7. *One or more ILFs or EIFs are referenced.* For example, when adding an employee, the currency EIF is referenced for the correct U.S. dollar conversion rate to determine an employee's hourly rate.

   ■ If a business requirement results in referencing additional ILFs, EIFs, or DETs in an existing transaction, then the affected transaction would be counted as changed in the enhancement project functional size.

8. *Data or control information is retrieved.* For example, to view a list of employees, employee information is retrieved from a data function.

   ■ If the business requirement results in retrieving additional information in an existing transaction, then the affected transaction would be counted as changed in the enhancement project functional size.

9. *Derived data is created by transforming existing data to create additional data.* For example, to determine (derive) a patient's registration number (e.g., SMIJO01), the following data is concatenated: (1) the first three letters of the patient's last name (e.g., SMI for Smith); (2) the first two letters of the patient's first name (e.g., JO for John); (3) a unique two-digit sequence number (starting with 01).

   ■ If the business requirement results in changing how the transaction derives the data, then the affected transaction would be counted as changed in the enhancement project functional size.

10. *Behavior of the application is altered.* For example, the behavior of the elementary process of paying employees is altered when a change is made to pay them every other Friday vs. on the 15th and the last day of the month, resulting in 26 pay periods per year vs. 24.

    ■ If the business requirement results in altering the behavior of the system (e.g., in the example above, the transaction is changed so the pay date parameter affects only hourly employees, not all employees), then the affected transaction would be counted as changed in the enhancement project functional size.

11. *Prepare and present information outside the boundary.* For example, a list of employees is formatted and displayed for the user.

    ■ When the business requirement results in presenting additional DETs outside the boundary, then the affected transaction would be counted as changed in the enhancement project functional size.

    ■ Changes to literals, format, color, or other elements of the physical presentation are not considered changes to the processing logic and therefore are not part of an enhancement project functional size.

    ■ When the business requirement is to send an existing output file to a different or an additional application without a change to any other form of processing logic (e.g., selection criteria, calculations), there is no enhancement project functional size.

    ■ Rearranging data on a screen, report, or file by displaying an existing data element in a new position is not considered a change in processing logic and is not counted for an enhancement.

    ■ Changes to the characteristics (e.g., length, type, precision) of an attribute crossing the boundary must have a change to another form of processing logic (e.g., validations, calculations) to be counted.

    ■ When a new or changed screen function requires additional or modified help, a change to the existing Help function is not counted because there are only new or updated text or values.

12. *Capability exists to accept data or control information that enters the boundary of the application.* For example, a user enters information to add a customer order to the application.

    ■ When the business requirement results in different DETs that enter the boundary, the affected transaction would be counted as changed in the enhancement project functional size.

- When the business requirement is to accept an existing input file from a different or an additional application without changes to any other form of processing logic (e.g., validations, calculations), there is no impact on the enhancement project functional size.
- Changes to the characteristics (e.g., length, type, precision) of an attribute crossing the boundary must have changes to another form of processing logic (e.g., validations, calculations) to be counted.

13. *Sorting or arranging a set of data.* This form of processing logic does not impact the identification of the type or contribute to the uniqueness of an elementary process; that is, the orientation of the data does not constitute uniqueness. For example, a list of employees is sorted in either alphabetical or location order, or, on an order entry screen, the order header information is arranged at the top of the screen and the order details are placed below. *Note:* Changes in sort sequence are typically counted; changes in arrangement by themselves are not typically counted.

- When the business requirement results in changing the existing sort sequence (e.g., user now requests the above-referenced list of employees in location order instead of alphabetical order), the affected transaction would be counted as changed in the enhancement project functional size.
- On an order entry screen, the user requests order header information to be placed to the left of the order detail information instead of above. There is no count for this change.
- The user requests that the Last Name attribute on the Employee Assignment screen be placed to the left of Middle Initial and First Name. There is no change counted for the repositioning. If the requirement is also to prepopulate data based on last name as it is entered, then there is a change to another form of processing logic and the Employee Assignment function is counted.
- The user requests an additional report of the same data (list of employees) sorted by location. A new transaction would not be counted, but a change to the existing transaction would be included in the enhancement project functional size.

Considerations and Hints

Enhancement vs. Maintenance Considerations[6]

Once an application has been developed and installed, it must then be maintained (modified) in order for it to continue to meet the needs of an ever-changing business and technical environment. This maintenance includes a wide range of activities that are performed during this phase of the application life cycle, some of which involve functional changes that are applicable to function point analysis.

Categories of Maintenance

The Institute of Electrical and Electronics Engineers (IEEE) defines three categories of maintenance:

- *Adaptive maintenance*—Software maintenance performed to make a computer program usable in a changed environment.
- *Corrective maintenance*—Software maintenance performed to correct faults in hardware or software.
- *Perfective maintenance*—Software maintenance performed to improve the performance, maintainability, or other attributes of a computer program.

The International Organization for Standardization (ISO) and the International Electrotechnical Commission (IEC) define three categories of maintenance:

- *Adaptive maintenance*—The modification of a software product, performed after delivery, to keep a software product usable in a changed or changing environment. Adaptive maintenance provides enhancements necessary to accommodate changes in the environment in which a software product must operate. These changes are those that must be made to keep pace with the changing environment (ISO/IEC 14764:2006). For example, the operating system might be upgraded and some changes may be made to accommodate the new operating system.
- *Corrective maintenance*—The reactive modification of a software product performed after delivery to correct discovered problems. The modification repairs the software product to satisfy requirements (ISO/IEC 14764:2006). For example, the following fall into a corrective maintenance category:

---

[6] Refer to IFPUG, *Function Point Counting Practices Manual* (CPM), Release 4.3, Part 3, page 4-20.

- Abends
- Incorrect results
- Screen and report formatting errors
- Incorrect calculations
- Incorrect sequence of processing
- Missing data
- Runtime improvements required to meet application specifications
- Usability problems

■ *Perfective maintenance*—Modification of a software product after delivery to detect and correct latent faults in the software product before they are manifested as failures. Perfective maintenance provides enhancements for users, improvement of program documentation, and recoding to improve software performance, maintainability, or other software attributes. Contrast with adaptive maintenance or corrective maintenance (ISO/IEC 14764:2006). For example, the following fall into a perfective maintenance category:
- Changes not required by the customer to avert foreseeable problems
- Application and database changes to improve performance

Functional Size Measurement quantifies the size of business requirements. In an enhancement environment, it measures the effects of changes to those business requirements. Therefore, Functional Size Measurement is applicable to a subset of adaptive maintenance. This includes the software functionality added, changed, or deleted, as well as the software functionality provided to convert data and meet other implementation requirements (e.g., conversion reports).

Other responsibilities that might be categorized outside of application maintenance into the broad area of production support include:

■ Maintenance and monitoring of operations, including the data center, servers, PCs, telecommunications, etc.
■ Support of customer, including help desk and training
■ Package and system software upgrades
■ *Ad hoc* reporting

Further Reading

The rules included in this chapter have been extracted from Part 3, Chapter 4, of the IFPUG *Function Point Counting Practices Manual* (CPM), Release 4.3. A review of that chapter is recommended before taking the CFPS exam. The formulas used to size enhancements and applications after enhancements are included in Chapter 10 of this book.

Exam Guidance

■ Read and study this chapter, including all related examples.
■ Know the various maintenance categories:
- Adaptive
- Corrective
- Perfective
■ Understand how to measure data functions in enhancement projects.
■ Understand how to measure conversion in enhancement projects.
■ Understand how to measure transactional functions in enhancement projects when processing logic has been altered.
■ Familiarize yourself with the related examples in this chapter, as well as CPM 4.3, Part 3, Chapter 4 (Enhancement Projects and Maintenance Activities).
■ Become familiar with the enhancement guidance contained in the CPM 4.3, Part 5, Appendix C (Adjusted Functional Size), because it is unlikely that you will have time to look up everything during the exam
■ Complete the practice questions in this chapter, and go back to determine why you answered any question incorrectly.

Sample Exam Questions

1. A definition of adaptive maintenance is:
   A. Software maintenance performed to make a computer program usable in a changed environment
   B. The reactive modification of a software product performed after delivery to correct discovered problems
   C. Modification of a software product after delivery to detect and correct latent faults in the software product before they are manifested as failures
   D. None of the above

2. A definition of corrective maintenance is:
   A. The reactive modification of a software product performed after delivery to correct discovered problems
   B. The modification of a software product performed after delivery to keep a software product usable in a changed or changing environment
   C. Software maintenance performed to improve the performance, maintainability, or other attributes of a computer program
   D. None of the above

3. The enhancement project functional size measures the project's modifications to the existing installed application that:
   A. Add user functions
   B. Change user functions
   C. Delete user functions
   D. All of the above

4. Which of the following is true of perfective maintenance?
   A. It provides enhancements for users, improvement of program documentation, and recoding to improve software performance, maintainability, or other software attributes
   B. It is a modification of a software product after delivery to detect and correct latent faults in the software product before they are manifested as failures
   C. The modification repairs the software product to satisfy requirements
   D. A and B

5. Suggested steps for performing an enhancement project functional size can include which of the following:
   A. Determine complexity of the function prior to change
   B. Determine complexity of the function after change
   C. Identify and evaluate any conversion or one-time functionality required to implement this enhancement
   D. All of the above

6. Which of the following is a valid condition for a data function to be counted as a changed function?
   A. If the change involves only the addition of new records to a logical file or new values in an existing attribute within that logical file
   B. If a data function is changed because an attribute is added and that attribute is not used by the application being measured
   C. If a data function is structurally altered (e.g., adding or removing an attribute or changing the characteristics of the attribute)
   D. All of the above

7. Which of the following is true for measuring transactions in an enhancement project?
   A. When processing logic has been altered within an application to meet business requirements, the elementary process that embodies that logic should be identified and counted as being changed
   B. A single change in processing logic always affects all related transactions
   C. When an edit or validation change is made to input processing logic and Add, Delete, Update and Implied Inquiry transactions exist, all four transactions (Add, Update, Delete, and Implied Inquiry) are counted for the enhancement
   D. All of the above

Chapter 9

Conversion

Introduction

This chapter provides guidelines and examples of the conversion of application data and describes what should be measured when we transfer existing business application data to a new or enhanced application's Internal Logical Files (ILFs). The conversion process executes against existing data in a separate application to populate one or more logical files in the application being sized in order to fulfill specific user requirements for that application data. The conversion process could require additional data elements to be populated in the process. Conversion considers the source data, the logical files being populated, and the process used for conversion.

Assume that we are populating a customer file in a new application (or we are populating an existing customer file in an application being enhanced). We could have a customer service representative add a customer through a standardized process (the application's transaction to add a customer); however, if we have an existing file of hundreds or thousands of customers, it would take an immense amount of time to enter the data manually. In a conversion process, we write code for a temporary process that will read existing data files, take the attributes from those files, edit and validate those attributes, and place them into the customer file of the application being sized.

When conversion requirements are defined, it is customary to define the data requiring conversion in user terms such as "all customer data," which implies all attributes or data fields encompassed in the logical customer database. The individual Data Element Types (DETs) and Record Element Types (RETs) are the source of the data to be converted. The process of converting the data is not a complete elementary process as defined by the IFPUG *Function Point Counting Practices Manual* (CPM) until all data representing the logical file has been converted and is available for use within the new (or enhanced) application's ILFs. The elementary process

as defined by the CPM includes any exception reports, error reports, conversion reports, or control reports required to ensure the integrity of the data being converted. The new application's ILFs are populated by the converted data, and its user requirements dictate what is required from the existing (old) applications to meet the functional requirements of the new (enhanced) application.

- *Development project functional size* is a measure of the functionality provided to the users with the first release of the software, as measured by the development project function point count by the activity of applying the IFPUG Functional Size Measurement (FSM) Method. The functional size of a development project may include the size of conversion functionality. Count any conversion functionality required by the users to convert data that resided in other existing data files to the new application data files.[1]
- *Enhancement project functional size* is a measure of the functionality added, changed, or deleted at the completion of an enhancement project, as measured by the enhancement project function point count by the activity of applying the IFPUG Functional Size Measurement (FSM) Method. It measures the project's modifications to the existing installed application that add, change, or delete user functions. The functional size of an enhancement project can include the size of conversion functionality. Count any conversion functionality required by the users to convert data that resided in data files of other applications to the new (or enhanced) data files.[2]

---

[1] Refer to IFPUG, *Function Point Counting Practices Manual* (CPM), Release 4.3, Part 1, page 3; Part 2, page 4-2; Part 5, page G-1.

[2] Refer to IFPUG, *Function Point Counting Practices Manual* (CPM), Release 4.3, Part 1, page 4; Part 2, page 4-2; Part 3, page 4-2; Part 5, page G-3.

■ *Application functional size* is a measure of the functionality that an application provides to the user, determined by the application function point count by the activity of applying the IFPUG Functional Size Measurement (FSM) Method. An organization's total installed application function point count represents the sum of the application counts for all installed applications that are currently being utilized and maintained. Do not include conversion functionality in an application count.[3]

Conversion

Conversion functionality is transactional or data functions provided to convert data and/or provide other user-specified conversion requirements. Conversion of application data is based on the user view of the data.[4]

■ The user view of the data encompasses all of the attributes associated with the group of data as defined in the application.
■ This user-recognizable group of data and the associated data attributes become the basis for a logical group of data that fulfills a specific user requirement.
■ This logical file requires all of its data attributes to be maintained as part of the whole (linked and not independent).

New or changed business requirements could require additional attributes. As part of the enhancement project, it might be necessary to convert and populate newly added data attributes. The view of the conversion process is based on all of the following:

■ The original application
■ The logical files being converted
■ The data requirements of the new application

When counting conversion functionality, be aware of the following:

■ When an ILF is added or changed, there is a possibility that a conversion process might be required to populate the new ILFs or DETs in an existing ILF.
■ Part of the analysis is to identify what is crossing the boundary.
■ For new development, the existing data stores or ILFs of the system being replaced are considered to be crossing the boundary.

■ For enhancements involving a changed ILF where processing logic is required to populate the new attribute, the existing ILF is considered to be crossing the boundary as an external input (EI).
■ If a new attribute in an ILF is populated with only a default or null value, conversion should not be counted because data is not crossing the boundary.

Apply the standard elementary process identification rules to identify the conversion functionality, including:

■ Any exception reports
■ Any error reports
■ Any conversion reports
■ Any control reports required to ensure the integrity of the data being converted

The new or enhanced application's ILFs are populated by the converted data, and its user requirements dictate what is required from the old application(s) to meet the Functional User Requirements of the project. The conversion process executes against all data as viewed by the user to create an updated logical file that fulfills specific user requirements for the new or converted application data.

What Is Not Conversion Functionality[5]

Do not count the following as conversion functionality:

■ Software upgrades due to the installation of a revised version of vendor packages
■ The migration of an application to a new platform
■ The conversion of data accomplished via an existing Load utility (no functionality was developed to accomplish the conversion)
■ A changed EIF for the application being measured (only the application that has counted the data function as an ILF can count conversion functionality)

Scenario 1. Enhancement Project Data Conversion

The project involves incorporating data into an existing customer file from an application file of a recently acquired division. This one-time requirement will capture customer data of the recently acquired division and populate those data attributes into the existing corporate customer file ILF.

---

[3] Refer to IFPUG, *Function Point Counting Practices Manual* (CPM), Release 4.3, Part 1, page 2; Part 2, page 4-2; Part 5, page G-3.
[4] Refer to IFPUG, *Function Point Counting Practices Manual* (CPM), Release 4.3, Part 3, page 5-2.

[5] Refer to IFPUG, *Function Point Counting Practices Manual* (CPM), Release 4.3, Part 3, page 5-4.

Count the existing customer data to be imported as an EI. Control and error reports will be produced to ensure the integrity of the migration.

One elementary process initially populates the new data attributes into the existing corporate customer file ILF, including the control and error reports. The conversion process is counted as an EI and is included in the enhancement project function point count but not the application function point count because it is a one-time process. The error and control reports are not counted separately, as they cannot be produced independently from processing the conversion data to which they relate.

Scenario 2. Data Conversion with EIFs Referenced

The user has requested that an ILF (or part of an ILF) be populated from an ILF in another application. In this example, validation is required against yet another ILF from a third application. This conversion is specified as a one-time process, and the data referenced in the third application will not be utilized in the future. The attributes to be loaded serve as an input transaction to populate the receiving ILF that is counted as an EI. The data referenced in the third application for validation is counted as an EIF and an additional File Type Referenced (FTR). The receiving ILF is also considered as an FTR for the conversion transaction. Both the EI and the EIF are counted as conversion functionality for the project but not added to the application functional size.

Scenario 3. Assigning Default Values

An enhancement project requires the addition of an attribute (DET) to an existing human resources personnel ILF. The new DET will be populated with a specific default value of "00005." Although the human resources personnel ILF and any modified transactions utilizing that attribute are counted as changed, no conversion functionality is counted. No data is crossing the application boundary to establish the default value.

Further Reading

The rules included in this chapter have been extracted from Part 3, Chapter 5, of IFPUG *Function Point Counting Practices Manual* (CPM), Release 4.3. A review of this chapter is recommended before taking the CFPS exam.

Exam Guidance

- Read and study this chapter, including all related examples and scenarios.
- Memorize the various definitions and terminology:
  - Development project functional size
  - Enhancement project functional size
  - Application functional size
- Know what is and is not conversion functionality.
- Know what is included in the elementary process of conversion functionality.
- Know how to accurately count a conversion scenario, as it is extremely likely one will be on the exam.
- Familiarize yourself with the related examples and scenarios in this chapter as well as CPM 4.3, Part 3, Chapter 5 (Data Conversion Activity), because it is unlikely that you will have time to look up everything during the exam.
- Complete the practice questions in this chapter, and go back to determine why you answered any question incorrectly.

Sample Exam Questions

1. Which of the following is true of conversion functionality?
   A. It consists of functions used after software installation to satisfy the ongoing business needs of the user
   B. Conversion of application data is based on the user view of the data
   C. It is determined by using the 14 General System Characteristics to rate the application functional complexity
   D. None of the above

2. Which of the following should not be counted as conversion functionality?
   A. Migration of an application to a new platform
   B. Software upgrades due to the installation of a revised version of vendor packages
   C. Conversion of data accomplished via an existing load utility
   D. All of the above

3. Which of the following is true of conversion functionality?
   A. The new or enhanced application's ILF(s) are populated by the converted data, and its user requirements dictate what is required from the old application(s) to meet the Functional User Requirementss of the project

    B.   The elementary process includes any exception reports, error reports, conversion reports, or control reports required to ensure the integrity of the data being converted

    C.   If an EIF for the application being measured is changed, count it as conversion functionality

    D.   A and B

4. The view of the conversion process is based on:

    A.   The original application

    B.   The logical files being converted

    C.   The data requirements of the new application

    D.   All of the above

5. An enhancement project requires populating new data attributes in an ILF of a system and producing control and error reports for this population process. What is counted as conversion functionality?

    A.   One EI and two EQs

    B.   One EI and one EQ

    C.   One EI

    D.   Nothing is counted

Chapter 10

Calculating and Applying Functional Size

The purpose and counting scope shall be considered when selecting and using the appropriate formula to calculate the functional size.

Rules for Calculating New Development[1]

A development project functional size is calculated using the following formula:

$$DFP = ADD + CFP \qquad (10.1)$$

where:

- DFP is the development project functional size.
- ADD is the size of the functions to be delivered to the user by the development project.
- CFP is the size of the conversion functionality.

For example, a development project includes 5 high complexity external inputs (EIs), 20 average complexity EIs, and 10 low complexity EIs; 6 high complexity external queries (EQs), 12 average complexity EQs, and 5 low complexity EQs; and 3 average complexity Internal Logical Files (ILFs) and 8 low complexity ILFs. One low complexity EI for conversion is also included. Using the formula to calculate the development project functional size (Equation 10.1), for this development project:

ADD = 30 + 80 + 30 + 36 + 48 + 15 + 30 + 56 = 325
CFP = 3
DFP = 325 + 3 = 328

Rules for Calculating Application Size[2]

An application functional size from a measurement after the development project or at any time during the application's life cycle shall be calculated using the following formula:

$$AFP = ADD \qquad (10.2)$$

where:

- AFP is the application functional size.
- ADD is the size of the functions to be delivered to the user by the development project (excluding the size of any conversion functionality) or the functionality that exists whenever the application is counted.

Note: Only the size of the application functionality installed for the user is included in the initial application functional size.

In the previous example, the development project delivered 5 high complexity EIs, 20 average complexity EIs, and 10 low complexity EIs; 6 high complexity EQs, 12 average complexity EQs, and 5 low complexity EQs; and 3 average complexity ILFs and 8 low complexity ILFs. One low complexity EI for conversion was also included. Using the formula to calculate the application functional size (Equation 10.2), for this application:

ADD = 30 + 80 + 30 + 36 + 48 + 15 + 30 + 56 = 325
AFP = 325

---

[1] Refer to IFPUG, *Function Point Counting Practices Manual* (CPM), Release 4.3, Part 1, page 20.

[2] Refer to IFPUG, *Function Point Counting Practices Manual* (CPM), Release 4.3, Part 1, page 20; Part 3, page 4-18.

Rules for Calculating Enhancement Projects

An enhancement project functional size shall be calculated using the following formula:[3]

$$EFP = ADD + CHGA + CFP + DEL \qquad (10.3)$$

where:

- EFP is the enhancement project functional size.
- ADD is the size of the functions being added by the enhancement project.
- CHGA is the size of the functions being changed by the enhancement project (as they are and/or will be after implementation).
- CFP is the size of the conversion functionality.
- DEL is the size of the functions being deleted by the enhancement project.

In the previous example, the application consisted of 5 high complexity EIs, 20 average complexity EIs, and 10 low complexity EIs; 6 high complexity EQs, 12 average complexity EQs, and 5 low complexity EQs; and 3 average complexity ILFs and 8 low complexity ILFs for an initial application functional size of 325. The first enhancement project to this application will add 3 low complexity EIs, 1 low complexity EQ, and 3 average complexity external outputs (EOs). One average complexity EQ is deleted. One of the low complexity ILFs will be revised to an average complexity ILF. One average complexity EI for conversion is also included. Using the formula to calculate the enhancement project functional size (Equation 10.3), for this enhancement project:

$$
\begin{aligned}
ADD &= 9 + 3 + 15 = 27 \\
CHGA &= 10 \\
CFP &= 4 \\
DEL &= 4 \\
EFP &= 27 + 10 + 4 + 4 = 45
\end{aligned}
$$

An application functional size after an enhancement project shall be calculated using the following formula:[4]

$$AFPA = (AFPB + ADD + CHGA) - (CHGB + DEL) \quad (10.4)$$

where:

- AFPA is the application functional size after the enhancement project.
- AFPB is the application functional size before the enhancement project.
- ADD is the size of the functions being added by the enhancement project.
- CHGA is the size of the functions being changed by the enhancement project (as they are and/or will be after implementation).
- CHGB is the size of the functions being changed by the enhancement project (as they are and/or were before the project commenced).
- DEL is the size of the functions being deleted by the enhancement project.

Continuing with the previous example after the enhancement project, the enhancement project delivered 3 low complexity EIs, 1 low complexity EQ, and 3 average complexity EOs. One average complexity EQ was deleted. One of the low complexity ILFs was revised to an average complexity ILF. One average complexity EI for conversion is included. The application functional size before the project (the initial application size in this case) was 325. Using the formula to calculate the application functional size after the enhancement project (Equation 10.4), for this application after the enhancement:

$$
\begin{aligned}
AFPB &= 325 \\
ADD &= 9 + 3 + 15 = 27 \\
CHGA &= 10 \\
CHGB &= 7 \\
DEL &= 4 \\
AFPA &= (325 + 27 + 10) - (7 + 4) = 362 - 11 = 351
\end{aligned}
$$

Rules for Calculating Adjusted Functional Size

Some individuals may apply a Value Adjustment Factor (VAF), which considers 14 General System Characteristics (GSCs). For guidance in the use of the VAF and GSCs and the rules and formulas used in calculating adjusted functional size, refer to Chapter 11 of this book.

Further Reading

The rules included in this chapter have been extracted from Part 1 and Part 3, Chapter 4, of the IFPUG *Function Point Counting Practices Manual* (CPM), Release 4.3. A review of these chapters is recommended before taking the CFPS exam.

---

[3] Refer to IFPUG, *Function Point Counting Practices Manual* (CPM), Release 4.3, Part 1, page 21; Part 3, page 4-17.
[4] Refer to IFPUG, *Function Point Counting Practices Manual* (CPM), Release 4.3, Part 1, page 21; Part 3, page 4-19.

Exam Guidance

- Read and study this chapter, including all related examples.
- Become familiar with the formula changes between CPM Release 4.2.1 and CPM Release 4.3, making sure you know what the various acronyms represent (e.g., AFPA, AFPB, ADD, CFP, CHGA, CHGB, DEL, DFP, EFP).
- Make sure you are familiar with and know how to apply the various functional size formulas.
- Familiarize yourself with the related examples in this chapter as well as CPM 4.3, Part 1 (FSM), and Part 3, Chapter 4 (Enhancement Projects and Maintenance Activity), because it is unlikely that you will have time to look up everything during the exam.
- Use the formulas and examples in CPM 4.3, Part 5, Appendix C (Adjusted Functional Size), when using the General System Characteristics and Value Adjustment Factor.
- Complete the practice questions in this chapter, and go back to determine why you answered any question incorrectly.

Sample Exam Questions

1. Which of the following is the correct formula for calculating development project functional size?
   A. EFP = ADD + CHGA + CFP + DEL
   B. DFP = ADD + CFP
   C. AFP = ADD
   D. AFPA = (AFPB + ADD + CHGA) – (CHGB + DEL)

2. Which of the following is the correct formula for calculating an application functional size from a measurement after the development project or at any time during the application's life cycle?
   A. EFP = ADD + CHGA + CFP + DEL
   B. DFP = ADD + CFP
   C. AFP = ADD
   D. AFPA = (AFPB + ADD + CHGA) – (CHGB + DEL)

3. Which of the following is the correct formula for calculating an application functional size after an enhancement project?
   A. EFP = ADD + CHGA + CFP + DEL
   B. DFP = ADD + CFP
   C. AFP = ADD
   D. AFPA = (AFPB + ADD + CHGA) – (CHGB + DEL)

4. Which of the following is the correct formula for calculating an enhancement project functional size?
   A. EFP = ADD + CHGA + CFP + DEL
   B. DFP = ADD + CFP
   C. AFP = ADD
   D. AFPA = (AFPB + ADD + CHGA) – (CHGB + DEL)

Chapter 11

Value Adjustment Factors

Introduction

This chapter introduces General System Characteristics (GSCs) and the Value Adjustment Factor (VAF). The function point counter should keep in mind that neither the GSCs nor the VAF are included in the IFPUG Functional Size Measurement (FSM) Method, and they are considered optional in the IFPUG *Function Point Counting Practices Manual*, Release 4.3. This chapter, however, includes definitions and examples of each GSC as well as the formulas used in computing the VAF and an adjusted functional size (aFP).

When reporting functional size measured using the IFPUG method, the unadjusted functional size is reported which excludes the use of the VAF. When using the GSCs and the resulting VAF to compute an adjusted functional size, the reported size is adjusted and is reported as aFPs, with the lower case "a" denoting "adjusted." The function point counter should always identify the functional size as FP or aFP.

The text that follows has been extracted predominately from Part 5, Appendix C, of the IFPUG *Counting Practices Manual* (CPM), Release 4.3, in order to retain the rules and definitions that may be included in the certified function point specialist exam. Please refer to the CPM for complete definitions, examples, and formulas relevant to adjusting the functional size of projects and applications.

Value Adjustment Factor Determination[1]

- The Value Adjustment Factor is based on 14 General System Characteristics that rate the general functionality of the application being measured.

- Each characteristic has associated descriptions that help determine the Degree of Influence of that characteristic.
- The Degree of Influence for each characteristic is measured on a scale from 0 to 5 (no influence to strong influence).
- The 14 General System Characteristics are summarized in the Value Adjustment Factor.
- When applied, the Value Adjustment Factor adjusts the unadjusted functional size ±35% to produce the adjusted functional size.

Procedures to Determine the VAF[2]

Table 11.1 outlines the procedures to determine the Value Adjustment Factor.

General System Characteristics

The General System Characteristics are a set of 14 questions that evaluate the overall complexity of the application.[3] The 14 General System Characteristics are:

1. Data Communications
2. Distributed Data Processing
3. Performance
4. Heavily Used Configuration

---

[1] Refer to IFPUG, *Function Point Counting Practices Manual* (CPM), Release 4.3, Part 5, Appendix C, page C-4.

[2] Refer to IFPUG, *Function Point Counting Practices Manual* (CPM), Release 4.3, Part 5, Appendix C, page C-4.

[3] Refer to IFPUG, *Function Point Counting Practices Manual* (CPM), Release 4.3, Part 5, Appendix C, page C-5.

Table 11.1 Procedures to Determine the VAF

Step	Action
1.	Evaluate each of the 14 General System Characteristics on a scale from 0 to 5 to determine the Degree of Influence (DI).
2.	Add the Degrees of Influence for all 14 General System Characteristics to produce the Total Degree of Influence (TDI).
3.	Insert the TDI into the following equation to produce the Value Adjustment Factor: $$VAF = (TDI \times 0.01) + 0.65$$ For example, the following Value Adjustment Factor is calculated if there are 3 Degrees of Influence for each of the 14 GSC descriptions (3×14): $$VAF = (42 \times 0.01) + 0.65 = 1.07$$

5. Transaction Rate
6. On-Line Data Entry
7. End-User Efficiency
8. On-Line Update
9. Complex Processing
10. Reusability
11. Installation Ease
12. Operational Ease
13. Multiple Sites
14. Facilitate Change

Degrees of Influence[4]

Based on the stated user requirements, each General System Characteristic must be evaluated in terms of its Degree of Influence (DI) on a scale of 0 to 5 (see Table 11.2).

Guidelines to Determine Degree of Influence for GSCs

Each of the following General System Characteristic descriptions includes guidelines to determine the Degree of Influence. Each GSC guideline contains a definition of the GSC, rules for determining the score, and, in situations where the rule requires further clarification, hints have been provided to help apply the rules consistently across all platforms. Hints are not intended to cover all situations but are meant to provide additional guidance in determining the appropriate score.

Table 11.2 Degrees of Influence

Score as	System Influence
0	Not present or no influence
1	Incidental influence
2	Moderate influence
3	Average influence
4	Significant influence
5	Strong influence throughout

Data Communications[5]

Definition

Data Communications describes the degree to which the application communicates directly with the processor. The data and control information used in the application are sent or received over communication facilities. Devices connected locally to the control unit are considered to use communication facilities. *Protocol* is a set of conventions that permit the transfer or exchange of information between two systems or devices. All data communication links require some type of protocol.

Score

See Table 11.3.

Hints

Protocol examples include FTP, dial-up, Token Ring, Ethernet, SNA, TCP/IP, IPX/SPX, HTTP, XML, WAP, NTP, ICQ, and NETBEUI. This list should *not* be considered exhaustive.

Hints to Rules 1 and 2

■ Remote devices might include a 3270 terminal connected to a mainframe computer that allows only simple edits (numeric vs. alpha) or printers connected via parallel port (the user can specify where to direct the output).

■ The entry of data does not involve reading or writing directly to an Internal Logical File (ILF). Data is entered on-line, but the transactions are stored in a temporary file for batch update of ILFs at a later time.

---

[4] Refer to IFPUG, *Function Point Counting Practices Manual* (CPM), Release 4.3, Part 5, Appendix C, page C-6.

[5] Refer to IFPUG, *Function Point Counting Practices Manual* (CPM), Release 4.3, Appendix C, page C-7.

Table 11.3   Data Communications

Score as	Descriptions to Determine Degree of Influence
0	Application is pure batch processing or a stand-alone application.
1	Application is batch but has remote data entry *or* remote printing.
2	Application is batch but has remote data entry *and* remote printing
3	Application includes on-line data collection or TP (teleprocessing) front end to a batch process or query system.
4	Application is more than a front end but supports only *one type* of TP communications.
5	Application is more than a front end and supports *more than one type* of TP communication protocol.

Table 11.4   Distributed Data Processing

Score as	Descriptions to Determine Degree of Influence
0	Data is not transferred or processed on another component of the system.
1	Data is prepared for transfer then are transferred and processed on another component of the system for user processing.
2	Data is prepared for transfer then is transferred and processed on another component of the system, *not* for user processing.
3	Distributed processing and data transfer are on-line and in *one* direction only.
4.	Distributed processing and data transfer are on-line and in *both* directions.
5	Distributed processing and data transfer are on-line and are dynamically performed on the most appropriate component of the system.

Hints to Rule 3

■ Simple business rules and minimal edits (e.g., alpha/numeric, range check, required data) may be performed. When this data is eventually processed by the application, additional edits are performed.

■ The entry of data does not involve reading or writing directly to an ILF. Data is entered on-line, but the transactions are stored in a temporary file for batch update of ILF(s) at a later time.

Hints to Rule 4

■ Data for the application is collected and may directly update ILF(s) or be stored for future processing using an input device that performs edits based on business rules.

■ Only one communication protocol is used. Typically, when the data is processed by the application, no further edits are required.

■ The entry of data involves reading or writing to an ILF.

■ Examples include client–server data entry or Internet data entry, but not both.

Hints to Rule 5

■ Same as for Rule 4; however, data collection is performed using multiple telecommunication protocols.

■ Examples include client–server data entry and Internet data entry of the same transaction.

Typically

■ Batch applications receive a score of 0 to 3.
■ On-line applications receive a score of 4.
■ Web-based applications receive a score of 4 or 5.
■ Real-time, telecommunication, or process control systems receive a score of 4 or 5.

Distributed Data Processing[6]

Definition

Distributed Data Processing describes the degree to which the application transfers data among physical components of the application. Distributed data or processing functions are a characteristic of the application within the application boundary.

Score

See Table 11.4.

---

[6] Refer to IFPUG, *Function Point Counting Practices Manual* (CPM), Release 4.3, Part 5, Appendix C, page C-9.

Hints

Distributed Data Processing, by definition, is not an application that is contained on a central processor that sends data to other applications. In a distributed environment, the application is viewed as requiring multiple components (hardware) on which certain processing or data resides. A knowledgeable user would usually recognize this configuration.

Hint to Rule 0

Presentation, processing, and I/O components are all in the same place (i.e., stand-alone applications).

Hints to Rule 1

- Application downloads data to a user's client machine so the user can use Excel® or other reporting tools to prepare graphs and perform other analysis.
- Process transfers data from the mainframe to an external component for user processing. This transfer is performed using a simple protocol such as FTP.
- Data is transferred to a user for processing.

Hints to Rule 2

- Process transfers data from the mainframe to mid-tier—for example, processing with SAS-PC.
- Application sends data to the client or server. The data is then processed or used to produce reports, etc. No data or confirmation is sent back to the client or server.
- Data is transferred to a component for processing.

Hint to Rule 3

- Data is sent between the client and server in *one* direction only. The data is then processed or used to produce reports, etc. by the receiving application. This data typically includes transactions that update an ILF on the client or server.
- Examples include client–server or Web-enabled applications.

Hint to Rule 4

- Data is sent between client and server in *either* direction. This data is then processed or used to produce reports, etc. by the receiving application. The data typically includes transactions that update an ILF on the client or server.
- Examples include client–server or Web-enabled applications.

- The application runs under an operating system that automatically handles the allocation between components; however, the use of the operating system did not influence the design and implementation of the application.

Hint to Rule 5

- The developer must consider special application software that looks at multiple processors and runs the application on a specific type of processor. This is invisible to the user.
- The application runs under an operating system that automatically handles the dynamic allocation between components, and the use of the operating system specifically influenced the design and implementation of the application.

Typically

- Many applications, including legacy applications, receive a score of 0.
- Primitive distributed applications that include batch applications in which data is not transferred on-line receive a score of 1 to 2.
- Client–server or Web-based applications receive a score of 3 to 4.
- It is uncommon to score 5.
- There must be multiple servers or processors, each of which would be selected dynamically on the basis of its real-time availability, to score 5.

Performance[7]

Definition

Performance describes the degree to which response time and throughput performance considerations influenced the application development. Application Performance objectives, stated or approved (or implied) by the user, in either response or throughput, influence (or will influence) the design, development, installation, and support of the application.

Score

See Table 11.5.

---

[7] Refer to IFPUG, *Function Point Counting Practices Manual* (CPM), Release 4.3, Part 5, Appendix C, page C-11.

Table 11.5 Performance

Score as	Descriptions to Determine Degree of Influence
0	No special Performance requirements were stated by the user.
1	Performance and design requirements were stated and reviewed but no special actions were required.
2	Response time or throughput is critical during *peak* hours. No special design for CPU utilization was required. Processing deadline is for the next business cycle.
3	Response time or throughput is critical during *all* business hours. No special design for CPU utilization was required. Processing deadline requirements with interfacing systems are constraining.
4	In addition, stated user Performance requirements are stringent enough to require Performance analysis tasks in the design phase.
5	In addition, Performance analysis tools were used in the design, development, and/or implementation phases to meet the stated user Performance requirements.

Table 11.6 Heavily Used Configuration

Score as	Descriptions to Determine Degree of Influence
0	No explicit or implicit operational restrictions are included.
1	Operational restrictions do exist but are less restrictive than a typical application. No special effort is needed to meet the restrictions.
2	Operational restrictions do exist but are typical for an application. Special effort through controllers or control programs is needed to meet the restrictions.
3	Stated operational restrictions require special constraints on *one* piece of the application in the central processor or a dedicated processor.
4	Stated operational restrictions require special constraints on the *entire* application in the central processor or a dedicated processor.
5	In addition, there are special constraints on the application in the distributed components of the system.

Hints

■ The General System Characteristics of Performance, Heavily Used Configuration, and Transaction Rate (GSCs 3, 4, and 5) are somewhat related. For this GSC, think in terms of: "How fast can we make the application go and how much did/does that impact the design, development, and/or implementation?"

■ The users may require real-time access to their data, stating or implying standards for response time and throughput capacity.

■ Response time typically relates to interactive processing; throughput relates to batch processing

Typically

■ Batch applications receive a score of 0 to 4.
■ On-line (including interactive client–server or Web-enabled) applications receive a score of 0 to 4.
■ Web-based applications receive a score of 4 or 5.
■ Most MIS on-line systems receive a score of 2.

■ Real-time, telecommunication, or process control systems receive a score of 0 to 5.
■ A score of 5 requires the use of performance analysis tools.

Heavily Used Configuration[8]

Definition

Heavily Used Configuration describes the degree to which computer resource restrictions influenced the development of the application. A heavily used operational configuration may require special considerations when designing the application; for example, the user wants to run the application on existing or committed equipment that will be heavily used.

Score

See Table 11.6.

---

[8] Refer to IFPUG, *Function Point Counting Practices Manual* (CPM), Release 4.3, Part 5, Appendix C, page C-13.

Hints

- The General System Characteristics of Performance, Heavily Used Configuration, and Transaction Rate (GSCS 3, 4, and 5) are somewhat related.
- For this GSC, think in terms of: "How much does the infrastructure influence the design?"

Examples

Examples of operational restrictions may include the following (not an exhaustive list):

- This question indicates that the application must run on a computer that is underpowered and cannot adequately handle the new or changed functionality and that somehow the developers can overcome this by developing the application differently.
- More than one application accessing the same data can create operational restrictions.
- Applications competing for the same resources and technologies with the potential deadlocks must be tuned and constrained to avoid performance degradation.

Typically

- Most applications receive a score of 2.
- Client–server, Web-enabled, real-time, telecommunication, or process control systems receive a score of 3 to 5, but then you would need either a dedicated processor or multiple processors processing the same transactions and searching for the most expeditious means of processing.

Transaction Rate[9]

Definition

The *Transaction Rate* describes the degree to which the rate of business transactions influenced the development of the application. The Transaction Rate is high, and it influences the design, development, installation, and support of the application. Users may require what they regard as normal response time even during times of peak volume.

Table 11.7 Transaction Rate

Score as	Descriptions to Determine Degree of Influence
0	No peak transaction period is anticipated
1	Low Transaction Rates have minimal effect on the design, development, and installation phases.
2	Average Transaction Rates have some effect on the design, development, and installation phases.
3	High Transaction Rates affect the design, development, and/or installation phases.
4	High Transaction Rates stated by the user in the application requirements or service-level agreements are high enough to require Performance analysis tasks in the design, development, and/or installation phases.
5	High Transaction Rates stated by the user in the application requirements or service-level agreements are high enough to require Performance analysis tasks and, in addition, the use of Performance analysis tools in the design, development, and/or installation phases.

Score

See Table 11.7.

Hints

- The General System Characteristics of Performance, Heavily Used Configuration, and Transaction Rate (GSCs 3, 4, and 5) are somewhat related. For this GSC, think in terms of: "How many transactions can be processed by the application in a given period of time?"
- Often this score is the same as the score for the Performance GSC because Transaction Rates often influence Performance requirements.

Typically

- Batch applications receive a score of 0 to 3.
- On-line (including interactive client–server or Web-enabled) applications receive a score of 0 to 4.
- Real-time, telecommunication, or process control systems receive a score of 0 to 5.
- A score of 5 requires the use of performance analysis tools.

---

[9] Refer to IFPUG, *Function Point Counting Practices Manual* (CPM), Release 4.3, Part 5, Appendix C, page C-15.

Table 11.8   On-Line Data Entry

Score as	Descriptions to Determine Degree of Influence
0	All transactions are processed in batch mode.
1	1 to 7% of transactions are interactive.
2	8 to 15% of transactions are interactive.
3	16 to 23% of transactions are interactive.
4	24 to 30% of transactions are interactive.
5	More than 30% of transactions are interactive.

On-Line Data Entry[10]

Definition

On-Line Data Entry describes the degree to which data is entered or retrieved through interactive transactions. On-line user interfaces for data entry, control functions, reports, and queries are provided in the application.

Score

See Table 11.8.

Hint

This refers to types of transactions, not volumes. For example, if an application has 45 external inputs (EIs), external outputs (EOs), and external inquiries (EQs), what percent of the EIs, EOs, and EQs are accomplished via on-line transactions?

Typically

■ Batch applications receive a score of 0 to 1.
■ On-line, real-time, telecommunication, or process control systems receive a score of 5.
■ Most contemporary on-line (including interactive client–server or Web-enabled) applications receive a score of 5.
■ Batch systems with on-line features may have a lot of batch transactions, but there must be at least 71% batch to receive a score of less than 5.

End-User Efficiency[11]

Definition

End-User Efficiency describes the degree of consideration for human factors and ease of use for the user of the application measured. The on-line functions provided emphasize a design for user efficiency (human factor/user friendliness). The design includes:

■ Navigation aids (e.g., function keys, jumps, dynamically generated menus, hyperlinks)
■ Menus
■ On-line help and documents
■ Automated cursor movement
■ Scrolling
■ Remote printing (via on-line transmissions)
■ Preassigned function keys (e.g., clear screen, request help, clone screen)
■ Batch jobs submitted from on-line transactions
■ Drop-down list box
■ Heavy use of reverse video, highlighting, colors, underlining, and other indicators
■ Hard-copy documentation of on-line transactions (e.g., screen print)
■ Mouse interface
■ Pop-up windows
■ Templates and/or defaults
■ Bilingual support (supports two languages; count as four items)
■ Multilingual support (supports more than two languages; count as six items)

Score

See Table 11.9.

Hints

■ Use a convention of a score of 4 whenever the application is deployed in a graphical user interface (GUI) environment (unless it scores 5).
■ Usually, only software environments that prepare applications for mass-market or nontechnical users score 5, and then only if they have ergonomics specialists and/ or usability studies as part of their process.

---

[10] Refer to IFPUG, *Function Point Counting Practices Manual* (CPM), Release 4.3, Part 5, Appendix C, page C-16.

[11] Refer to IFPUG, *Function Point Counting Practices Manual* (CPM), Release 4.3, Part 5, Appendix C, page C-17.

Table 11.9   End-User Efficiency

Score as	Descriptions to Determine Degree of Influence
0	None of the components listed.
1	One to three of the components listed.
2	Four to five of the components listed.
3	Six or more of the components listed, but there are no specific user requirements related to efficiency.
4	Six or more of the components listed, and stated requirements for user efficiency are strong enough to require *design tasks* for human factors to be included.
5	Six or more of the components listed, and stated requirements for user efficiency are strong enough to require *use of special tools and processes* in order to demonstrate that the objectives have been achieved.

Table 11.10   On-Line Update

Score as	Descriptions to Determine Degree of Influence
0	None.
1	On-Line Update of one to three control files is included. Volume of updating is low and recovery is easy.
2	On-Line Update of four or more control files is included. Volume of updating is low and recovery is easy.
3	On-Line Update of major Internal Logical Files is included.
4	In addition, protection against data loss is essential and has been specially designed and programmed in the system.
5	In addition, high volumes bring cost consideration into the recovery process. Highly automated recovery procedures with minimum human intervention are included.

Typically

- Pure batch applications receive a score of 0.
- Character mode user interface receives a score of 1 or possibly a 2.
- GUI to be used for low-volume transactions receives a score of 3.
- GUI Web interface to be used for high-volume transactions and most Web *Intranet* user interfaces receive a score of 4 (requires design tasks for human factors).
- Web *Internet* user interfaces receive a score of 5 (requires special tools and processes to demonstrate that the objectives have been achieved).

On-Line Update[12]

Definition

On-Line Update describes the degree to which Internal Logical Files (ILFs) are updated on-line. The application provides On-Line Update for the ILFs.

Score

See Table 11.10.

Hints

- On-Line Update usually requires a keyed file or database.
- Automatic recovery provided by the operating system counts if it impacts the application.

Typically

- Pure batch applications receive a score of 0.
- On-Line Updates of files that modify the way an application processes or validates data receive a score of 1 or 2.
- On-Line Updates of user persistent data receive a score of 3.
- MIS applications receive a score of 3 or less.
- Most GUI-type applications receive a score of 3 or above.
- Applications that use programmed recovery, such as SQL roll back and commit, receive a score of 4. Operational/routine back-up is not considered protection against data loss.
- Applications required to recover data, reboot, or perform other self-contained functions in the event of a system error receive a score of 5. Recovery may require a human to press enter or perform some other minimal function to initiate this process.

---

[12]Refer to IFPUG, *Function Point Counting Practices Manual* (CPM), Release 4.3, Part 5, Appendix C, page C-19.

Table 11.11 Complex Processing

Score as	Descriptions to Determine Degree of Influence
0	None of the components listed.
1	Any one of the components listed.
2	Any two of the components listed.
3	Any three of the components listed.
4	Any four of the components listed.
5	All five of the components listed.

Complex Processing[13]

Definition

Complex Processing describes the degree to which processing logic influenced the development of the application. The following components are present:

- Sensitive control and/or application-specific security processing
- Extensive logical processing
- Extensive mathematical processing
- Much exception processing, resulting in incomplete transactions that must be processed again
- Complex Processing to handle multiple input/output possibilities

Score

See Table 11.11.

Hints

- Sensitive control or security processes (e.g., individual users would have different access authority to screens where they could view and/or change data) may include special audit processing (audit data would be captured whenever the data was viewed and/or changed and reported).
- Application-specific security processing may include internally developed security processing or the use of purchased security packages.
- Extensive logical processing is Boolean logic (use of AND, OR) of greater than average difficulty or a minimum of four nested conditional (IF, CASE) statements. Extensive logical processing does not occur in most MIS applications.

Table 11.12 Reusability

Score as	Descriptions to Determine Degree of Influence
0	No reusable code.
1	Reusable code is used within the application.
2	Less than 10% of the application code developed is intended for use in more than one application.
3	10% or more of the application code developed is intended for use in more than one application.
4	Application was specifically packaged and/or documented to ease reuse, and application is customized at the source code level.
5	Application was specifically packaged and/or documented to ease reuse, and application is customized for use by means of user parameter maintenance.

- Extensive mathematical processing is arithmetic that is beyond the capability of a four-function calculator (add, subtract, multiply, divide). This is usually not present in most MIS applications; however, an engineering application may qualify.
- Exception processing includes incomplete ATM transactions caused by TP interruption, missing data values, failed validations, or cycle redundancy checks, which can be used to recreate lost pieces of data.
- Multiple input/output possibilities include multimedia, device independence, voice, OCR readers, barcode reading, retinal scanning, and breathalyzer analysis.

Typically

Scoring is not platform dependent.

Reusability[14]

Definition

Reusability describes the degree to which the application and the code in the application have been specifically designed, developed, and supported to be usable in *other* applications.

Score

See Table 11.12.

---

[13] Refer to IFPUG, *Function Point Counting Practices Manual* (CPM), Release 4.3, Part 5, Appendix C, page C-20.

[14] Refer to IFPUG, *Function Point Counting Practices Manual* (CPM), Release 4.3, Part 5, Appendix C, page C-22.

Hints

Hints for Rule 1

- A score of 1 is awarded for reusing code regardless of where it was developed.
- Code developed specifically for reuse within the application and used more than once within the application counts, as well as code retrieved from a central library and available for general use.

Hints for Rule 2

- To score 2 or more, the code must be developed for use in more than one application, stored and managed in a central library, and available for general use. Code from one application that is cut and pasted into another application is not considered reuse.
- The reusable code would be supported by documentation that enables and eases the reuse.

Hints for Rule 5

- Examples of applications customized through use of parameters include PeopleSoft® and SAP® and would generally receive a score of 5.
- Reused code may be slightly modified in the receiving application.
- Examples of reuse include objects or other static code maintained in an object/code library.

Typically

Scoring is not platform dependent.

Installation Ease[15]

Definition

Installation Ease describes the degree to which conversion from previous environments influenced the development of the application. Conversion and Installation Ease are characteristics of the application. A conversion and installation plan and/or conversion tools were provided and tested during the system test phase.

Score

See Table 11.13.

---

[15] Refer to IFPUG, *Function Point Counting Practices Manual* (CPM), Release 4.3, Part 5, Appendix C, page C-23.

Table 11.13 Installation Ease

Score as	Descriptions to Determine Degree of Influence
0	No special considerations were stated by the user, *and* no special setup is required for installation.
1	No special considerations were stated by the user, *but* special setup is required for installation.
2	Conversion and installation requirements were stated by the user, and conversion and installation guides were provided and tested. The impact of conversion on the project *is not* considered to be important.
3	Conversion and installation requirements were stated by the user, and conversion and installation guides were provided and tested. The impact of conversion on the project *is* considered to be important.
4	In addition to 2 above, automated conversion and installation tools were provided and tested.
5	In addition to 3 above, automated conversion and installation tools were provided and tested.

Hints

- Conversion and installation includes converting preexisting data into new data files, loading files with actual data, and/or developing special installation software, such as porting.
- Purchased or developed software must be used in order to take credit for installation and conversion.

Hint for Rule 1

Most business applications require some special setup to install the application and receive a score of 1.

Hint for Rule 2

If the application has conversion and installation requirements and installation guides were provided, and providing these functions and guides were not on the critical path of the project, score a 2.

Hint for Rule 3

If the application has conversion and installation requirements and installation guides were provided, and providing these functions and guides were on the critical path of the project, score a 3.

Hint for Rule 4 and 5

If the application has conversion and installation requirements and can be installed with no external intervention, score a 4 or 5, depending on the other requirements for the scoring of 2 or 3.

Typically

Scoring is not platform dependent.

Operational Ease[16]

Definition

Operational Ease describes the degree to which the application attends to operational aspects, such as start-up, back-up, and recovery processes. Operational Ease is a characteristic of the application. The application minimizes the need for manual activities, such as tape mounts, paper handling, and direct on-location manual intervention.

Score

See Table 11.14.

Hints

Hint for Rule 1-4a

Application has the ability to perform start-up, back-up, and recovery; however, human response is required to initiate the function.

Hint for Rule 1-4b

Application has the ability to perform start-up, back-up, and recovery, and no human response is required to initiate the function.

Hints for Rule 1-4c

■ The application minimizes the need to access data that is not immediately available.
■ This may include importing data from a distributed processor to the local processor prior to execution to eliminate access delays.

Table 11.14 Operational Ease

Score as	Descriptions to Determine Degree of Influence
0	No special operational considerations other than the normal back-up procedures were stated by the user.
1–4	One, some, or all of the following items apply to the application. Select all that apply. Each item has a point value of one, except as noted otherwise: • Start-up, back-up, and recovery processes were provided, but human intervention is required. • Start-up, back-up, and recovery processes were provided, but *no* human intervention is required (count as two items). • The application minimizes the need for tape mounts and/or remote data access requiring human intervention. • The application minimizes the need for paper handling.
5	The application is designed for unattended operation. Unattended operation means *no human intervention* is required to operate the system other than to start up or shut down the application. Automatic error recovery is a feature of the application.

Hints for Rule 1-4d

■ The application has been designed to provide the user with data in a condensed format or via a media other than paper.
■ This could include elimination of detailed printed information or access to on-line reports, inquiries, microfiche, CD, or other such media.

Hints for Rule 5

■ A score of 5 is assigned to an application that runs and recovers automatically from errors, on its own—an unattended operation.
■ Unattended operation may include unmanned satellites, nuclear reactors, or air traffic control.

Typically

Scoring is not platform dependent.

---

[16] Refer to IFPUG, *Function Point Counting Practices Manual* (CPM), Release 4.3, Part 5, Appendix C, page C-25.

Table 11.15 Multiple Sites

Score as	Descriptions to Determine Degree of Influence
0	The needs of *only one* installation site were considered in the design.
1	The needs of more than one installation site were considered in the design, and the application is designed to operate only under *identical* hardware and software environments.
2	The needs of more than one installation site were considered in the design, and the application is designed to operate only under *similar* hardware and/or software environments.
3	The needs of more than one installation site were considered in the design, and the application is designed to operate under *different* hardware or software environments.
4	Documentation and support plans are provided and tested to support the application at multiple installation sites and the application is as described by 2.
5	Documentation and support plans are provided and tested to support the application at multiple installation sites and the application is as described by 3.

Multiple Sites[17]

Definition

Multiple Sites describes the degree to which the application has been developed for different hardware and software environments.

Score

See Table 11.15.

Hints

The term *Multiple Sites* is a logical term and is not necessarily physical. There can be Multiple Sites within the same physical location. The determining factor is based on the needs of the various installations.

Hint for Rule 0

Most mainframe applications would probably score 0; however, if an application is installed on multiple mainframe computers with significantly different configurations or different operating systems, it would receive a score of greater than 0.

Hint for Rule 1

An example would be Windows® NT on hardware with exactly the same configuration.

Hints for Rule 2

■ Examples include Windows® 95, 98, and NT on hardware with a similar configuration.
■ Variations could include different memory sizes, various storage capability, different processor speeds, and different printer types.

Hints for Rule 3

■ Examples include Windows®, Mac OS® X, UNIX®, Linux™, and VOS3 on different types of hardware.
■ Differences could include Intel®-based PCs, Mac®, Tandem, Sun, and AS400.

Typically

Scoring is dependent on the number of different platforms.

Facilitate Change[18]

Definition

Facilitate Change describes the degree to which the application has been developed for easy modification of processing logic or data structure. The following characteristics can apply for the application:

A. Flexible Query
   ■ A Flexible Query and Report facility is provided that can handle simple requests (count as 1 item).
   ■ A Flexible Query and Report facility is provided that can handle requests of average complexity (count as 2 items).
   ■ A Flexible Query and Report facility is provided that can handle complex requests (count as 3 items).

---

[17] Refer to IFPUG, *Function Point Counting Practices Manual* (CPM), Release 4.3, Part 5, Appendix C, page C-27.

[18] Refer to IFPUG, *Function Point Counting Practices Manual* (CPM), Release 4.3, Part 5, Appendix C, page C-29.

Table 11.16 Facilitate Change

Score as	Descriptions to Determine Degree of Influence
0	None of the items listed.
1	A total of one of the items listed.
2	A total of two of the items listed.
3	A total of three of the items listed.
4	A total of four of the items listed.
5	All five of the items listed.

Table 11.17 Calculating Adjusted Functional Size

Step	Action
1	Determine the functional size using the rules in the CPM 4.3 and addressed in previous chapters of this book.
2	Determine the Value Adjustment Factor using the guidance contained in Appendix C of the CPM 4.3 and addressed in this chapter.
3	Calculate the adjusted functional size in accordance with the formulas contained in Appendix C of the CPM 4.3 and addressed in this chapter.

B. Business Control Data
   ■ Business Control Data is kept in tables that are maintained by the user with on-line interactive processes, but changes take effect only on the next business cycle (count as 1 item).
   ■ Business Control Data is kept in tables that are maintained by the user with on-line interactive processes, and the changes take effect immediately (count as 2 items).

Score

See Table 11.16.

Hints for Flexible Query and Reporting

- A Flexible Query and Report facility means more than a list of choices in a "canned" query or report.
- It is the ability of the user to control the data, data source, sequence, and format of their query or report request.
- It means freedom to design screen layout, horizontal and vertical sorting, data item display formats, and selection criteria for both files and data items.
- It includes true user programming for inquiries and is sometimes referred to as *ad hoc* query or reporting.
- Using filters that control the amount of data viewed or printed in a fixed format is not considered to be a Flexible Query and Report facility.
- Query and/or report writer capability is often provided by languages such as SQL or Focus or by some of the more dynamic *ad hoc* reporting tools (e.g., Crystal Reports®).

Hint for Rule A1

Simple requests may include AND/OR logic applied to only one Internal Logical File.

Hint for Rule A2

Requests of average complexity may include AND/OR logic applied to more than one Internal Logical File.

Hint for Rule A3

Complex requests may include AND/OR logic combinations on one or more Internal Logic Files.

Hints for Business Control Data

- Business Control Data (Reference Data) is stored to support the business rules for maintenance of the Business Data (e.g., in a payroll application it would be the data stored on the government tax rates for each wage scale and the date the tax rate became effective).
- See Code Data (CPM Part 3, Chapter 1) for additional information.

Typically

Scoring is not platform dependent.

Calculating the Adjusted Functional Size[19]

Table 11.17 includes the functional size analysis steps extended to provide adjusted functional size.

---

[19] Refer to IFPUG, *Function Point Counting Practices Manual* (CPM), Release 4.3, Part 5, Appendix C, page C-3.

Adjusted Development Project Functional Size (aDFP)[20]

Application Functionality

Application functionality consists of functions used after software installation to satisfy the ongoing business needs of the user.

Conversion Functionality

Conversion functionality consists of functions provided only at installation to convert data and/or provide other user-specified conversion requirements, such as special conversion reports.

Application Value Adjustment Factor

The Value Adjustment Factor is determined by using the 14 General System Characteristics to rate the application functional complexity.

Formula

Use the following formula to calculate the adjusted development project functional size.

$$\text{aDFP} = \text{DFP} \times \text{VAF} \qquad (11.1)$$

where:

- aDFP is the adjusted development project functional size.
- DFP is the development project functional size (DFP = ADD + CFP, where ADD is the size of the functions being added by the development project, and CFP is the size of the conversion functionality).
- VAF is the Value Adjustment Factor.

Example

A small development project includes 20 average complexity EIs, 10 low complexity EIs, 12 average complexity EQs, and 8 low complexity ILFs. One low complexity EI is included for conversion. The VAF is equal to 1.10. Using the formula to calculate the adjusted development project functional size (Equation 11.1), for this development project:

$$ADD = 80 + 30 + 48 + 56 = 214$$
$$CFP = 3$$
$$VAFA = 1.10$$
$$aDFP = (214 + 3) \times 1.10$$
$$aDFP = 217 \times 1.10 = 238.7$$

---

[20] Refer to IFPUG, *Function Point Counting Practices Manual* (CPM), Release 4.3, Part 5, Appendix C, page C-32.

Adjusted Enhancement Project Functional Size (aEFP)[21]

The adjusted enhancement project functional size consists of three components:

- Application functionality included in the user requirements for the project
- Conversion functionality included in the user requirements for the project
- Application Value Adjustment Factor

Enhancement Project GSC Considerations

The optional 14 General System Characteristics should be reviewed for change. Small enhancements do not normally require such a review. Examples of changes that may indicate a need to review the GSCs include:

- Addition of on-line functions to a batch application
- Increased transaction volumes and/or degraded response times now requiring performance design and testing activities
- Additional usability features requested
- Addition of a Web interface to an existing on-line application
- Addition of a new communication protocol to an existing application

Application Functionality

Application functionality consists of:

- Function points identified from the functionality added by the enhancements
- Function points measured because existing functionality is changed during the enhancement project
- Function points measured for functionality deleted during the enhancement project

Conversion Functionality

The conversion functionality consists of function points delivered because of any conversion functionality required by the user.

Value Adjustment Factor

The two Value Adjustment Factors are the:

---

[21] Refer to IFPUG, *Function Point Counting Practices Manual* (CPM), Release 4.3, Part 5, Appendix C, pages C-37 and C-38.

- Application Value Adjustment Factor before the enhancement project begins
- Application Value Adjustment Factor after the enhancement project is complete

Formula

Use the following formula to calculate the adjusted enhancement project functional size. *Note:* Data conversion requirements are included in this calculation.

$$aEFP = [(ADD + CHGA + CFP) \times VAFA] + (DEL \times VAFB) \quad (11.2)$$

where:

- aEFP is the adjusted enhancement project functional size.
- ADD is the size of the functions being added by the enhancement project.
- CHGA is the size of the functions being changed by the enhancement project (as they are or will be after implementation).
- CFP is the size of the conversion functionality.
- VAFA is the Value Adjustment Factor of the application after the enhancement project is complete.
- DEL is the size of the functions being deleted by the enhancement project.
- VAFB is the Value Adjustment Factor of the application before the enhancement project begins.

Example

A small enhancement project adds 2 average complexity EIs, 1 low complexity EI, 1 average complexity EQ, and 1 low complexity ILF. One low complexity EO is revised, so it is now average complexity. One low complexity EI is included for conversion. One low complexity EQ is deleted. The VAF before is equal to 1.00, and the VAF after is equal to 1.01. Using the formula to calculate the adjusted enhancement project functional size (Equation 11.2) after the enhancement project:

$$ADD = 8 + 3 + 4 + 7 = 22$$
$$CHGA = 5$$
$$CFP = 3$$
$$VAFA = 1.01$$
$$DEL = 3$$
$$VAFB = 1.00$$
$$aEFP = [(22 + 5 + 3) \times 1.01] + (3 \times 1.00)$$
$$aEFP = (30 \times 1.01) + 3$$
$$aEFP = 30.3 + 3 = 33.3$$

Adjusted Application Functional Size[22]

This section provides the formulas to calculate the adjusted application functional size. The two variations of this formulas are:

- Formula to establish the initial adjusted functional size for an application
- Formula to reestablish the adjusted functional size for an application after an enhancement project has changed the application functionality

Formula: Initial Adjusted Application Functional Size (aAFP)

Use the formula in this section to establish the initial adjusted functional size for an application. Initially, the user is receiving new functionality. There are no changes to the existing functionality or deletions of obsolete or unneeded functionality. The adjusted application functional size does not include conversion requirements.

$$aAFP = ADD \times VAF \quad (11.3)$$

where:

- aAFP is the initial adjusted application functional size.
- ADD is the size of the functions changed by the development project to be delivered to the user or the functionality that exists whenever the application is measured.
- VAF is the Value Adjustment Factor of the application.

Formula: Application Functional Size after Enhancement Projects

When an enhancement project is installed, the existing application functional size must be updated to reflect modifications to the application. The functionality for the application can be altered in one or more ways:

- Added (new) functionality increases the size of the application.
- Changed functionality increases, decreases, or has no effect on the size of the application.
- Deleted functionality decreases the application size.
- Changes to the Value Adjustment Factor increase or decrease the application size.

---

[22]Refer to IFPUG, *Function Point Counting Practices Manual* (CPM), Release 4.3, Part 5, Appendix C, page C-43.

Note: Because conversion functionality does not affect the adjusted application functional size, any conversion functionality associated with an enhancement project is omitted entirely from the adjusted application functional size calculation.

Use the following formula to calculate the adjusted application functional size after an enhancement project:[23]

$$aAFPA = [(AFPB + ADD + CHGA) - (CHGB + DEL)] \times VAFA \quad (11.4)$$

where:

- aAFPA is the adjusted application functional size after the enhancement project.
- AFPB is the application functional size before the enhancement project begins.
- ADD is the size of the functions being added by the enhancement project.
- CHGA is the size of the functions being changed by the enhancement project (as they are and/or will be after implementation).
- CHGB is the size of the functions being changed by the enhancement project (as they are and/or were before the project commenced).
- DEL is the size of the functions being deleted by the enhancement project.
- VAFA is the Value Adjustment Factor of the application after the enhancement project is complete.

Note: If the AFPB is unavailable, it can be calculated using the formula AFPB = aAFPB/VAFB, where aAFPB is the adjusted application functional size before the enhancement project and VAFB is the Value Adjustment Factor of the application before the enhancement project.

Example

Refer to our previous enhancement project that added 2 average complexity EIs, 1 low complexity EI, 1 average complexity EQ, and 1 low complexity ILF. One low complexity EO was revised, so it is now average complexity. One low complexity EQ was deleted. One low complexity EI was included for conversion. The VAF before was equal to 1.00, and the VAF after was equal to 1.01. Assume that the application functional size before the enhancement project began (AFPB) was 400. Using the formula to calculate the adjusted application functional size after the enhancement project (Equation 11.4):

---

[23]Refer to IFPUG, *Function Point Counting Practices Manual* (CPM), Release 4.3, Part 5, Appendix C, page C-44.

AFPB = 400
ADD = 8 + 3 + 4 + 7 = 22
CHGA = 5
CHGB = 4
VAFA = 1.01
DEL = 3
aAFPA = [(400 + 22 + 5) − (4 + 3)] × VAFA
aAFPA = (427 − 7) × 1.01
aAFPA = 420 × 1.01 = 424.2

Further Reading

The rules included in this chapter have been extracted from Part 5, Appendix C, of the IFPUG *Function Point Counting Practices Manual* (CPM), Release 4.3. A review of this chapter is recommended before taking the CFPS exam.

Exam Guidance

- Read and study this chapter, including all related examples.
- Even though the GSCs, Value Adjustment Factor, and adjusted functional size have been moved to Part 5, Appendix C, of CPM 4.3, there may still be questions on the exam covering these topics.
- Become very familiar with the 14 General System Characteristics so you can quickly look up the information on the GSC Quick Reference Card or in Part 5, Appendix C, of the CPM.
- Make sure you are familiar with and know how to apply the various adjusted functional size formulas.
- Become familiar with the formula changes between CPM Release 4.2.1 and CPM Release 4.3, making sure you know what the various acronyms represent (e.g., aAFP, aAFPA, aDFP, aEFP, AFPB, ADD, CFP, CHGA, CHGB, DEL, DFP, VAF, VAFA, VAFB).
- Memorize the Value Adjustment Factor determination components.
- Familiarize yourself with the related examples in this chapter as well as CPM 4.3 Part 5, Appendix C (Adjusted Functional Size), because it is unlikely that you will have time to look up everything during the exam.
- Complete the practice questions in this chapter, and go back to determine why you answered any question incorrectly.

Sample Exam Questions

1. The Degree of Influence (DI) for each General System Characteristic ranges on a scale of:
   A. 0 to 4
   B. 1 to 5
   C. 0 to 5
   D. 1 to 4

2. The degree to which the rate of business transactions influenced the development of the application is which General System Characteristic:
   A. Heavily Used Configuration
   B. Performance
   C. Operational Ease
   D. Transaction Rate

3. Which of the following are characteristics of Operational Ease:
   A. The application minimizes the need for tape mounts or remote data access requiring human intervention
   B. Conversion and Installation Ease are characteristics of the application
   C. Start-up, back-up, and recovery processes were provided, but human intervention is required
   D. A and C

4. A score of 2 for Degree of Influence indicates:
   A. Incidental influence
   B. Moderate influence
   C. Average influence
   D. Significant influence

5. What is the Degree of Influence if an application has provided a Flexible Query and Report facility that can handle requests of average complexity and has business control data kept in tables that are maintained by the user with on-line interactive processes, and the changes take effect immediately:
   A. 1
   B. 2
   C. 3
   D. 4

6. The formula for Value Adjustment Factor is:
   A. VAF = (TDI × 0.01) + 0.65
   B. VAF = TDI + 0.65
   C. VAF = TDI × 0.01
   D. None of the above

7. When applied, the Value Adjustment Factor adjusts the unadjusted functional size:
   A. ±30% to produce the adjusted functional size
   B. ±35% to produce the adjusted functional size
   C. ±60% to produce the adjusted functional size
   D. ±65% to produce the adjusted functional size

8. Multiple Sites describes:
   A. The degree to which the computer resource restrictions influenced the development of the application
   B. The degree to which the application has been developed for different hardware and software environments
   C. The degree to which the application transfers data among physical components of the application
   D. The degree to which computer resource restrictions influenced the development of the application

9. What is the Degree of Influence if the needs of more than one installation site were considered in the design, the application is designed to operate under different hardware or software environments, and the documentation and support plan are provided and tested to support the application at multiple installation sites and the application:
   A. 1
   B. 2
   C. 3
   D. 5

10. Which of the following are characteristics of End-User Efficiency:
    A. Batch jobs submitted from on-line transactions
    B. Drop-down list box
    C. Flexible query
    D. A and B

11. Multilingual support counts as how many items:
    A. 1
    B. 2
    C. 4
    D. 6

12. An application would receive a score of 3 for On-Line Data Entry if:
    A. 1 to 7% of transactions are interactive
    B. 8 to 15% of transactions are interactive
    C. 16 to 23% of transactions are interactive
    D. 24 to 30% of transactions are interactive

13. Sensitive control or application-specific security processing is a characteristic of:
    A. End-User Efficiency
    B. On-Line Update
    C. Complex Processing
    D. Reusability

14. What is the Value Adjustment Factor if the Total Degree of Influence is equal to 45:
    A. 1.00
    B. 1.10
    C. 1.05
    D. .95

15. The total Degree of Influence is between:
    A. 0 and 70
    B. .65 and 1.35
    C. 0 to 5
    D. 1 to 5

16. The Value Adjustment Factor (VAF):
    A. Is the measure of the functionality provided to the user by the project or application
    B. Rates the general functionality of the application being measured
    C. Is calculated based on an assessment of the 14 General System Characteristics for an application
    D. B and C

17. Which of the following formulas is used to calculate the adjusted application functional size after enhancement:
    A. aAFP = ADD × VAF
    B. aEFP = [(ADD + CHGA + CFP) × VAFA] + (DEL × VAFB)
    C. aAFPA = [(AFPB + ADD + CHGA) – (CHGB + DEL)] × VAFA
    D. aDFP = DFP × VAF

18. Which of the following formulas is used to calculate the adjusted development project functional size:
    A. aAFP = ADD × VAF
    B. aEFP = [(ADD + CHGA + CFP) × VAFA] + (DEL × VAFB)
    C. aAFPA = [(AFPB + ADD + CHGA) – (CHGB + DEL)] × VAFA
    D. aDFP = (ADD + CFP) × VAF

19. Which of the following formulas is used to establish the initial adjusted application functional size:
    A. aAFP = ADD × VAF
    B. aEFP = [(ADD + CHGA + CFP) × VAFA] + (DEL × VAFB)

C. aAFPA = [(AFPB + ADD + CHGA) – (CHGB + DEL)] × VAFA
D. aDFP = DFP × VAF

20. Which of the following formulas is used to calculate the adjusted enhancement project functional size:
    A. aAFP = ADD × VAF
    B. aEFP = [(ADD + CHGA + CFP) × VAFA] + (DEL × VAFB)
    C. aAFPA = [(AFPB + ADD + CHGA) – (CHGB + DEL)] × VAFA
    D. aDFP = DFP × VAF

21. CHGB in the formula aAFPA = [(AFPB + ADD + CHGA) – (CHGB + DEL)] × VAFA:
    A. Is the size of the functions being deleted by the enhancement project
    B. Is the size of the functions being changed by the enhancement project (as they are/were before the project commenced)
    C. Is the size of the functions being changed by the enhancement project (as they are/will be after implementation)
    D. Is the size of the functions being added by the enhancement project

22. CHGB in the formula aAFPA = [(AFPB + ADD + CHGA) – (CHGB + DEL)] × VAFA:
    A. Is the size of the functions being deleted by the enhancement project
    B. Is the size of the functions being changed by the enhancement project (as they are/were before the project commenced)
    C. Is the size of the functions being changed by the enhancement project (as they are/will be after implementation)
    D. Is the size of the functions being added by the enhancement project

23. In the formula aAFPA = [(AFPB + ADD + CHGA) – (CHGB + DEL)] × VAFA, the lower case "a":
    A. Denotes "application"
    B. Denotes "after"
    C. Denotes "adjusted"
    D. None of the above

Chapter 12

Preparing for the Certified Function Point Specialist (CFPS) Exam

The Certification Process

The Certified Function Point Specialist (CFPS) designation formally recognizes an individual's level of expertise in function point analysis (FPA). Candidates are examined for both their knowledge of and their ability to apply the International Function Point Users Group (IFPUG) counting rules in accordance with the IFPUG *Function Point Counting Practices Manual* (CPM). A CFPS is acknowledged as having the skills necessary to perform consistent and accurate function point counts and comprehending the current counting rules, definitions, and procedures.

An individual who passes the CFPS exam receives a certificate from IFPUG stating: "IFPUG certifies that [name] has met the requirements as specified by the standards and guidelines of the International Function Point Users Group to qualify as a Certified Function Point Specialist (CFPS) for the [version/series] of the *Counting Practices Manual*." The certificate is signed by the Certification Committee Chair, as an authorized representative of IFPUG, and indicates the month and year the exam was taken, as well as the month and year the certification expires. The CFPS certificate is valid for a period of 3 years; however, membership in IFPUG is required to hold the CFPS designation. All individuals must be members of IFPUG to sit for the CFPS exam or to apply for the Certification Extension Program, and they must remain members in good standing for the duration of their CFPS certification period. CFPS certificates for individuals who pass the CFPS exam or who successfully extend their certification via the Certification Extension Program expire at the end of each IFPUG fiscal year (i.e., each June 30). New certificates are then issued throughout the duration of the overall certification period to individuals whose IFPUG member dues are paid in full. CFPS certification will expire for individuals who allow their IFPUG membership to lapse. An individual may remain certified by either taking the CFPS exam in the third year of certification or applying for extensions through the CFPS Certification Extension Program. Always refer to the IFPUG website (www.IFPUG.org) for the current rules and regulations concerning certification.

Recommendations for Exam Preparation

- Study the current version of the IFPUG *Counting Practices Manual*. Remember to thoroughly review the counting examples.
- Count! The more you count, the better your chances of achieving a passing grade.
- Count a variety of application types and count types (development, application, and enhancement). A limited use of function point analysis in an organization can lead to a limited amount of the experience necessary to perform well on all parts of the exam.
- Read the CFPS Overview and Helpful Hints documents at http://www.ifpug.org/certification/.
- Consult with other exam candidates regarding their experiences via the IFPUG website Bulletin Board.
- IFPUG Case Studies are available and can be used as a study aid for both applying the rules and practicing casework. Be sure that the case studies used are applicable to the CPM version of the test that you are taking.

- Consider contacting vendors that provide CFPS exam preparation training. This training does not guarantee that an individual will pass the exam; however, it can better prepare you for the actual CFPS exam.
- Go through the sample questions provided at the end of each chapter in this book until you can answer (and understand) every question correctly.
- *Take the practice exams provided in this book several times. The more you practice, the better prepared you will be!*

Review of the IFPUG *Counting Practices Manual* (CPM)[1]

The *Counting Practices Manual*, Release 4.3, complies with ISO/IEC 14143-1:2007 (Information technology—Software measurement—Functional size measurement—Part 1: Definition of concepts). The five major parts in the CPM include:

1. FSM
2. The Bridge—Applying the IFPUG Functional Size Measurement Method
3. Counting Practices
4. Examples
5. Appendices and Glossary

Part 1. FSM

Part 1 covers the IFPUG Functional Size Measurement (FSM) Method and contains the rules. To speak a language as a native, learning the grammar and the words alone is not sufficient, as they provide only a framework. You need language experience to understand how the language is spoken in practice, how the grammar rules should be applied, what idiomatic expressions are common, and so on. The same is true for FPA. The knowledge of process and rules as reflected in Part 1 is a necessity, but the knowledge alone is not a sufficient condition to apply FPA correctly, thus the need for the remaining parts of the CPM.

Part 2. The Bridge

Part 2 provides guidance for sizing software following the IFPUG Functional Size Measurement (FSM) Method provided in Part 1.

---

[1] Refer to IFPUG, *Function Point Counting Practices Manual* (CPM), Release 4.3, Part 0, page x.

Part 3. Counting Practices, and Part 4. Examples

Parts 3 and 4 provide detailed examples to explain counting practices concepts and rules. Each example should be considered on its own merits. Because each example is intended to illustrate a specific scenario, variations may exist between examples. Although the examples throughout the manual deal with similar subject matter, they are not intended to represent a single set of user requirements.

Part 5. Appendices and Glossary

Part 5 contains valuable additional information in such appendices as Functional Size Calculation Table, The Change from Previous Version (transition from CPM 4.2.1 to CPM 4.3), Adjusted Functional Size (when using the General System Characteristics) and IFPUG Glossary.

What to Know/What to Look Up During Exam

- Memorize or at least be very familiar with the definitions and rules in the CPM, because it is unlikely that you will have time to look up everything during the exam. However, you do have time to verify some of your less certain answers. Do so. A few definitions are found on the Quick Reference Card, but many more are found in the Glossary.
- Use the Glossary when you do need to locate definitions. Remember to use the "Find" capability on the electronic document, if needed, but the Glossary is in alphabetical order and it may be faster not to search. Some questions, however, may provide descriptions of the term rather than asking for the meaning of the term itself. In this case, a search of the Glossary may be necessary to locate candidate answers.
- Do not try to memorize the formulas and matrices; instead, look these up on the Quick Reference Card or, better still, where you copied them on to the grease board provided. You may be limited in how much space you will have on the grease board; use that space carefully.
- Do not try to memorize the General System Characteristics (GSCs). Use the "Find" capability on the electronic GSC Quick Reference Card.
- Know which formula to use in any given situation, and know how to do the actual calculations.

The Exam

The exam is structured so both the knowledge and the ability to apply the definitions and rules as published in the current CPM are tested. The 3-hour exam currently is composed of three sections: Definition, Implementation, and Case Study. You may request an exam duration extension of 30 minutes if English is not your first language and the exam is not available in your native or business language. Refer to the IFPUG website for more information on requesting the extension. The three sections are summarized below:

■ The Definition section consists of 50 multiple-choice questions. This section specifically tests the individual's knowledge of definitions and rules.
■ The Implementation section consists of 50 multiple-choice questions. This section indirectly tests the individual's knowledge of definitions and rules and directly tests the individual's ability to apply the definitions and rules through small story problems.
■ The Case Study section directly tests the individual's ability to apply the definitions and rules of the CPM using various case topics. The written exam case study section consists of two to three case studies with 50 to 55 associated line items. The automated exam (see the following section) has 10 cases with 50 associated line items.

A successful exam requires a score of at least 90% overall correct, with at least 80% correct on each section of the exam.

Helpful Hints for Taking the Exam

■ Ask where the bathroom is before starting the exam and go! The nearest bathroom might not be convenient.
■ Provide answers for *all* multiple-choice questions, as blanks will be counted as incorrect answers. Fortunately, on the automated exam, you have an option to review all unanswered questions before submitting the exam for grading. Also, on the automated exam, you can mark questions to return to later, and these are identified for you in a summary as you are reviewing the exam before submitting it.
■ Mark questions you may be unsure of for later review.
■ Do not spend too much time on Parts 1 and 2; typically, you will need a longer amount of time for the Case Studies in Part 3.
■ Read and answer the questions carefully.
■ Do not make assumptions; do not count something if it is not presented (e.g., an error file as an FTR or an action key on batch).

■ Conversely, make sure you do count a DET for the capability to return a message if it is stated that the functionality is present.
■ Make sure you count a DET for the action key for on-line functionality.
■ Double-check your calculations (especially if your answer is not represented in the choices)!
■ Comment on any questions or answer options that are unclear. Comments will be collected and reviewed by the Certification Committee.

Exam Automation

If you are sitting for the automated exam, it is imperative that you review the following documents at http://www.ifpug.org/certification/cfps.htm:

■ Automated Exam Day Rules and Hints for Success
■ Automated CFPS Exam FAQ

These documents are prepared and updated by the IFPUG's Certification Committee.

Automated Exam Format and Scoring

An advantage of the automated exam process is that you receive your exam results immediately after completing the exam. In addition, you will be provided with printed exam results before leaving the test center. This report contains your overall final score, as well as scores for each of the three sections of the exam.

The Case Section on the automated exam is very different from the written exam. It consists of 10 multiple-choice, multiple part/possible question and answer sets, worth 5 points each. Every question *must* include an answer. When one part/possible answer does not apply, choose the N/A (not applicable) radio button.

The Case Section contains two types of question sets, based on the provided scenario. The first type of question set asks that you to identify function types. The second question set type asks that you determine the complexity for a group of function types. Each question set has text and/or graphics displayed on the left side of the screen to describe the scenario. The answer boxes for the question set are displayed on the right side of the screen. A statement at the end of each question set specifies the action you should take, such as identify the data function types or determine the complexity of the transactional function types. The practice exam questions in this book are very similar to the actual automated exam questions.

Helpful Hints for Taking the Automated Exam

- You are *not* permitted to take anything into the exam, so leave everything in your car except your picture ID and one other form of identification. The test center may or may not have accommodations to secure your possessions.

- Take some earplugs to the test site to block out any noise around you.

- The CPM, Quick Reference Cards, and calculator are electronic. You are *not* permitted to take in your own.

- The Reference drop-down menu has selections for the various parts of the CPM as well as the Quick Reference Cards. Make sure you are familiar with what is in each part of the CPM and what is on the Quick Reference Cards prior to taking the exam so you know which one to open.

- The electronic calculator is quick and easy to use. Use the number keys on the keyboard instead of clicking on the numbers on the calculator. The number keys are faster.

- Get familiar with the IFPUG Quick Reference Cards that are available on the IFPUG website, as these are the ones provided with the exam. The two cards for CPM 4.3 are the Function Point Quick Reference Card and the GSC Quick Reference Card.

- The English language references are separate PDF documents, each accessed independently. If you open a reference, remember that as soon as you answer a question the reference closes in the current implementation of the exam.

- You will be provided with a small grease board or something similar on which to make notes. The board might smear, so try to keep your hands off what you have written.

- As soon as you begin the CFPS exam, to save time open the Quick Reference Cards and write the matrices and formulas on your grease board.

- Use the "Find" feature in the CPM PDF. Some of the questions may be verbatim from the CPM, so type a few words in the "Find" area to go straight to the answer.

- Take the tutorial on the PC at the test site before beginning the CFPS exam so you can get the feel of things.

- A 3-hour countdown clock is provided on the upper right-hand screen. You are notified when there are 15 minutes left and when there are 5 minutes left.

- The answer choices are radio button selections. Click on one to mark or unmark it.

- You can mark a question to review. Do so if you think you need to check your answer. At the end, if time remains, you will be provided with a list of all the question numbers along with information regarding whether the question was answered or unanswered, as well as if it was marked. Click on the question number to be taken back to it.

- Provide comments using the "Comment" button, should you believe any questions or answer options are unclear. Comments will be collected and reviewed by the Certification Committee.

- Schedule your exam at a time that you are at your best, whether that is early in the morning or later in the afternoon.

- Use preparation techniques that have worked for you in the past. Most of us do not do well on an empty stomach. Some of us perform better with legal stimulants such as caffeine. Remember that you cannot take beverages into many test centers, so you may have to consume your food or drink of choice prior to entering the exam room. If cramming and sleepless nights work for you, consider your preferences ahead of time. In addition, unless you perform better under stress, relax.

Good luck!

Appendix 1

Formulas and Matrices

Matrices

See Tables A1.1 through A1.8.

Table A1.1 Internal Logical File (ILF) and External Interface File (EIF) Complexity Matrix

	1 to 19 DETs	20 to 50 DETs	51 or More DETs
1 RET	Low	Low	Average
2 to 5 RETs	Low	Average	High
6 or More RETs	Average	High	High

Table A1.2 Internal Logical File (ILF) Translation Table

Functional Complexity Rating	Function Points
Low	7
Average	10
High	15

Table A1.3 External Interface File (EIF) Translation Table

Functional Complexity Rating	Function Points
Low	5
Average	7
High	10

Table A1.4 External Input (EI) Complexity Matrix

	1 to 4 DETs	5 to 15 DETs	16 or More DETs
0 to 1 FTR	Low	Low	Average
2 FTRs	Low	Average	High
3 or More FTRs	Average	High	High

Table A1.5 External Output (EO) and External Inquiry (EQ) Complexity Matrix

	1 to 5 DETs	6 to 19 DETs	20 or More DETs
0 to 1 FTR	Low	Low	Average
2 to 3 FTRs	Low	Average	High
4 or More FTRs	Average	High	High

Note: An EQ has a minimum of 1 FTR.

Table A1.6 External Input (EI) and External Inquiry (EQ) Translation Table

Functional Complexity Rating	Function Points
Low	3
Average	4
High	6

Table A1.7 External Output (EO) Translation Table

Functional Complexity Rating	Function Points
Low	4
Average	5
High	7

Formulas

Functional Size Formulas

Enhancement Project Functional Size

$$EFP = ADD + CHGA + CFP + DEL$$

where:

- EFP is the enhancement project function point count.
- ADD is the size of the functions being added by the enhancement project.
- CHGA is the size of the functions being changed by the enhancement project (as they are/will be after implementation).

- CFP is the size of the conversion functionality.
- DEL is the size of the functions being deleted by the enhancement project.

Initial Application Functional Size

$$AFP = ADD$$

where:

- AFP is the application function point count.
- ADD is the size of the functions to be delivered to the user by the development project (excluding the size of any conversion functionality) or the functionality that exists whenever the application is measured.

Application Functional Size Measurement to Reflect Enhancements

$$AFPA = (AFPB + ADD + CHGA) - (CHGB + DEL)$$

where:

Table A1.8 Functional Size Calculation Table

Function Type		Functional Complexity		Complexity Totals	Function Type Totals
ILF	_____	Low	× 7 =	_____	
	_____	Average	× 10 =	_____	
	_____	High	× 15 =	_____	
EIF	_____	Low	× 5 =	_____	
	_____	Average	× 7 =	_____	
	_____	High	× 10 =	_____	
EI	_____	Low	× 3 =	_____	
	_____	Average	× 4 =	_____	
	_____	High	× 6 =	_____	
EQ	_____	Low	× 3 =	_____	
	_____	Average	× 4 =	_____	
	_____	High	× 6 =	_____	
EO	_____	Low	× 4 =	_____	
	_____	Average	× 5 =	_____	
	_____	High	× 7 =	_____	
Total functional size					

- AFPA is the application function point count after the enhancement project.
- AFPB is the application function point count before the enhancement project.
- ADD is the size of the functions being added by the enhancement project.
- CHGA is the size of the functions being changed by the enhancement project (as they are/will be after implementation).
- CHGB is the size of the functions being changed by the enhancement project (as they are/were before the project commenced).
- DEL is the size of the functions being deleted by the enhancement project.

Adjusted Functional Size Formulas

Value Adjustment Factor (VAF)

$$VAF = (TDI \times 0.01) + 0.65$$

where TDI is the Total Degree Of Influence obtained by summing the degrees of influence for each General System Characteristic.

Adjusted Development Project Functional Size (aDFP)

$$aDFP = DFP \times VAF$$

where:

- aDFP is the adjusted development project functional size.
- DFP is the development project functional size (DFP = ADD + CFP).
- VAF is the Value Adjustment Factor.

Adjusted Enhancement Project Functional Size (aEFP)

$$aEFP = [(ADD + CHGA + CFP) \times VAFA] + (DEL \times VAFB)$$

where:

- aEFP is the adjusted enhancement project functional size.
- ADD is the size of the functions being added by the enhancement project.
- CHGA is the size of the functions being changed by the enhancement project (as they are/will be after implementation).
- CFP is the size of the conversion functionality.
- VAFA is the Value Adjustment Factor of the application after the enhancement project is complete.

- DEL is the size of the functions being deleted by the enhancement project.
- VAFB is the Value Adjustment Factor of the application before the enhancement project begins.

Adjusted Application Functional Size

This section provides the formulas to calculate the adjusted application functional size. There are two variations of this formula:

- Formula to establish the initial adjusted functional size for an application
- Formula to reestablish the adjusted functional size for an application after an enhancement project has changed the application functionality

Initial Adjusted Application Functional Size (aAFP)

$$aAFP = ADD \times VAF$$

where:

- aAFP is the initial adjusted application functional size.
- ADD is the size of the functions by the development project to be delivered to the user or the functionality that exists whenever the application is measured.
- VAF is the Value Adjustment Factor of the application.

Adjusted Application Functional Size After Enhancement Projects (aAFPA)

$$aAFPA = [(AFPB + ADD + CHGA) - (CHGB + DEL)] \times VAFA$$

where:

- aAFPA is the adjusted application functional size after the enhancement project.
- AFPB is the application functional size before the enhancement project begins.
- ADD is the size of the functions being added by the enhancement project.
- CHGA is the size of the functions being changed by the enhancement project (as they are/will be after implementation).
- CHGB is the size of the functions being changed by the enhancement project (as they are/were before the project commenced).
- DEL is the size of the functions being deleted by the enhancement project.
- VAFA is the Value Adjustment Factor of the application after the enhancement project is complete.

Appendix 2

Practice Exam 1

Part 1. Definitions and Rules

1. Steps in the function point counting procedure include:
   A. Gather the available documentation
   B. Document and report
   C. Calculate the functional size
   D. All of the above

2. The following guidance applies when counting FTRs for EQs:
   A. Count one FTR for each ILF maintained
   B. Count one FTR for each ILF or EIF read
   C. Count only one FTR for each ILF that is both maintained and read
   D. All of the above

3. An associative entity is:
   A. An entity type that further describes one or more characteristics of another entity type
   B. Often created by the data modeler to resolve some of the business rules required to relate two separate entities
   C. Used to associate two or more entities as a way of defining the many-to-many relationship
   D. B and C

4. The application boundary
   A. Acts as a "membrane" through which data processed by transactions pass into and out from the application
   B. Is independent of technical and/or implementation considerations
   C. Is a conceptual interface between the software under study and its users
   D. All of the above

5. Application functional size:
   A. Measures an installed application
   B. Includes the functionality that will be measured in the initial application function point count, as well as any functionality required for data conversion
   C. Measures modifications to existing applications
   D. A and B

6. Functional User Requirements are:
   A. Detailed design specifications
   B. Requirements that specify what the software will do in terms of tasks and services
   C. A subset of the user requirements
   D. B and C

7. Business Data may also be referred to as:
   A. Core Data
   B. Business Objects
   C. List Data
   D. A and B

8. Code Data are sometimes referred to as:
   A. List Data
   B. Core Data
   C. Translation Data
   D. A and C

9. Entity independence is:
   A. An entity that is meaningful or significant to the business, in and of itself without the presence of other entities
   B. A fundamental thing of relevance to the user, about which a collection of facts is kept
   C. An entity that is not meaningful or is not significant to the business, in and of itself without the presence of other entities
   D. A and C

10. A refresh is:
    A. The process of recreating a set of data to make it current with its source
    B. Activity associated with mapping data or programs from one format to another
    C. Initiated by business requests to add, change, or delete business functionality
    D. To read data from a source, leaving the source data unchanged, and to write the same data elsewhere in a physical form that may differ from that of the source

11. A data function:
    A. Represents functionality provided to the user to meet internal and external data storage requirements
    B. Represents functionality provided to the user to create internal data storage requirements
    C. Is either an Internal Logical File or an External Interface File
    D. A and C

12. The smallest unit of activity that is meaningful to the user is the definition of:
    A. Functional size
    B. Function point
    C. Processing logic
    D. An elementary process

13. The two types of subgroups for Record Element Types are:
    A. Mandatory and logical
    B. Mandatory and optional
    C. Optional and logical
    D. Mandatory and operational

14. Software maintenance performed to correct faults in hardware or software is the definition of:
    A. Adaptive maintenance
    B. Perfective maintenance
    C. Corrective maintenance
    D. Preventive maintenance

15. Software maintenance performed to improve the performance, maintainability, or other attributes of a computer program is the definition of:
    A. Adaptive maintenance
    B. Perfective maintenance
    C. Corrective maintenance
    D. Preventive maintenance

16. Business Data:
    A. May also be referred to as Core User Data or Business Objects
    B. Reflects the information needed to be stored and retrieved by the functional area addressed by the application

C. Usually represents a significant percentage of the entities identified
    D. All of the above

17. Which of the following defines the set of functional requirements to be included in the function point count?
    A. Elementary process
    B. Purpose of the count
    C. Counting scope
    D. Scope creep

18. An application:
    A. Is a cohesive collection of automated procedures and data supporting a business objective
    B. Consists of one or more components, modules, or subsystems
    C. Is a group of related items treated as a unit
    D. A and B

19. An elementary process that processes data or control information sent from outside the boundary is an:
    A. EI
    B. EO
    C. EQ
    D. All of the above

20. Which of the following is true about an external output?
    A. It is an elementary process that sends data or control information outside the application's boundary and includes additional processing beyond that of an external inquiry
    B. The primary intent is to present information to a user through the retrieval of data or control information
    C. The processing logic contains no mathematical formula or calculation
    D. A and B

21. A File Type Referenced is:
    A. A unique, user-recognizable, nonrepeated attribute
    B. An elementary process that provides functionality to the user to process data
    C. A data function read and/or maintained by a transactional function
    D. None of the above

22. No prior or subsequent processing steps are needed to initiate or complete the functional requirements is the definition of:
    A. An elementary process
    B. Maintain
    C. Constant Data
    D. Self-contained

23. Which of the following statement(s) is true for conversion?
    A. Transactional or data functions provided to convert data
    B. To read data from a source, leaving the source data unchanged, and to write the same data elsewhere in a physical form that may differ from that of the source
    C. Transactional or data functions that provide other user-specified conversion requirements
    D. A and C

24. To read data from a source, leaving the source data unchanged, and to write the same data elsewhere in a physical form that may differ from that of the source is the definition of:
    A. Load
    B. Copy
    C. Refresh
    D. Image

25. To copy computer instructions or data from external storage to internal storage is the definition of:
    A. Load
    B. Copy
    C. Refresh
    D. Image

26. The process of recreating a set of data to make it current with its source is the definition of:
    A. Load
    B. Copy
    C. Refresh
    D. Image

27. Which of the following are transactional functions?
    A. EI, EIF
    B. EI, EO, ILF
    C. EI, EO, EQ
    D. EI, EO, EIF

28. Which of the following are data functions?
    A. EI, ILF
    B. ILF, EIF
    C. EI, EO, EQ
    D. EI, EIF

29. What type of data provides a list of available values for an attribute of one or more business object types?
    A. Business Data
    B. Constant Data
    C. Reference Data
    D. Valid Values Data

30. What type of data are stored to support the business rules for the maintenance of the Business Data?
    A. Code Data
    B. Constant Data
    C. Reference Data
    D. Valid Values Data

31. What type of data rarely change?
    A. Code Data
    B. Constant Data
    C. Reference Data
    D. Valid Values Data

32. What type of data provides a list of valid values that a descriptive attribute may have?
    A. Code Data
    B. Constant Data
    C. Reference Data
    D. Business Data

33. An enhancement project:
    A. Is a project to develop and deliver the first release of a software application
    B. Is a project to develop and deliver adaptive maintenance
    C. Includes repair, minor enhancement, conversion, user support, and preventive maintenance activities
    D. B and C

34 Maintenance activities include:
    A. Defect removal
    B. Hardware or software upgrades
    C. Optimization or quality improvement
    D. All of the above

35. Any of the requirements specifically requested by the user to complete an elementary process, such as validations, algorithms, or calculations, and reading or maintaining a file, is the definition of:
    A. Maintenance
    B. Control information
    C. Conversion
    D. Processing logic

36. A Data Element Type is:
    A. A unique, user-recognizable, nonrepeated attribute
    B. A data function read and/or maintained by a transactional function
    C. A user-recognizable subgroup of Data Element Types within a data function
    D. None of the above

37. A Record Element Type is:
    A. A unique, user-recognizable, nonrepeated attribute
    B. A data function read and/or maintained by a transactional function
    C. A user-recognizable subgroup of Data Element Types within a data function
    D. None of the above

38. A File Type Referenced is:
    A. A unique, user-recognizable, nonrepeated attribute
    B. A data function read and/or maintained by a transactional function
    C. A user-recognizable subgroup of Data Element Types within a data function
    D. None of the above

39. The features or capabilities of an application as seen by the user is the definition of:
    A. Attribute
    B. User view
    C. Elementary process
    D. Function

40. Which of the following is true of an External Interface File?
    A. It is a user-recognizable group of logically related data or control information that is referenced by the application being measured but which is maintained within the boundary of another application
    B. The primary intent is to hold data referenced through one or more elementary processes within the boundary of the application measured
    C. An EIF counted for an application must be in an ILF in another application
    D. All of the above

41. Which of the following is true of an external output?
    A. It may maintain one or more ILFs and/or alter the behavior of the system
    B. It may not contain derived data
    C. It may not contain calculations
    D. It may not maintain one or more ILFs and/or alter the behavior of the system

42. Data in an ILF or EIF that exists because the user requires a relationship with another ILF or EIF is the definition of:
    A. Foreign key
    B. Primary key
    C. Secondary key
    D. None of the above

43. The unique ID of an entity is the definition of:
    A. Foreign key
    B. Primary key
    C. Secondary key
    D. None of the above

44. The definition of primary intent is:
    A. The smallest unit of activity that is meaningful to the user
    B. An elementary process that provides functionality to the user to process data
    C. Intent that is first in importance
    D. Requirements for processes and/or data that are agreed upon, and understood by, both the user(s) and software developer(s)

45. Adaptive maintenance:
    A. Is modification of a software product, performed after delivery, to keep a software product usable in a changed or changing environment
    B. Provides enhancements necessary to accommodate changes in the environment in which a software product must operate
    C. Changes are those that must be made to keep pace with the changing environment
    D. All of the above

46. Quality includes:
    A. Usability
    B. Reliability
    C. Efficiency
    D. All of the above

47. The result of a normalization process that transforms groups of data so they have a unique identifier, one or more attributes, and no repeating attributes is:
    A. First normal form
    B. Second normal form
    C. Third normal form
    D. None of the above

48. Entity dependence is:
    A. An entity that is meaningful or significant to the business, in and of itself without the presence of other entities
    B. A fundamental thing of relevance to the user, about which a collection of facts is kept
    C. An entity that is not meaningful or is not significant to the business, in and of itself without the presence of other entities
    D. A and B

49. A group of related items that is treated as a unit is a:
    A. Record
    B. File
    C. File system
    D. Function

50. The activity of sequencing attributes in a transactional function is the definition of:
    A. Sorting
    B. Loading
    C. Refreshing
    D. Arranging

Part 2. Implementation

1. How many DETs are counted on an external output that has a pie chart with a category label and a numerical equivalent in a graphical output?
   A. 1
   B. 2
   C. 0
   D. 3

2. An external input that has six DETs and two FTRs has how many function points?
   A. 3
   B. 4
   C. 5
   D. 6

3. What is the application functional size of an application that has five low external inputs, one high external output, three average external inquiries, and one average Internal Logical File?
   A. 40
   B. 42
   C. 44
   D. 49

4. Which of the following would be a high complexity?
   A. An external input with 3 FTRs and 4 DETs
   B. An external output with 4 FTRs and 5 DETs
   C. An external inquiry with 3 FTRs and 19 DETs
   D. None of the above

5. An enhancement project added a low external input, deleted an average external inquiry, and added two average external outputs. What is the enhancement project functional size?
   A. 13
   B. 17
   C. 19
   D. 20

6. Put the following steps in the function point counting procedure in order:
   a. Determine counting scope and boundary and identify Functional User Requirements
   b. Document and report
   c. Measure data functions
   d. Measure transactional functions
   e. Calculate the functional size
   f. Gather the available documentation
   A. b, f, a, c, d, e
   B. f, b, d, c, a, e
   C. f, a, c, d, e, b
   D. f, b, c, d, e, b

7. Application A and Application B both modify the same ILF. Application A added four fields to this ILF. Application A populates these new fields by changing an existing external input to include these four fields. There was no impact to transactions in Application B. What is counted?
   A. A changed ILF for Applications A and B; a changed transaction for Application A
   B. A changed ILF and a changed transaction for Application A
   C. A changed ILF for Applications A and B; a changed transaction for Applications A and B
   D. A changed transaction for Application A

8. Currency Exchange-Rate Table (Country and Current Exchange Rate) is an example of what type of data?
   A. Code Data
   B. Constant Data
   C. Reference Data
   D. Valid Values Data

9. Airport code and airport name are examples of what type of data?
   A. Code Data
   B. Constant Data
   C. Reference Data
   D. Valid Values Data

10. Application A has added two external inputs (add employee and change employee), each having two record types (employee basic information and employee address information). How many external inputs are counted?
    A. 4
    B. 2
    C. 1
    D. 3

11. An application's function points before an enhancement is 200. The enhancement added three low EIs, two high EIs, four average EQs, and one average EO. What is the enhancement project functional size?
    A. 242
    B. 42
    C. 246
    D. 46

12. Which of the following formulas is used to calculate an enhancement project functional size?
    A. DFP = ADD + CFP
    B. EFP = ADD + CHGA + CFP + DEL
    C. AFPA = (AFPB + ADD + CHGA) – (CHGB + DEL)
    D. None of the above

13. DETs that cross the boundary include:
    A. Attributes the user enters via a screen as well as those displayed on a report or screen
    B. Attributes in an electronic file that enter or exit the boundary
    C. Attributes that enter the application boundary and are required to specify when, what, and/or how the data is to be retrieved or generated by the elementary process
    D. All of the above

14. Which of the following are not counted as DETs on a transaction?
    A. Attributes generated within the boundary by a transactional function and saved to an ILF without exiting the boundary
    B. Attributes retrieved or referenced from an ILF or EIF for participation in the processing without exiting the boundary
    C. Attributes provided by, or presented to, the user of the transactional function
    D. A and B

15. Which of the following types of transactions may alter the behavior of the application?
    A. EI
    B. EO
    C. EQ
    D. A and B

16. Which of the following is/are a form of processing logic?
    A. Sorting or arranging a set of data
    B. Conditions are analyzed to determine which are applicable
    C. Validations are performed
    D. All of the above

17. In an enhancement project, the size of the functions being added is 10, the size of the functions being deleted is 10, the size of the functions being changed as they are/will be after implementation is 20, and the size of the functions being changed as they are/were before the project commenced is 15. What is the enhancement project functional size?
    A. 55
    B. 45

C. 40
D. 35

18. An invoice data function has a header section of the customer information (customer name; account number; purchase order number; billing street address, city, state, and Zip Code; shipping street address, city, state, and Zip Code; phone number; e-mail address; fax number) and line items of the purchases (item number; description; price; weight; color; quantity ordered). The invoice data store is updated in the application being measured. What is the size of this data function?
    A. 5
    B. 7
    C. 10
    D. 15

19. A transaction whose primary intent is maintaining an ILF is being added to an application. This transaction has 15 unique DETs, updates one ILF, and reads two EIFs. What is the functional size of this transaction?
    A. 4
    B. 5
    C. 6
    D. 7

20. The ability to initiate a transactional function can be done by the clicking on the enter key, the PF2 key, or the OK button. How many DETs are counted for initiating the action?
    A. 0
    B. 1
    C. 2
    D. 3

21. Presenting information to a user is the primary intent of which transaction(s)?
    A. External input
    B. External output
    C. External inquiry
    D. B and C

22. Transforming existing data to create additional data is a form of which processing logic?
    A. Equivalent values are converted
    B. Sorting or arranging a set of data
    C. Derived data
    D. Mathematical formulas and calculations are performed

23. Classify an elementary process as an EI if:
    A. It has a primary intent of either maintaining one or more ILFs or altering the behavior of the application
    B. It has the primary intent of presenting information to the user

C. It includes processing logic to accept data or control information that enters the application boundary

D. A and C

24. Functional User Requirements may include which of the following?
    A. Data transformation
    B. Quality constraints
    C. Environmental constraints
    D. None of the above

25. Which of the following formulas is used to calculate an application functional size after an enhancement project?
    A. DFP = ADD + CFP
    B. EFP = ADD + CHGA + CFP + DEL
    C. AFPA = (AFPB + ADD + CHGA) – (CHGB + DEL)
    D. AFP = ADD

26. After an enhancement project, the application functional size may be updated to reflect changed functionality. This changed functionality may:
    A. Increase the application functional size
    B. Decrease the application functional size
    C. Have no effect on the application functional size
    D. All of the above

27. The formula DFP = ADD + CFP is used to calculate which of the following?
    A. Application functional size
    B. Development project functional size
    C. Application functional size after an enhancement project
    D. None of the above

28. A transaction to add an employee has the ability to return 10 unique error messages and two unique confirmation messages. How many DETs are counted for the error and confirmation messages?
    A. 12
    B. 11
    C. 2
    D. 1

29. In the formula AFPA = (AFPB + ADD + CHGA) – (CHGB + DEL), CHGB is:
    A. The application functional size before the enhancement project
    B. The application functional size after the enhancement project
    C. The size of the functions being changed by the enhancement project (as they are/will be after implementation)

D. The size of the functions being changed by the enhancement project (as they are/were before the project commenced)

30. An application functional size before an enhancement project was 100. The enhancement project added two low EIs, deleted one high EO, and changed one EQ from a low to an average. What is the application functional size after the enhancement project?
    A. 100
    B. 107
    C. 113
    D. 104

31. An application functional size before an enhancement project was 100. The enhancement project added two low EIs, deleted one high EO, and changed one EQ from a low to an average. What is the enhancement project functional size?
    A. 16
    B. 17
    C. 10
    D. 9

32. A new logon function requires the entry of the fields User Identifier and User Password. When the user logs on, the Security file is read to validate the user identifier and password as well as to determine the windows the user can access and maintain. If the fields do not pass edits, error messages are generated and incorrect fields are highlighted. Two error messages and one confirmation message are included for the security logon transaction. The security logon transactions is counted as an:
    A. EI
    B. EO
    C. EQ
    D. It is not counted

33. During construction of the Payroll application, a requirement for help functionality was added. Help information is not maintained in any application. How is help counted in the Payroll application?
    A. ILF
    B. EIF
    C. EQ
    D. It is not counted

34. A user requires that an application print a monthly report automatically every month. This report lists all employees by department and contains employee name and employee ID. This report is counted as an:
    A. EI
    B. EQ
    C. EO
    D. It is not counted

35. The user requires the ability to perform the following activities:
    - Enter a report definition that includes a unique report identifier, a report name, attributes used on the report, and calculations to generate the report.
    - Reuse the defined report at any time, changing the definition if necessary.
    - View and print a report using the report definition.
    - Inquire on existing report definitions by report name or report identifier.

    What data functions are counted for these activities?
    A. ILF, EI, EQ
    B. ILF, EI, EO
    C. ILF
    D. EIF

36. A user needs to inquire on report definitions using the report name as the key to finding the desired definition. To satisfy the user requirement, an alternate index is created using the report name as the key. This alternate index is counted as:
    A. An ILF
    B. An EIF
    C. A RET on the report definition ILF
    D. It is not counted

37. The user requires the ability to view a list of states. The list is retrieved from a file containing state code and state description. No other data is stored on the file. The retrieved list is counted as an:
    A. EQ
    B. EI
    C. EO
    D. It is not counted

38. At the end of each day, Application A sends a Daily Check file to Application B listing the check numbers and the amount and date of each check printed for the day. Application B uses the file to update a data function maintained within its boundaries. This transactional function is counted as:
    A. An EQ for Application A and an EQ for Application B
    B. An EQ for Application A and an EI for Application B
    C. An EO for Application A and an EI for Application B
    D. An EQ for Application A and nothing for Application B

39. Application A maintains the following information in the Vendor data function: vendor ID, vendor name, vendor phone number, vendor fax number, and vendor address, which includes floor, street, city, state, and Zip Code. Application B requires the ability to produce mailing labels for each vendor by retrieving the vendor address from the Vendor data function. The Vendor data function is counted as:
    A. An ILF with 5 DETs for Application A and an EIF with 5 DETs for Application B
    B. An ILF with 9 DETs for Application A and an EIF with 5 DETs for Application B
    C. An ILF with 9 DETs for Application A and an EIF with 1 DET for Application B
    D. An ILF with 9 DETs for Application A and an ILF with 1 DET for Application B

40. When a user adds a customer record in Application A, a validation is done on the Zip Code by sending the city, state, and Zip Code to Application B. By reading a maintained Zip Code data function, Application B validates that the Zip Code is a valid Zip Code for the city and state and sends a success or failure message back to Application A. If a success message is received, Application A adds the record to the Customer data function. If a failure message is received, Application A does not add the record and sends an error message back to the user that the Zip Code is invalid for the city/state. Identify all of the functions to be counted in this scenario for Application A.
    A. An ILF for the Customer data function and an EQ for the Zip Code validation
    B. An EI for adding a customer record, an ILF for the Customer data function, and an EQ for the Zip Code validation
    C. An ILF for the Customer data function and an EIF for the Zip Code data function
    D. An EI for adding a customer record, an ILF for the Customer data function, and an EIF for the Zip Code data function

41. A development project has five average complexity EIs and two high complexity EIs; two average complexity EOs; two average complexity EQs and one high complexity EQ; one low complexity ILF and one high complexity ILF; one low complexity EIF; and one average complexity conversion EI. What is the application count after the development project is installed?
    A. 85
    B. 87
    C. 80
    D. 83

42. Which of the following is not considered conversion functionality?
    A. Software upgrades due to the installation of a revised version of vendor packages
    B. An enhancement project requires the addition of a DET to an existing ILF and the new DET will be populated with a specific default value
    C. A changed EIF for the application being measured
    D. All of the above

43. Identify the transactional functions in the following scenario: A batch feed of new customer data from another application must be accepted. The customer data must be validated and saved to the Customer file; an error report is produced containing any identified errors. The business office is notified via e-mail with processing summary data.
    A. One EI, one EO, and one EQ
    B. One EI and two EQs
    C. One EI and one EO
    D. One EI only

44. An enhancement project adds six high complexity EIs and two average complexity EQs, deletes one high complexity EQ, and changes three EOs from low to high complexity. If the application count is 1000 before the enhancement, what is the value of the enhancement count?
    A. 1059
    B. 1047
    C. 71
    D. 62

45. The user requires the ability to delete a customer from the Customer ILF. Via an on-line screen, the user enters the customer ID and clicks on the delete button. If the customer ID is invalid, an error message is returned and the Customer ILF is not updated. If the customer ID is valid, the status field on the Customer ILF is updated with an "I," the system date is entered in the Effective Date on the Customer ILF, and a confirmation message is returned. What is counted for this transactional function?
    A. An EI with 1 FTR and 5 DETs
    B. An EI with 1 FTR and 6 DETs
    C. An EI with 1 FTR and 3 DETs
    D. An EI with 1 FTR and 4 DETs

46. Application A generates a Monthly PO file at the end of each month and sends it to Application B. During the creation of the Monthly PO file, the total number of purchase orders and the total dollar amount of those purchase orders for the month are calculated.

Application B uses this file to update a data function within its boundaries. What transactional functions are counted?
    A. An EQ for Application A and an EI for Application B
    B. An EO for Application A and an EI for Application B
    C. An EQ for Application A; nothing for Application B
    D. An EO for Application A; nothing for Application B

47. A development project has two low complexity EIs, two average complexity EIs, two low complexity EOs, two high complexity EQs, two low complexity ILFs, and one low complexity conversion EI. What is the development count?
    A. 49
    B. 50
    C. 51
    D. 53

48. An application's functional size before an enhancement is 100. The enhancement added two low EIs and deleted one average EO. What is the application size after the enhancement project is delivered?
    A. 100
    B. 101
    C. 110
    D. 111

49. The user has requested that an ILF (or part of an ILF) be populated from an ILF in another application. Validation is required against yet another ILF from a third application. This processing is specified as a one-time process and the data referenced in the third application will not be utilized in the future. What is counted for the conversion functionality?
    A. An EIF and an EI with two FTRs
    B. An ILF and an EI with one FTR
    C. An ILF only
    D. An ILF, an EQ, and an EI with one FTR

50. Application A generates an image copy with no additional processing logic and sends it to Application B; Application B loads a copy with no additional processing logic. What is counted?
    A. An ILF for Application A and an ILF for Application B
    B. An EIF for Application A and an EIF for Application B
    C. An ILF for Application A and an EIF for Application B
    D. An ILF for Application A and an EI for Application B

Part 3. Case Studies

Case Study 1

An Employee batch file enters Application A with three attributes (Employee ID, Employee Hire Date, and Employee Job Assignment). There are two transaction types: Add Employee and Update Employee. The Employee Job Assignment attribute on the input record is validated against the Job Assignment logical file maintained in Application C; this is the only attribute accessed in the Job Assignment logical file by Application A; however, the Job Assignment logical file has 51 attributes within Application C. If the validation passes, the Employee logical file is updated in Application A; a total of 12 fields are maintained and/or referenced in the Employee logical file within Application A. If the validation fails, no update is made and an error report is produced.

Identify the functional complexity of the possible function types by choosing the correct radio buttons in Table A2.1.

Case Study 2

Use the screen in Figure A2.1 to identify the functions present (see Table A2.2). Note that the "Add Customer" button causes the Customer data maintained inside the application boundary to be updated with the fields entered by the user. The "Clear Screen" button causes all of the fields to

Table A2.1

Names of Possible Function Types	Enter Complexity			
	Low	Average	High	N/A
Add Employee	O	O	O	O
Update Employee	O	O	O	O
Error Listing	O	O	O	O
Employee ILF	O	O	O	O
Job Assignment EIF	O	O	O	O

Table A2.2

Names of Possible Function Types	Identify the Function Used					
	ILF	EIF	EI	EO	EQ	N/A
Add Customer	O	O	O	O	O	O
Clear Screen	O	O	O	O	O	O
Error Message Window	O	O	O	O	O	O
Customer Data	O	O	O	O	O	O
Zip Code Data	O	O	O	O	O	O

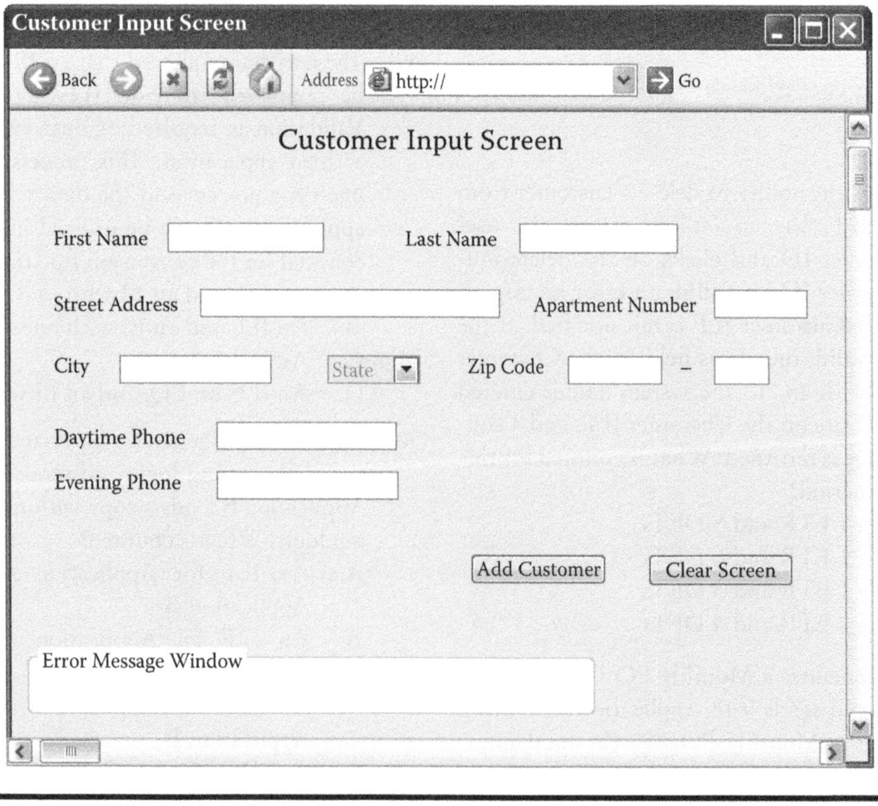

Figure A2.1   Customer input screen.

be erased. The "Error Message Window" displays any errors associated with validations performed against an externally maintained Zip Code Data file after the "Add Customer" button is pressed.

Case Study 3

A retail store has developed a new application, Frequent Buyer Program (FBP), to track customer purchases. The customer fills out a paper application and gives it to the store clerk. The clerk then adds the customer's information on-line. The clerk can also list customers, view a customer's detailed information, and change a customer's information. A report is produced daily listing customers that were added with their addresses.

Identify the functions of the FBP application by choosing the correct radio buttons in Table A2.3.

Case Study 4

Use the data flow diagram in Figure A2.2 to identify the functions in the HR application and the Mail Distribution application (see Table A2.4).

Table A2.3

Names of Possible Function Types	Identify the Function Used					
	ILF	EIF	EI	EO	EQ	N/A
Add Customer	O	O	O	O	O	O
Change Customer's Information	O	O	O	O	O	O
List Customers	O	O	O	O	O	O
View Customer's Detail Information	O	O	O	O	O	O
Customer Report	O	O	O	O	O	O

Case Study 5

SME is implementing a Customer Relations Management (CRM) application. The Web Info (WI) application, an existing application, will be required to send information to the CRM each evening by retrieving all Requests for Information (RFI) submitted that day and currently maintained in the RFI logical file within the WI application. The

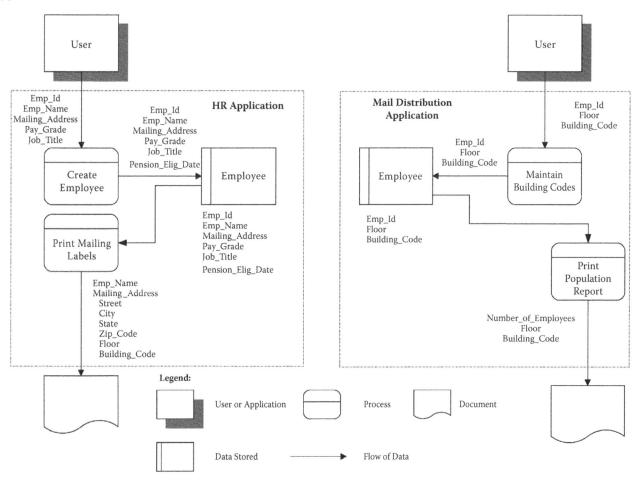

Figure A2.2 HR and mail distribution applications.

Table A2.4

Names of Possible Function Types	Identify the Function Used					
	ILF	*EIF*	*EI*	*EO*	*EQ*	*N/A*
Create Employee	O	O	O	O	O	O
Print Mailing Labels	O	O	O	O	O	O
Maintain Building Codes	O	O	O	O	O	O
Print Population Report	O	O	O	O	O	O
Employee	O	O	O	O	O	O

Table A2.5

Names of Possible Function Types	Enter Complexity			
	Low	*Average*	*High*	*N/A*
RFI Daily Feed	O	O	O	O
Potential Customer logical file	O	O	O	O
State Report	O	O	O	O
Retrieve/View Customer Information	O	O	O	O
Update Requested Information	O	O	O	O

Table A2.6

Names of Possible Function Types	Enter Complexity			
	Low	*Average*	*High*	*N/A*
Customer logical file	O	O	O	O
Orders logical file	O	O	O	O
CUSTID logical file	O	O	O	O
Add Bulk Orders	O	O	O	O
Change Bulk Orders	O	O	O	O

following information is sent on this daily feed: requestor ID; requestor's first, middle, and last name; requestor's organization; requestor's address (street address, city, state, and Zip Code); date of request; requested items; and quantities for requested items. The CRM application will validate and process the daily feed into a new Potential Customer logical file.

Separate reports by state will be generated each morning by the CRM application and delivered to state sales coordinators. The printout will contain all of the information on the Potential Customer logical file as well as a total number of requests for information, which is calculated at the time the report is produced. The state code and state name, retrieved from a code table, will also be printed on each report.

Each state sales coordinator will have the ability to retrieve via screen all information maintained in the Potential Customer logical file by entering the requestor ID and action key; hard-coded error messages will be returned if the requestor ID is not found.

Using that screen, the state coordinator can revise the requested items and/or quantities using the requestor ID and a preassigned function key; hard-coded error messages may be returned if the newly assigned requested item is not contained in the Inventory logical file maintained by the Inventory application, or a hard-coded confirmation message will occur.

Identify the complexity of the functions for the CRM application by choosing the correct radio buttons in Table A2.5.

Case Study 6

A company is creating a new application called Sales Order System (SOS). This application will have the following logical files:

■ CUSTOMER contains the company name; street address, city, state, and Zip Code; customer code; region; sales agent; and billing street address, city, state, and Zip Code.

■ ORDERS contains: (a) Record One (Ship to) contains customer code, record ID, "attention to" name (first name, middle initial, last name), street address, city, state, Zip Code, carrier code, and date to be shipped. (b) Record Two (Details) contains customer code, record ID, item code, item quantity, item dollar amount, bulk order discount code, total order dollar amount, tax code, tax amount, and date order placed. (c) Record Three (Billing) contains customer code, record ID, company code, billing street address, city, state, Zip Code, and orderer's name (first name, middle initial, last name).

■ CUSTID contains the same information as CUSTOMER but sorted by customer code and is used in processing outputs.

Bulk orders are entered into the SOS via the Bulk Order file from the regional system. The transaction contains 29 attributes and updates the ORDERS logical file. One of the attributes contains an action field with the values A (add) or C (change).

Identify the complexity of the functions for the SOS application by choosing the correct radio buttons in Table A2.6.

Case Study 7

An insurance company offers several product lines, including homeowner's and auto insurance. A new marketing strategy is to offer a discount on the purchase of auto insurance to a policyholder who already has homeowner's insurance with the company. To provide this service, enhancements must be made:

- The Policyholder logical file that is maintained by both the Homeowner's Insurance application and the Auto Insurance application will have two fields added to it: Multipolicy Discount Indicator and Discount Amount.
- Processing logic must be changed in the Auto Insurance application. During the nightly batch processing of new auto policies, the Policyholder logical file must be checked to see if the policyholder has homeowner's insurance with the company. If so, the two new fields in the Policyholder logical file will be updated. In addition, the confirmation report that is produced from the batch process will be changed to include a message that the discount was applied.
- The Homeowner's Insurance application must also be changed. During the nightly batch process of cancelled homeowner's policies, the Policyholder logical file must be checked to see if the policyholder has been receiving the multipolicy discount on auto insurance. If so, the Multipolicy Discount Indicator will be set to "C" for "Cancelled."
- The nightly batch process in the Auto Insurance application must also be changed to check each record on the Policyholder logical file for cancelled homeowner's insurance. If the Multipolicy Discount Indicator is a "C," it will be changed to an "N," the Discount Amount will be set to zero, the new auto insurance premium will be calculated, and a letter outlining the changes will be produced and mailed to the policyholder.

Identify the new and changed functions of the Homeowner's Insurance and Auto Insurance applications by choosing the correct radio buttons in Table A2.7.

Case Study 8

Company XYZ plans to enhance its Accounts Payable (AP) application. The current application interfaces with existing banking, help, and purchase order (PO) applications. This is a menu-driven system. To enter the AP application, the user must make selections from a main menu. The menu has the following options:

Table A2.7

Names of Possible Function Types	Identify the Function Used					
	ILF	EIF	EI	EO	EQ	N/A
Policyholder logical file	O	O	O	O	O	O
New Auto Policy	O	O	O	O	O	O
New Auto Policy Confirmation Report	O	O	O	O	O	O
Cancelled Homeowner's Policy	O	O	O	O	O	O
Policyholder Letter	O	O	O	O	O	O

Table A2.8

Names of Possible Function Types	Identify the Function Used					
	ILF	EIF	EI	EO	EQ	N/A
Add Vendor	O	O	O	O	O	O
Change Vendor	O	O	O	O	O	O
Delete Vendor	O	O	O	O	O	O
Display Vendor Information	O	O	O	O	O	O
Vendor logical file	O	O	O	O	O	O

- Invoices
  - Add an invoice
  - Display an invoice
  - Change an invoice
  - Delete an invoice
- Payments
  - Retrieve payments due
  - Record payments

Invoices and payments are maintained in the Invoice logical file in AP. The enhancement will allow users to maintain Vendor information in the AP application. The following is being added to the AP menu:

- Vendor
  - Add a vendor
  - Display vendor information
  - Change vendor information

The Vendor information will be maintained in a new Vendor logical file in the AP application.

Identify the enhanced functions of the AP application by choosing the correct radio buttons in Table A2.8.

Case Study 9

A new file is to be passed from the Accounts Payable (AP) application to the Banking application at the close of every business day. This file contains the payment date required, payment amount, PO number, vendor name, and vendor billing street address, city, state, and Zip Code. The Banking application must now be enhanced to process this incoming file and to generate the appropriate checks.

The Banking application will process the incoming file from the AP application without any edits or validation into two user-maintained logical files: Checking Account and Disbursements. The Checking Account logical file previously had 2 RETs and 19 DETs. This change will require the addition of the PO number to the Checking Account logical file. All other attributes were previously included. The Disbursements logical file will not require any changes as a result of this enhancement.

The current process to generate checks to pay invoices is to be modified. Checks now will be generated with the PO number as a separate memo attribute by the banking system. Previously, checks contained the following information: preprinted name and address for the company, preprinted check numbers, payment date, payment amount, payee (same as vendor's name), and payee street address, city, state, and Zip Code. Checks previously did not include a memo attribute. These checks reference only the Checking Account logical file when they are created. The Checking Account logical file is updated internally to indicate payment as part of the check generation elementary process.

A printed report will be generated from the Checking Account logical file if checks were not produced because of

Table A2.9

Names of Possible Function Types	Enter Complexity			
	Low	Average	High	N/A
Payment file from AP	O	O	O	O
Checking Account logical file	O	O	O	O
Disbursement logical file	O	O	O	O
Checks	O	O	O	O
Report of Insufficient Funds	O	O	O	O

an inadequate balance. The Report of Insufficient Funds will contain the following attributes: insufficient funds for payment date, payee, PO number, payment amount, total number of payees, and total payment amount (total attributes are calculated when the report is produced).

Identify the complexity of the enhanced functions for the Banking application by choosing the correct radio buttons in Table A2.9.

Case Study 10

Students enrolling in a course at a local university have the ability to do so on-line by accessing the Course Registration application. When the student selects File: New, the Course Registration screen shown in Figure A2.3 appears. The

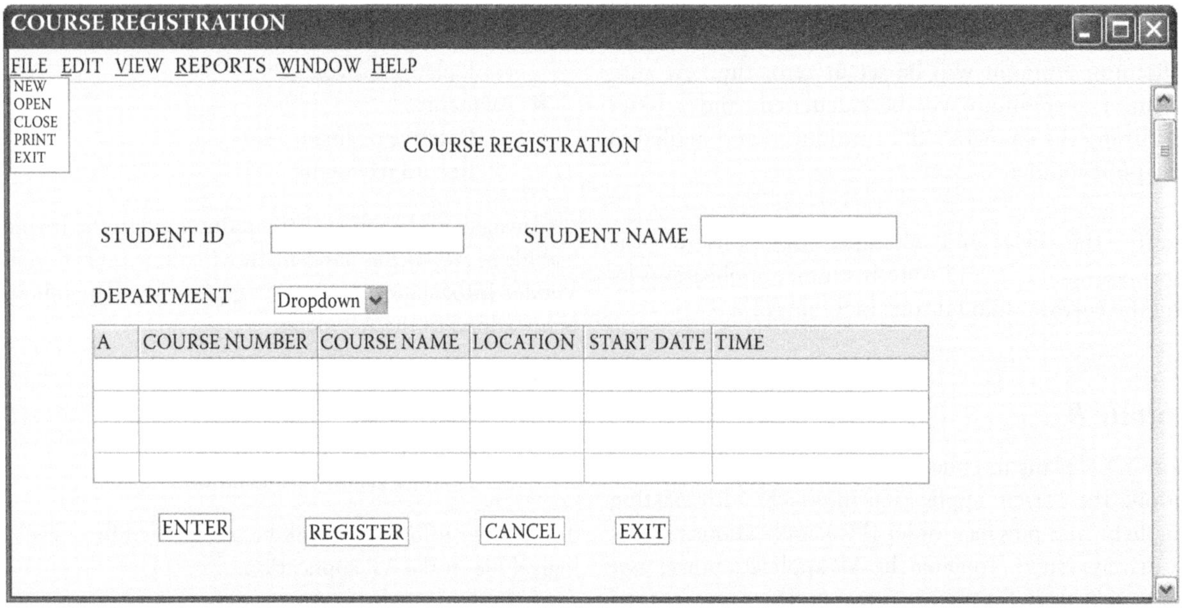

Figure A2.3   Course registration.

student then enters his or her student ID and clicks "Enter." If the entered student ID has no match on the Student logical file, an error message is returned, and the student may either try again or click "Cancel" to exit the application. If a match is found on the student's ID, the student's name is retrieved from the Student logical file and displayed on the screen. The student then selects a department from the drop-down list box, and a list of all courses offered by that department is retrieved from the Course logical file that is maintained in another application. Displayed on the list are course number, course name, location, start date, and time. To register for a course, the student enters "X" in Column A next to the desired course and clicks "Enter" or "Register." A validation on the Course logical file is made to ensure that the class still has openings. If there are no openings, an error message is displayed on the screen. If there are openings, a validation is made on the Student logical file to ensure that the student is eligible to enroll for the course. If ineligible, an error message is displayed on the screen. Otherwise, the Student logical file is updated, and a confirmation message

Table A2.10

Names of Possible Function Types	Identify the Function Used					
	ILF	EIF	EI	EO	EQ	N/A
Student logical file	O	O	O	O	O	O
Course logical file	O	O	O	O	O	O
Register for Course	O	O	O	O	O	O
Department Drop-Down List Box	O	O	O	O	O	O
Cancel	O	O	O	O	O	O

is displayed. The student can then either register for another course by repeating the process or click on "Exit" to end the process.

Identify the functions for the Course Registration application by choosing the correct radio buttons in Table A2.10.

Appendix 3

Practice Exam 2

Part 1. Definitions and Rules

1. Translation Data is sometimes referred to as:
   A. User Metacode Data
   B. Substitution Data
   C. Code Data
   D. None of the above

2. Examples of repair include:
   A. Missing functions that do not result in application failure (external design error)
   B. Errors resulting in a stop-run situation (code error)
   C. Both A and B
   D. Neither A nor B

3. Steps in the Functional Size Measurement Method procedure include:
   A. Gather the available documentation
   B. Report quality metrics
   C. Calculate the technical size
   D. Both A and B

4. The application area:
   A. Acts as a "membrane" through which data processed by transactions pass into and out from the application
   B. Is a general term for a grouping of applications that handle a specific business area
   C. Corresponds to an administrative level for management purposes
   D. Both B and C

5. The smallest unit of activity that is meaningful to the user is the definition of:
   A. An elementary unit
   B. A single function point
   C. An elementary process
   D. A functional unit

6. An elementary process that processes data or control information sent from outside the boundary is an:
   A. EO
   B. EI
   C. EQ
   D. Both A and C

7. Business Data may also be referred to as:
   A. Personal User Data
   B. Core Objects
   C. List Data
   D. None of the above

8. The Value Adjustment Factor (VAF) is:
   A. A measure of the functional vs. technical ratio in a given application
   B. The factor that indicates the general functionality provided to the user of the application
   C. The factor of value delivered to the end user by the application
   D. None of the above

9. Entity subtype:
   A. Is a subdivision of entity type
   B. Inherits all the attributes and relationships of its parent entity type
   C. May have additional, unique attributes and relationships
   D. All of the above

10. The process of recreating a set of data to make it current with its source is the definition of:
    A. Reload
    B. Copy

C. Refresh

D. Image Load

11. General System Characteristics (GSCs) are:

A. A set of 14 questions that quantify the degree of quality for the application

B. A set of 14 questions that evaluate the overall complexity of the application

C. Both A and B

D. None of the above

12. Total Degree of Influence (TDI) is:

A. ±35%

B. The sum of the 14 degrees of influence

C. A score between 0 and 70

D. Both B and C

13. The two types of subgroups for record element types are:

A. Obligatory and arbitrary

B. Mandatory and optional

C. Optional and indispensable

D. Compulsory and discretionary

14. Corrective maintenance is:

A. The modification of a software product performed after delivery to account for scope creep

B. The modification of a software product performed after delivery to introduce product enhancements

C. The reactive modification of a software product performed after delivery to correct discovered problems

D. All of the above

15. Flexible query/report capability is accounted for in which of the following GSCs:

A. Complex Processing

B End-User Efficiency

C. Facilitate Change

D. Operational Ease

16. Internal Logical Files (ILFs) can:

A. Be hard coded

B. Be counted in more than one application

C. Contain multiple FTRs

D. Both B and C

17. Counting scope:

A. Includes the effect of scope creep

B. Defines the set of Functional User Requirements to be included inside of the application boundary

C. Defines the set of Functional User Requirements to be included in the function point count

D. Both A and C

18. An application:

A. Is a cohesive collection of automated procedures and data supporting a business objective

B. Consists of one or more components, modules, or subsystems

C. Is a group of related items treated as a unit

D. A and B

19. The formula for Value Adjustment Factor is:

A. VAF = (TDI × 0.01) + 0.65

B. VAF = TDI + 0.65

C. VAF = TDI × 0.01

D. None of the above

20. Which GSC describes the degree to which the application and the code in the application have been specifically designed, developed, and supported to be usable in other applications:

A. Installation Ease

B. Operational Ease

C. Reusability

D. Multiple Sites

21. A File Type Referenced is:

A. A data function maintained by an elementary process

B. A data function maintained by a transactional function

C. A data function read and/or maintained by a transactional function

D. None of the above

22. Which of the following can be counted as one or more ILFs in a project:

A. Application data

B. Application security data

C. Control data

D. All of the above

23. What do most mainframe applications score for the Multiple Sites GSC:

A. 3

B. 2

C. 1

D. 0

24. On-line applications typically receive a score of _____ for the Data Communications GSC.

A. 3

B. 4

C. 5

D. None of the above

25. The IEEE definition of load is:
    A. To copy computer instructions or data from external storage to internal storage
    B. To read data from a source, leaving the source data unchanged, and to write the same data elsewhere in a physical form that may differ from that of the source
    C. The process of recreating a set of data to make it current with its source
    D. None of the above

26. The process of recreating a set of data to make it current with its source is the definition of:
    A. Load
    B. Copy
    C. Refresh
    D. Image

27. Which of the following are exclusively transactional functions:
    A. EI, EIF
    B. EI, EO, ILF
    C. ILF, EIF
    D. None of the above

28. Which of the following are data functions:
    A. ILF, ELF
    B. ILF, EIF
    C. EI, EO, EQ
    D. None of the above

Refer to Figure A3.1 for questions 29 through 31.

29. What is the number of the step corresponding to "calculate functional size":
    A. 2
    B. 3
    C. 4
    D. 5

30. What is the number of the step corresponding to "measure data functions":
    A. 2
    B. 3
    C. 4
    D. None of the above

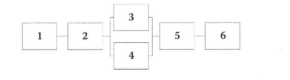

Figure A3.1   Steps in function point counting procedure.

31. The last step of the functional size measurement method procedure labeled 6 in the figure is:
    A. Measure data functions
    B. Calculate functional size
    C. Measure transactional functions
    D. None of the above

32. A score of 2 for degree of influence indicates:
    A. Incidental influence
    B. Moderate influence
    C. Average influence
    D. Significant influence

33. The degree to which the rate of business transactions influenced the development of the application is which General System Characteristic:
    A. Transaction Rate
    B. Heavily Used Configuration
    C. Operational Ease
    D. Performance

34. A project used to develop and deliver adaptive maintenance is:
    A. A development project
    B. An enhancement project
    C. Not measurable using function point analysis
    D. An application function point count

35. Hardware or software upgrades are an example of:
    A. Planned obsolescence
    B. An enhancement project
    C. System upgrades
    D. A maintenance activity

36. When applied, the Value Adjustment Factor adjusts the unadjusted functional size:
    A. ±30% to produce the adjusted functional size
    B. ±35% to produce the adjusted functional size
    C. ±60% to produce the adjusted functional size
    D. ±65% to produce the adjusted functional size

37. A unique, user-recognizable, nonrepeated attribute is:
    A. A Data Element Type
    B. A File Type Referenced
    C. A Record Element Type
    D. None of the above

38. Multilingual support counts as how many items:
    A. 1
    B. 2
    C. 4
    D. 6

39. The Total Degree of Influence is between:
    A.   0 to 5
    B.   0 to 70
    C.   1 to 5
    D.   0.65 to 1.35

40. What is the Value Adjustment Factor if the TDI is equal to 45:
    A.   0.95
    B.   1.00
    C.   1.05
    D.   1.10

41. Which of the following statements is false:
    A.   An ILF is a user-recognizable group of logically related data or control information that is referenced by the application being measured but which is maintained within the boundary of another application
    B.   The primary intent of an EIF is to hold data referenced through one or more elementary processes within the boundary of the application measured
    C.   An EIF counted for an application must be in an ILF in another application
    D.   All of the above are true

42. Processing logic for EIs may include:
    A.   Validations are performed
    B.   Equivalent values are converted
    C.   One or more ILFs are updated
    D.   All of the above

43. A record is equivalent to the relational database term:
    A.   A row
    B.   A column
    C.   A tuple
    D.   Both A and C

44. Attributes designed to provide fast access to the information is the definition of:
    A.   Foreign key
    B.   Primary key
    C.   Secondary key
    D.   None of the above

45. When performing function point analysis, it is preferable to analyze the logical data model in:
    A.   First normal form
    B.   Second normal form
    C.   Third normal form
    D.   Fourth normal form

46. An average complexity EIF has a value of:
    A.   5
    B.   7

C.   10
D.   15

47. Functional size can be approximated but not measured during what stage:
    A.   Proposal
    B.   Requirements
    C.   Design
    D.   Maintenance

48. An EI can be invoked if the user hits the submit button on the GUI screen, presses the F10 key on the keyboard, or enters an "Add" command on a command line. How many DETs should be counted for these options:
    A.   1
    B.   3
    C.   0
    D.   None of the above

49. The Functional User Requirements as perceived by the user is:
    A.   Requirements view
    B.   Specification view
    C.   User view
    D.   Design view

50. A group of related items that is treated as a unit is a:
    A.   Record
    B.   File
    C.   File system
    D.   Function

Part 2. Implementation

1. An application includes 72 occurrences of field level help that are all maintained inside the application boundary. How many transactional functions are counted:
    A.   72 EQs
    B.   72 EOs
    C.   No transaction functions are counted
    D.   One transaction function

2. Which of the following is not an example of Reference Data:
    A.   Job rates
    B.   Tax tables
    C.   Discount rates
    D.   Airport Codes/Airport Names

3. Which of the following could be an EQ:
    A.   A menu screen providing only navigation
    B.   An output report containing derived data

Sales

4th Qtr 9%
3rd Qtr 10%
2nd Qtr 23%
1st Qtr 58%

Figure A3.2   Sales pie chart.

C.   Help text retrieved from an ILF
D.   An output containing a monthly total not retrieved from a data function

4.   Assuming the data shown have been calculated at the time of display, how would you count the pie chart shown in Figure A3.2:
A.   4 EOs
B.   1 EO with 4 DETs
C.   1 EO with 2 DETs
D.   1 EO with 8 DETs

5.   An enhancement project added three low external inputs, deleted two high external inquiries, and changed two average external outputs to low complexity. What is the enhancement project functional size:
A.   5
B.   20
C.   29
D.   None of the above

6.   The change in the value of the application functional size for the preceding question is:
A.   −20
B.   −5
C.   30
D.   42

7.   The function point value of an ILF with 20 DETs and 4 RETs is:
A.   5
B.   7
C.   10
D.   15

8.   An application has a Pantone color table that contains two data elements: color code and color description. This table is an example of what type of data:
A.   Code Data
B.   Constant Data
C.   Reference Data
D.   Valid Values Data

9.   Users have requested four tabs on a Web application to accomplish the elementary process of creating a purchase order. What is counted:
A.   1 EI
B.   4 EIs
C.   1 EI and 4 EQs
D.   4 EIs and 1 EQ

10.   In a count of DETs in an EO the following should be counted:
A.   System generated dates in the heading
B.   Calculated totals of sales data retrieved from an ILF
C.   Literals in the heading
D.   Both A and B

11.   An ILF is maintained by three separate applications. Where is it counted:
A.   In the application that maintains the most DETs
B.   In all three applications
C.   In the application that accesses the ILF with the greatest frequency
D.   In none of the applications because it cannot be shared

12.   Which of the following formulas is used to calculate an enhancement project functional size:
A.   DFP = ADD + CFP
B.   EFP = ADD + CHGA + DEL
C.   AFPA = (AFPB + ADD + CHGA) − (CHGB + DEL)
D.   None of the above

13.   Three user-defined groups of data are maintained by the application and exist in the same physical file. How many ILFs are counted:
A.   0
B.   1
C.   2
D.   3

14.   Which of the following cannot be counted as an EQ:
A.   Screens providing only navigation
B.   Reports that contain derived data
C.   A screen displaying data simply retrieved from an ILF
D.   A and B

15.   Which of the following types of transactions may perform validations:
A.   EI
B.   EO
C.   EQ
D.   All of the above

16. To be an EI, it is mandatory that you either update at least one ILF or do one of the following:
    A. Sort or arrange a set of data
    B. Perform validations
    C. Create derived data
    D. Alter the behavior of the application

17. In an enhancement project, the size of the functions being added is 30, the size of the functions being deleted is 15, the size of the functions being changed as they are/will be after implementation is 35, and the size of the functions being changed as they are/were before the project commenced is 20. What is the enhancement project functional size:
    A. 60
    B. 65
    C. 80
    D. None of the above

18. A data function stores customer information (customer name; account number; purchase order number; billing street address, city, state, and Zip Code; shipping street address, city, state, and Zip Code; phone number; e-mail address; fax number). The billing address and shipping address are each treated as a single unit. The customer information store is being updated by the application being measured. What type of data function is this and how many DETs are present:
    A. An EIF with 14 DETs
    B. An EIF with 8 DETs
    C. An ILF with 8 DETs
    D. An ILF with 14 DETs

19. A transaction whose primary intent is maintaining an ILF is being added to an application. This transaction has 15 unique DETs, updates one ILF, and reads one EIF. What is the functional size of this transaction:
    A. 4
    B. 5
    C. 6
    D. 7

20. When determining the Value Adjustment Factor for an enhancement project:
    A. Use the Value Adjustment Factor from the application functional size
    B. Use the Value Adjustment Factor from the most recent enhancement count
    C. Use the constant 1.0 as your Value Adjustment Factor
    D. None of the above

21. Which of the following activities are within the enhancement counting scope:
    A. Correction of production errors
    B. Perfective or preventative maintenance

C. Platform upgrades, new system software releases
D. None of the above

22. Which of the following is an EO:
    A. Confirmation messages displayed to the screen
    B. Error messages printed as a report
    C. A report containing derived data requested via an online menu
    D. Both B and C

23. Which of the following is not an EQ:
    A. Application level help
    B. A logon screen that does not reference a data function
    C. Navigation screen with no retrieved data
    D. Both B and C

24. Functional user requirements may include which of the following:
    A. Technical constraints
    B. Quality constraints
    C. Environmental constraints
    D. None of the above

25. Which of the following formulas is used to calculate an adjusted development project functional size:
    A. DFP = ADD + CFP
    B. EFP = ADD + CHGA + CFP + DEL
    C. aDFP = DFP × VAF
    D. aDFP = DFP + ADD + CHGA + CFP + DEL

26. After an enhancement project, the application functional size must be updated to reflect changed functionality. This changed functionality may:
    A. Increase the application functional size
    B. Decrease the application functional size
    C. Be unable to be determined
    D. Both A and B

27. Application A maintains an ILF that is also read by Application B. Application A should:
    A. Get credit for an ILF and an EIF
    B. Get credit for an ILF
    C. Get credit for an EQ
    D. Both B and C

28. In the previous question, Application B should:
    A. Get credit for an EIF and EI
    B. Get credit for an EI
    C. Get credit for an ILF
    D. Get credit for an EIF

29. A transaction to add an employee has the ability to return ten unique error messages and two unique confirmation messages. How many EQs are counted for the error and confirmation messages:
    A. 12
    B. 2

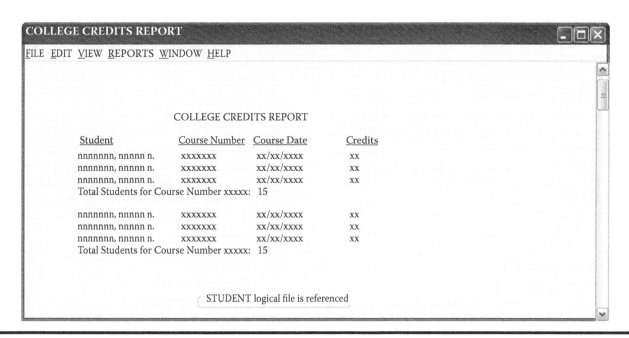

Figure A3.3   College Credits Report.

C.   1

D.   0

30. An application has three menus to navigate through the system. Each page of navigation contains 25 selections. How many DETs should be counted:
    A.   0
    B.   1
    C.   3
    D.   75

31. The maximum Total Degree of Influence is:
    A.   35
    B.   65
    C.   70
    D.   135

32. How would you count the College Credits Report shown in Figure A3.3? No totals are stored in the Student logical file.
    A.   1 low EQ
    B.   1 average EQ
    C.   1 low EO
    D.   1 average EO

33. An ILF has 50 DETs and 5 RETs. What is its functional size:
    A.   5
    B.   7
    C.   10
    D.   15

34. A user requires that an application print a monthly report automatically every month. This report lists all employees by department and contains employee name and employee ID. This report is generated automatically by the system, thus no DETs cross the application boundary to cause the report to print. This report is counted as an:
    A.   EI
    B.   EQ
    C.   EO
    D.   It is not counted

35. The functional complexity of EQs is determined by:
    A.   The number of FTRs and RETs
    B.   The number of DETs and RETs
    C.   The number of DETs and FTRs
    D.   None of the above

36. A report is printed with retrieved fields from a single ILF and a single EIF. A different ILF is updated with the time and date when the report was printed. What is counted:
    A.   2 EQs and 1 EI
    B.   1 EI and 1 EO
    C.   1 EQ
    D.   1 EO

37. A user-defined customer file is maintained in three database tables. These three tables are customer, address, and a hash table used to accelerate the search for a customer's data. How many ILFs are counted within this single application:
    A.   0
    B.   1
    C.   2
    D.   3

38. When counting DETs in an ILF, count:
    A. All DETs in the file
    B. Only those DETs maintained
    C. Only those DETs referenced
    D. Only those DETs maintained and/or referenced

39. An Accounts Payable application allows the user to extract information from an ILF and an EIF. The users enters an ID number and presses the submit key. A screen display provides a response screen with 19 retrieved data elements and no derived or calculated fields. What is counted:
    A. A low EI and an average EQ
    B. A low EI and a high EQ
    C. A high EQ
    D. An average EQ

40. Examples of EIs include:
    A. Batch input from another application that adds data to an ILF
    B. Control information that initiates the generation of a report
    C. Data referenced by another application
    D. Both A and B

41. A development project has four average complexity EIs and one high complexity EI; two average complexity EOs; three average complexity EQs and two high complexity EQs; three low complexity ILFs and one high complexity ILF; two low complexity EIFs; and four average complexity conversion EIs. What is the application functional size after the development project is installed:
    A. 86
    B. 90
    C. 102
    D. 118

42. For the above question, what is the development project functional size:
    A. 90
    B. 102
    C. 118
    D. None of the above

43. A screen containing a drop-down list with items retrieved from an ILF is displayed to the user. This drop-down list should be counted as:
    A. An EO only
    B. A DET on the count of the screen
    C. A EQ and a DET on the screen being counted
    D. An EQ only

44. An enhancement project adds six high complexity EIs and two average complexity EQs, deletes one high complexity EQ, changes three EOs from low to high complexity, and adds two high complexity EIs for conversion. If the application functional size is 1000 before the enhancement, what is the value of the conversion functionality:
    A. 1059
    B. 1047
    C. 71
    D. 12

45. The top right-hand corner of every application contains an "About" link that displays information about the application, including version number, product ID, and copyright information. This information is maintained in an application outside the boundary by a developer tool called Robot_Help. What should be counted for the "About" link:
    A. An EIF and an EQ
    B. Only an EQ
    C. An EI and an EQ
    D. Nothing is counted

46. Figure A3.4, from the IFPUG *Counting Practices Manual*, Release 4.3, illustrates what process:
    A. Screen scraping
    B. Image copy/load
    C. Static image copy
    D. Copy merge "refresh"

47. A development project has three low complexity EIs and four average complexity EIs, three average complexity EOs, four high complexity EQs, one low complexity ILF, and five low complexity conversion EIs. What is the development functional size:
    A. 16
    B. 71
    C. 86
    D. 89

48. An application's functional size before an enhancement is 100. The enhancement added four low complexity EIs, changed three EQs from low to average complexity, and deleted three average complexity EOs. What is the functional size of the application after the enhancement project is delivered:
    A. 97
    B. 100
    C. 115
    D. 124

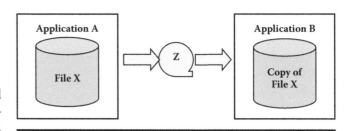

Figure A3.4 Shared data example.

49. The user has requested that an ILF (or part of an ILF) be populated from an ILF in another application. Validation is required against yet another ILF from a third application. This is specified as a one-time process, and the data reference in the third application will not be utilized in the future. What is counted for the conversion functionality:

    A. An EIF and an EI with two FTRs
    B. An ILF and an EI with one FTR
    C. An ILF and an EI with three FTRs
    D. An ILF, an EQ and an EI with one FTR

50. To avoid the overhead of Application C having to dynamically search the data from both Application A and Application B, the data is being copied from Application A and Application B and merged into a new data store in Application C. The user requires that the information from Applications A and B be refreshed daily for validation or reference purposes only. Unload, Merge, and Load utilities are used. There is no business processing logic involved. What is counted:

    A. An ILF for Application A, an ILF for Application B, and an EI for Application C
    B. An ILF and EQ for Application A, an ILF and EQ for Application B, and an EI for Application C
    C. An ILF for Application A, an ILF for Application B, and an EIF for Application C
    D. An ILF for Application A, an ILF for Application B, and an EI and EIF for Application C

Part 3. Case Studies

Case Study 1

SME is implementing a Customer Relations Management (CRM) application. The Web Info (WI) application, an existing application, will be required to send information to the CRM each evening by retrieving all Requests for Information (RFI) submitted that day and currently maintained in the RFI logical file within the WI application. The following information is sent on this daily feed: requestor ID; requestor's first, middle, and last name; requestor's organization; requestor's address: street address, city, state, and Zip Code; date of request; requested items; and quantities for requested items. The CRM application will validate and process the daily feed into a new Potential Customer logical file.

Separate reports by state will be generated each morning by the CRM application and delivered to state sales coordinators. The printout will contain all of the information on the Potential Customer logical file as well as a Total Number of Requests for Information, which is calculated at the time the report is produced. The state code and state name, retrieved from a code table, will also be printed on each report. Each state sales coordinator will have the ability to retrieve via screen all information maintained in the Potential Customer logical file by entering the requestor ID and action key; hard-coded error messages will be returned if the requestor ID is not found.

Using that screen, the state coordinator can revise the requested items and/or quantities using the requestor ID and a preassigned function key; hard-coded error messages may be returned if the newly assigned requested item is not contained in the Inventory logical file maintained by the Inventory application or a hard-coded confirmation message will occur.

Identify the data functions for the CRM application by choosing the correct radio buttons in Table A3.1.

Case Study 2

A university's Course Registration application is being enhanced so students can view a list of all of the courses for which they have registered in the past. The requirements are:

1. Upon entering the student ID, a list of courses for which that student has registered at any time at that university is retrieved from the Student logical file. A list of course numbers and the corresponding course date is displayed if any records are found; otherwise, a static error message is returned.

2. If a list of courses is returned, the student may view details of the course registration by selecting the course number and course date from the list and clicking the Enter button. The details displayed will be the student's name, student's ID, course number, course name, course date, and course location.

All information is retrieved from the Course Registration logical file (which is maintained in the Course Registration application) and the Student logical file (which is not

Table A3.1

Names of Possible Function Types	Identify the Function Used		
	ILF	EIF	N/A
Potential Customer logical file	O	O	O
RFI	O	O	O
Inventory logical file	O	O	O
Error Messages Table	O	O	O
State Code Table	O	O	O

Table A3.2

Names of Possible Function Types	Enter Complexity			
	Low	Average	High	N/A
List Courses	O	O	O	O
View Course Details	O	O	O	O
Student logical file	O	O	O	O
Course Registration File	O	O	O	O
Error File	O	O	O	O

Table A3.3

Names of Possible Function Types	Enter Complexity			
	Low	Average	High	N/A
Create Employee	O	O	O	O
Maintain Building Codes	O	O	O	O
Employee ILF	O	O	O	O
Print Mailing Labels	O	O	O	O
Print Population Report	O	O	O	O

maintained by the Course Registration application but is maintained in another application). No new attributes were added to Course Registration logical file, and no new attributes were retrieved from the Student logical file as a result of this enhancement.

Identify the complexity of the enhancement functions by choosing the correct radio buttons in Table A3.2.

Case Study 3

Use the data flow diagram in Figure A3.5 to determine the complexity for the functions in the Human Resources application and Mail Distribution application.

Indicate the complexity of the function types by selecting the correct radio buttons in Table A3.3.

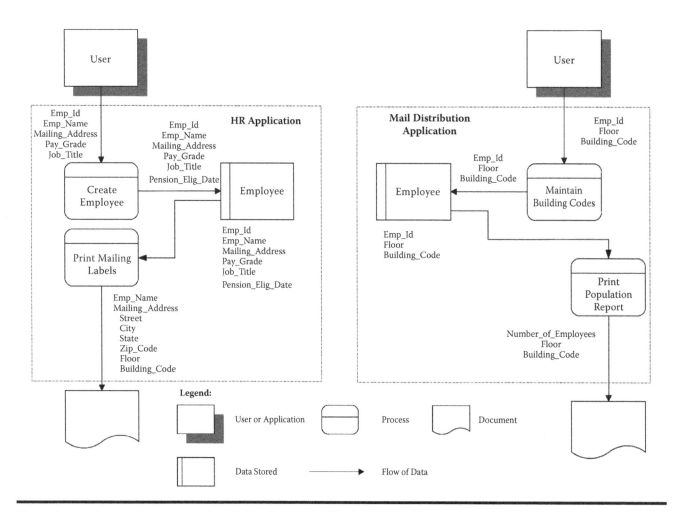

Figure A3.5   Human Resources and Mail Distribution applications.

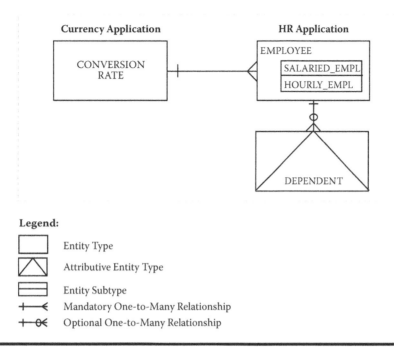

Figure A3.6   Human Resources and Currency applications.

Case Study 4

The user requires the Human Resources application to provide the following capabilities:

1. All hourly employees must be paid in U.S. dollars.
2. When the user adds or changes employee information, the Human Resources application must access the Currency application to retrieve a conversion rate. After retrieving the conversion rate, the HR application converts the employee's local standard hourly rate to a U.S. hourly rate using the following calculation: standard hourly rate ÷ conversion rate = U.S. dollar hourly rate.

Figure A3.6 shows the relationships for this example. The currency conversion rate information includes:

    CURRENCY
    Conversion_Rate_To_Base_Currency
    Currency

Identify the data functions for the Human Resources application by choosing the correct radio buttons in Table A3.4.

Case Study 5

The business users have requested a new Payroll Department application to track details of subcontractors' employment. These attributes will be maintained in a logical file called Contractor_Data that will be maintained inside the application boundary. Contractor_Data will include the contractor's first name, last name, home address, Social Security Number,

contract number, and ten additional user-specified attributes (not indicated here). An audit requirement has been imposed that requires that the application maintain audit data any time a change will be made to any of these attributes. The date of change, time of change, and User_ID of the user responsible for the change must be recorded together with "before" and "after" copies of the changed attributes. This data will be held in a file inside the application boundary in a table named Audit_Data. An audit report can be generated that will include the date of change, time of change, and User_ID of all changes in the last 30 days.

To place this new application into service, two single-use conversion processes will be run. The first conversion process will load a static attribute of "C" (indicating "Contractor") into one of the ten additional user-specified attributes specified earlier in the application's Contractor Data file. The second

Table A3.4

Names of Possible Function Types	Identify the Function Used		
	ILF	EIF	N/A
Currency Conversion Rate	O	O	O
Employee	O	O	O
Dependent	O	O	O
Hourly_Employee	O	O	O
Conversion Rate	O	O	O

Table A3.5

Names of Possible Function Types	Enter Complexity			
	Low	Average	High	N/A
Contractor_Data	O	O	O	O
Audit_Data	O	O	O	O
Audit Report	O	O	O	O
First Conversion	O	O	O	O
Second Conversion	O	O	O	O

Table A3.6

Names of Possible Function Types	Identify the Function Used					
	ILF	EIF	EI	EO	EQ	N/A
Locations	O	O	O	O	O	O
Transaction Data	O	O	O	O	O	O

Table A3.7

Names of Possible Function Types	Identify the Function Used					
	ILF	EIF	EI	EO	EQ	N/A
Locations	O	O	O	O	O	O
Transaction Data (Adds and Changes)	O	O	O	O	O	O
Transaction Data (Deletes)	O	O	O	O	O	O

conversion process will use the Social Security Number as a primary key to lookup data in a file named Sub_Contractors_Agreements maintained outside of the application boundary and load the returned the Contractor's First_Name, Last_Name, Home Address, and Social Security Number in the application's Contractor Data file.

Select the correct radio buttons in Table A3.5 to indicate the complexity of the function types listed.

Case Study 6

Application A retrieves a transaction file of changes named "Transaction Data" from an Internal Logical File named "Locations"; calculations are performed during the creation of this file. The transaction file contains three transaction types: Add, Change, and Delete; Application B processes the Transaction Data file based on the transaction type in updating its Internal Logical File, also named "Locations." Although they share the same physical name (Locations), the attributes maintained in Application A's Locations and those maintained Application B's Locations are different. Figure A3.7 shows this transfer.

Count the first two questions from Applications A's perspective (Table A3.6). Count the next three questions form Application B's perspective (Table A3.7).

Case Study 7

A data function (Main_Data) is maintained within the application boundary of a Patient Maintenance application. This table has 200 columns of data that store the functional

and nonfunctional data used by the application. The Patient Maintenance screen allows the user to add, change, or delete the following attributes of Main_Data:

a. Patient first name
b. Patient middle initial (optional)
c. Patient last name
d. Patient title (optional)
e. Patient ID number
f. Patient street address
g. Patient city
h. Patient state
i. Patient Zip Code
j. Patient home phone
k. Patient work phone
l. Patient blood type
m. Patient is organ donor (1 is stored for yes, 0 is stored for no)
n. Date of last patient checkup (stored as an integer starting from January 1, 1900)
o. Patient date of birth (stored as an integer starting from January 1, 1900)
p. Patient HIV status (1 is stored for positive, 0 is stored for negative)
q. Patient HIPPA consent (1, consent on file; 0 otherwise)

An optional subgroup of information is maintained that contains:

r. Patient advocate name
s. Patient advocate address (as one block of data)
t. Patient advocate phone

Other columns have been set aside for potential future use.

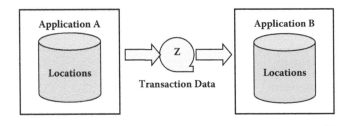

Figure A3.7   Data transfer.

Table A3.8

Names of Possible Function Types	Enter Complexity			
	Low	Average	High	N/A
Patient Maintenance Screen (Add)	O	O	O	O
Patient Maintenance Screen (Delete)	O	O	O	O
Main_Data	O	O	O	O
Initialize Reminders	O	O	O	O
Check-Up List	O	O	O	O

For an Add transaction, all of the attributes supplied by the user are saved in Main_Data; the next available patient ID is calculated at the time of the Add transaction and saved to Main_Data. For a Change transaction, the patient ID and any changed attributes will cross the application boundary. For a Delete transaction, only the patient ID crosses the application boundary.

The system clock kicks off an Initialize Reminders process at midnight every day that compares the Date of Last Patient Checkup to the current date and places a one-bit attribute in the DET Send Reminder Card in Main_Data if over one calendar year has passed. The user can generate a report by pressing the "Who Is Due for a Check-Up" button. The report extracts attributes a through i and n from the Main_Data and prints them with a heading and system-generated date and page numbers. The report name is "Check-Up List."

Identify the complexity of the functions by choosing the correct radio buttons in Table A3.8. Assume that there are no additional data functions or data elements used by the Patient Maintenance application for the above functions.

Case Study 8

(Refer to Figures A3.8 through A3.10.) Old Country Bank plans to enhance its online banking application. The current application interface allows customers to check balances, transfer funds, and apply for a bank debit card. To enter the online banking application, the user enters a preassigned user name and password. Once validated, the user gains access to a main menu, which is displayed in Figure A3.8. The bank plans to add a bill-payment option to its available services. After the enhancement, the menu screen will include the option for maintaining payee information and making payments, as displayed in Figure A3.9.

Payee data will be maintained by the online banking application in a Payee logical file through Add and Change transactions. Display Payee will retrieve data from the Payee logical file and will not include any calculations. Payment by an Old Country Bank check will be mailed to a designated payee when Make Payment has been selected and submitted; the payment date will be entered into the Payee logical file when the check is created. The functionality shown in Figure A3.10 is being added via the Bill Payment screen.

Identify the new functions of the application by choosing the correct radio buttons in Table A3.9.

Case Study 9

An online multilevel marketing company named New Age Distributors has developed an application to maintain profiles of members and record individual member sales. A clerk from New Age sets up a member's profile. The clerk can also list members with their profiles and change a member's information. A monthly customer report is produced that lists all members and calculates their year-to-date sales. Members who exceed total year-to-date sales of $5000 are

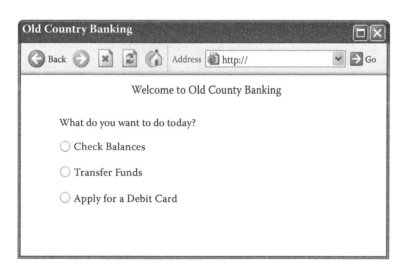

Figure A3.8   Main screen before enhancement.

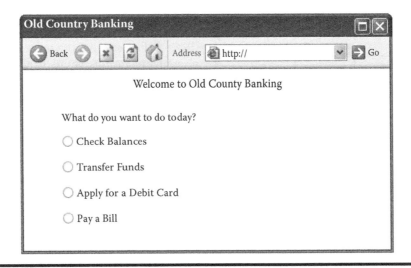

Figure A3.9 Main screen after enhancement.

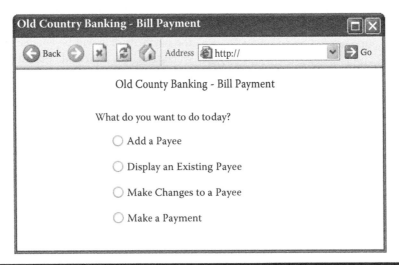

Figure A3.10 Screen added during enhancement.

indicated on the report as Diamond Club members. A copy of the monthly report appears in Figure A3.11.

Identify the functions of the FBP application by choosing the correct radio buttons in Table A3.10.

Case Study 10

A building access system sends a batch update with time-card data indicating when employees swipe their ID cards to enter and leave the building. This data enters the company's Time Management application and includes three attributes (employee ID, time of day, and in/out indicator). The employee ID attribute on the input record is validated against an Active Employees logical file maintained in the company's Employee Payroll application. If the validation passes, the Employee Hours logical file is updated in the Time Management application, and a confirmation message is printed. If the validation fails, no update is made, and an error listing is printed.

Table A3.9

Names of Possible Function Types	Identify the Function Used					
	ILF	EIF	EI	EO	EQ	N/A
Add Payee	O	O	O	O	O	O
Change Payee	O	O	O	O	O	O
Make Payment	O	O	O	O	O	O
Display Payee Information	O	O	O	O	O	O
Payee logical file	O	O	O	O	O	O

Identify the functional complexity of the functions in the Time Management application by choosing the correct radio buttons in Table A3.11.

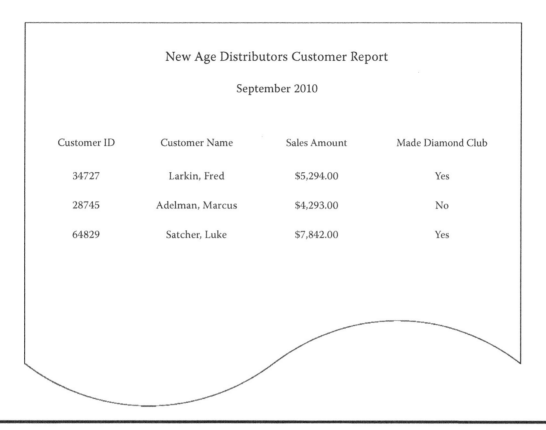

Figure A3.11   New Age Distributors customer report.

Table A3.10

Names of Possible Function Types	Identify the Function Used					
	ILF	EIF	EI	EO	EQ	N/A
Set Up Member's Profile	O	O	O	O	O	O
Change Member's Information	O	O	O	O	O	O
List Members	O	O	O	O	O	O
Membership logical file	O	O	O	O	O	O
Customer Report	O	O	O	O	O	O

Table A3.11

Names of Possible Function Types	Enter Complexity			
	Low	Average	High	N/A
Batch Update	O	O	O	O
Confirmation Message	O	O	O	O
Error Listing	O	O	O	O
Employee Hours ILF	O	O	O	O
Active Employees EIF	O	O	O	O

Appendix 4

Chapter 1 Sample Exam Answers

1. Organizations can apply the international standard of the IFPUG functional size measurement method known as function point analysis to measure the size of a software product to:
   A. Support quality and productivity analysis
   B. Provide a normalization factor for software comparison
   C. Estimate cost and resources required for software development, enhancement, and maintenance
   D. All of the above[1]

2. The objectives of function point analysis are to measure:
   A. Functionality implemented in software that the user requests and receives
   B. Nonfunctional, technical requirements
   C. Functionality impacted by software development, enhancement, and maintenance independently of technology used for implementation
   D. A and C[2]

3. The process of function point analysis is:
   A. Assisting users in determining the benefit of an application package to their organization by functionally sizing functions that specifically match their requirements
   B. A consistent measure among various projects and organizations
   C. Simple enough to minimize the overhead of the measurement process
   D. B and C[3]

4. A function point is:
   A. The smallest unit of activity that is meaningful to the user
   B. A unit of measure for functional size as defined within the international standard of the IFPUG Functional Size Measurement Method known as function point analysis[4]
   C. A unique, user-recognizable, nonrepeated attribute
   D. None of the above

5. Which of the following is true of the IFPUG Functional Size Measurement Method?
   A. It is known as function point analysis
   B. Its units of functional size are called function points
   C. It cannot provide a normalization factor for software comparison
   D. A and B[5]

---

[1] Refer to IFPUG), *Function Point Counting Practices Manual* (CPM), Release 4.3, Part 1, page iii.
[2] Refer to IFPUG), *Function Point Counting Practices Manual* (CPM), Release 4.3, Part 1, page iii.

[3] Refer to IFPUG), *Function Point Counting Practices Manual* (CPM), Release 4.3, Part 1, page iii.
[4] Refer to IFPUG, *Function Point Counting Practices Manual* (CPM), Release 4.3, Part 1, page 6.
[5] Refer to IFPUG, *Function Point Counting Practices Manual* (CPM), Release 4.3, Part 1, page iii.

Appendix 5

Chapter 2 Sample Exam Answers

1. A user view:
   A. Can be used to measure the functional size
   B. Can be used to measure the technical size
   C. Can be verbal statements made by the user as to what his or her view is
   D. A and C[1]

2. Steps in the function point counting procedure include:
   A. Measure the data functions
   B. Measure the transactional functions
   C. A and B[2]
   D. None of the above

3. The size of the software derived by quantifying the Functional User Requirements is the:
   A. Technical size
   B. Functional size[3]
   C. A and B
   D. None of the above

4. Functional User Requirements are:
   A. A subset of the user requirements
   B. Requirements that describe what the software should do, in terms of tasks and services
   C. A and B[4]
   D. None of the above

5. Functional User Requirements may include:
   A. Data storage
   B. Data transformation

   C. Data retrieval
   D. All of the above[5]

6. A user is:
   A. Any person who communicates or interacts with the software at any time
   B. Any thing that communicates or interacts with the software at any time
   C. A and B[6]
   D. None of the above

7. Technical Requirements may have one or more of the following characteristics:
   A. Lack of "utility" functionality
   B. Terminology that can be understood by both users and software developers
   C. Technology dependence[7]
   D. All of the above

8. Initial User Requirements
   A. Represent user requirements prior to the sessions between the users and the software developers
   B. Do not address the needs of all users of the application
   C. Lack "utility" functionality
   D. All of the above[8]

9. A user view:
   A. Can vary in physical form
   B. Is approved by the user

---

[1] Refer to IFPUG, *Function Point Counting Practices Manual* (CPM), Release 4.3, Part 2, page 3-2.

[2] Refer to IFPUG, *Function Point Counting Practices Manual* (CPM), Release 4.3, Part 2, page 2-2.

[3] Refer to IFPUG, *Function Point Counting Practices Manual* (CPM), Release 4.3, Part 2, page 1-3.

[4] Refer to IFPUG, *Function Point Counting Practices Manual* (CPM), Release 4.3, Part 2, page 1-3.

[5] Refer to IFPUG, *Function Point Counting Practices Manual* (CPM), Release 4.3, Part 2, page 1-3.

[6] Refer to IFPUG, *Function Point Counting Practices Manual* (CPM), Release 4.3, Part 2, page 3-2.

[7] Refer to IFPUG), *Function Point Counting Practices Manual* (CPM), Release 4.3, Part 2, page 3-5.

[8] Refer to IFPUG, *Function Point Counting Practices Manual* (CPM), Release 4.3, Part 2, page 3-4.

    C. Is the Functional User Requirements *as perceived* by the user

    D. All of the above[9]

10. Which of the following documentation is useful when conducting any functional size measurement?

    A. Class diagrams

    B. Data/object models

    C. Requirements

    D. All of the above[10]

---

[9] Refer to IFPUG, *Function Point Counting Practices Manual* (CPM), Release 4.3, Part 2, page 3-2.

[10] Refer to IFPUG, *Function Point Counting Practices Manual* (CPM), Release 4.3, Part 2, page 2-4.

Appendix 6

Chapter 3 Sample Exam Answers

1. Which of the following is not true of a boundary:
   A. **Is dependent on technical and/or implementation considerations**[1]
   B. Is dependent on the user's external business view of the application
   C. Encloses the logical data maintained by the application (ILFs)
   D. Assists in identifying the logical data referenced by but not maintained within this application (EIFs)

2. The scope of an enhancement project function point count includes:
   A. **All the functions being added, changed, and deleted, as well as conversion functions developed as part of the enhancement project**[2]
   B. Only the functions being added
   C. Only the functions being added and deleted
   D. Only the functions being changed

3. Which of the following is not true of counting scope:
   A. It is determined by the purpose for performing the function point count
   B. It defines the functionality that will be included in a particular function point count
   C. It defines a (sub)set of the software being sized
   D. **It can include only one application**[3]

4. The boundary:
   A. Defines what is external to the application
   B. Encloses the logical data maintained by the application (ILFs)
   C. Is dependent on the user's external business view of the application
   D. **All of the above**[4]

5. The boundary:
   A. Indicates the border between the software being measured and the user
   B. Defines what is external to the application
   C. Acts as a membrane through which data processed by transactions (EIs, EOs, and EQs) passes into and out from the application
   D. **All of the above**[5]

6. The purpose of a function point count is to:
   A. Determine the type of function point count and the scope of the required count to obtain the answer to the business problem under investigation
   B. Influence the positioning of the boundary between the software under review and the surrounding software
   C. None of the above
   D. **A and B**[6]

---

[1] Refer to IFPUG, *Function Point Counting Practices Manual* (CPM), Release 4.3, Part 2, page 5-4.
[2] Refer to IFPUG, *Function Point Counting Practices Manual* (CPM), Release 4.3, Part 2, page 5-3.
[3] Refer to IFPUG, *Function Point Counting Practices Manual* (CPM), Release 4.3, Part 2, page 5-3.
[4] Refer to IFPUG, *Function Point Counting Practices Manual* (CPM), Release 4.3, Part 2, page 5-4.
[5] Refer to IFPUG, *Function Point Counting Practices Manual* (CPM), Release 4.3, Part 2, page 5-4.
[6] Refer to IFPUG, *Function Point Counting Practices Manual* (CPM), Release 4.3, Part 2, page 5-2.

7. What are the types of function point counts?
   A. Development project function point count and enhancement project function point count
   B. Enhancement project function point count and application function point count
   C. Application function point count, development project function point count, and enhancement project function point count[7]
   D. Application function point count and development project function point count

8. A development project's functional size:
   A. Is a measure of the functionality added, changed, or deleted at the completion of an enhancement project, as measured by the enhancement project function point count by the activity of applying the IFPUG Functional Size Measurement (FSM) Method
   B. Is a measure of the functionality provided to the users with the first release of the software, as measured by the development project function point count by the activity of applying the IFPUG Functional Size Measurement (FSM) Method[8]
   C. Is a measure of the functionality that an application provides to the user, as measured by the application project function point count by the activity of applying the IFPUG Functional Size Measurement (FSM) Method
   D. Is associated with an installed application

9. An enhancement project's functional size:
   A. Is a measure of the functionality added, changed, or deleted at the completion of an enhancement project, as measured by the enhancement project function point count by the activity of applying the IFPUG Functional Size Measurement (FSM) Method[9]
   B. Is a measure of the functionality provided to the users with the first release of the software, as measured by the development project function point count by the activity of applying the IFPUG Functional Size Measurement (FSM) Method

   C. Is a measure of the functionality that an application provides to the user, as measured by the application project function point count by the activity of applying the IFPUG Functional Size Measurement (FSM) Method
   D. Is associated with an installed application

10. An application's functional size:
    A. Is a measure of the functionality added, changed, or deleted at the completion of an enhancement project, as measured by the enhancement project function point count by the activity of applying the IFPUG Functional Size Measurement (FSM) Method
    B. Is a measure of the functionality provided to the users with the first release of the software, as measured by the development project function point count by the activity of applying the IFPUG Functional Size Measurement (FSM) Method
    C. Is a measure of the functionality that an application provides to the user, as measured by the application project function point count by the activity of applying the IFPUG Functional Size Measurement (FSM) Method[10]
    D. Includes conversion functionality

11. A baseline or installed functional size is synonymous with:
    A. An application functional size[11]
    B. A development project function point count
    C. An enhancement project function point count
    D. A and B

12. Which is not true of an application's functional size:
    A. This size provides a measure of the current functions the application provides the user
    B. It includes conversion functionality[12]
    C. This number is initialized when the development project function point count is completed
    D. It is updated every time completion of an enhancement project alters the application's functions

---

[7] Refer to IFPUG, *Function Point Counting Practices Manual* (CPM), Release 4.3, Part 2, page 4-2.
[8] Refer to IFPUG, *Function Point Counting Practices Manual* (CPM), Release 4.3, Part 2, page 4-2.
[9] Refer to IFPUG, *Function Point Counting Practices Manual* (CPM), Release 4.3, Part 2, page 4-2.

[10] Refer to IFPUG, *Function Point Counting Practices Manual* (CPM), Release 4.3, Part 2, page 4-3.
[11] Refer to IFPUG, *Function Point Counting Practices Manual* (CPM), Release 4.3, Part 2, page 4-3.
[12] Refer to IFPUG, *Function Point Counting Practices Manual* (CPM), Release 4.3, Part 2, page 4-3.

Appendix 7

Chapter 4 Sample Exam Answers

1. An Internal Logical File (ILF) is a:
   A. User-recognizable group of logically related data or control information that is referenced by the application being measured but which is maintained within the boundary of another application
   B. Unique user-recognizable, nonrepeated attribute
   C. **User-recognizable group of logically related data or control information maintained within the boundary of the application being measured**[1]
   D. User-recognizable subgroup of data elements

2. An External Interface File (EIF) is a:
   A. **User-recognizable group of logically related data or control information that is referenced by the application being measured but which is maintained within the boundary of another application**[2]
   B. Unique user-recognizable, nonrepeated attribute
   C. User-recognizable group of logically related data or control information maintained within the boundary of the application being measured
   D. User-recognizable subgroup of data elements

3. A Data Element Type (DET) is a:
   A. User-recognizable group of logically related data or control information that is referenced by the application being measured but which is maintained within the boundary of another application
   B. **Unique user-recognizable, nonrepeated attribute**[3]

   C. User-recognizable group of logically related data or control information maintained within the boundary of the application being measured
   D. User-recognizable subgroup of data elements

4. A Record Element Type (RET) is a:
   A. User-recognizable group of logically related data or control information that is referenced by the application being measured but which is maintained within the boundary of another application
   B. Unique user-recognizable, nonrepeated attribute
   C. User-recognizable group of logically related data or control information that is maintained within the boundary of the application being measured
   D. **User-recognizable subgroup of Data Element Types within a data function**[4]

5. Mandatory subgroups are:
   A. Those that the user has the option of using one or none of during an elementary process that adds or creates an instance of the data
   B. **Subgroups where the user must use at least one during an elementary process that adds or creates an instance of the data**[5]
   C. Represent the functionality provided to the user to meet internal and external data requirements
   D. Unique user-recognizable, nonrepeated attributes

6. Data function types include:
   A. Internal Logical Files (ILFs)
   B. External Inputs (EIs)

---

[1] Refer to IFPUG *Function Point Counting Practices Manual* (CPM), Release 4.3, Part 2, page 6-2.
[2] Refer to IFPUG *Function Point Counting Practices Manual* (CPM), Release 4.3, Part 2, page 6-2.
[3] Refer to IFPUG, *Function Point Counting Practices Manual* (CPM), Release 4.3, Part 2, page 6-5.

[4] Refer to IFPUG, *Function Point Counting Practices Manual* (CPM), Release 4.3, Part 2, page 6-7.
[5] Refer to IFPUG, *Function Point Counting Practices Manual* (CPM), Release 4.3, Part 2, page 6-8.

C. **External Interface Files (EIFs)**[6]

D. A and C

7. The primary intent of an ILF is:
   A. **To hold data maintained through one or more elementary processes of the application being measured**[7]
   B. To hold data referenced through one or more elementary processes within the boundary of the application being measured
   C. A and B
   D. None of the above

8. The primary intent of an EIF is:
   A. To hold data maintained through one or more elementary processes of the application being measured
   B. **To hold data referenced through one or more elementary processes within the boundary of the application measured**[8]
   C. A and B
   D. None of the above

9. Which of the following counting rules must *not* apply for the information to be counted as an EIF?
   A. The group of data or control information is logical and user recognizable
   B. The group of data is referenced by, but not maintained by, the application being measured
   C. **The group of data is identified by the application being measured**[9]
   D. The group of data is maintained in an ILF of one or more other applications

10. The functional complexity of an ILF is based on:
    A. The number of DETs and FTRs
    B. **The number of DETs and RETs**[10]
    C. The number of FTRs and RETs
    D. The number of DETs, RETs, and FTRs

11. Which of the following rule(s) apply when counting RETs:
    A. Count one RET for each data function
    B. Count one additional RET for each additional logical subgroup of DETs (within the data function) that contains more than one DET

C. **A and B**[11]

D. None of the above

12. How many function points is a low complexity ILF?
    A. 5
    B. **7**[12]
    C. 10
    D. 15

13. How many function points is a low complexity EIF?
    A. **5**[13]
    B. 7
    C. 10
    D. 15

14. How many function points is a high complexity EIF?
    A. 5
    B. 7
    C. **10**[14]
    D. 15

15. Which of the following combinations would result in an average ILF?
    A. 1 RET and 5 DETs
    B. 2 RETs and 19 DETs
    C. 6 RETs and 20 DETs
    D. **5 RETs and 50 DETs**[15]

16. Which of the following combinations would result in an average EIF?
    A. 1 RET and 5 DETs
    B. 2 RETs and 19 DETs
    C. 6 RETs and 20 DETs
    D. **5 RETs and 50 DETs**[16]

17. What are the total function points for 2 low ILFs, 3 high ILFs, and 1 low EIF?
    A. 46
    B. **64**[17]
    C. 60
    D. 49

---

[6] Refer to IFPUG, *Function Point Counting Practices Manual* (CPM), Release 4.3, Part 2, page 6-1.

[7] Refer to IFPUG, *Function Point Counting Practices Manual* (CPM), Release 4.3, Part 2, page 6-2.

[8] Refer to IFPUG, *Function Point Counting Practices Manual* (CPM), Release 4.3, Part 2, page 6-2.

[9] Refer to IFPUG, *Function Point Counting Practices Manual* (CPM), Release 4.3, Part 2, page 6-5.

[10] Refer to IFPUG, *Function Point Counting Practices Manual* (CPM), Release 4.3, Part 2, page 6-5.

[11] Refer to IFPUG, *Function Point Counting Practices Manual* (CPM), Release 4.3, Part 2, page 6-7.

[12] Refer to IFPUG, *Function Point Counting Practices Manual* (CPM), Release 4.3, Part 2, page 6-8.

[13] Refer to IFPUG, *Function Point Counting Practices Manual* (CPM), Release 4.3, Part 2, page 6-8.

[14] Refer to IFPUG, *Function Point Counting Practices Manual* (CPM), Release 4.3, Part 2, page 6-8.

[15] Refer to IFPUG, *Function Point Counting Practices Manual* (CPM), Release 4.3, Part 2, page 6-8.

[16] Refer to IFPUG, *Function Point Counting Practices Manual* (CPM), Release 4.3, Part 2, page 6-8.

[17] Refer to IFPUG, *Function Point Counting Practices Manual* (CPM), Release 4.3, Part 2, page 6-8.

18. Data functions:
    A. **Represent the functionality provided to the user to meet internal and external data storage requirements**[18]
    B. Consist of one or more components, modules, or subsystems
    C. Are the functionality provided to the user to process data by an application
    D. Are unique user-recognizable, nonrepeated attributes

19. The primary difference between an Internal Logical File and an External Interface File is that:
    A. An EIF is maintained by the application being measured, but an ILF is not
    B. **An EIF is not maintained by the application being measured, but an ILF is**[19]
    C. An ILF can contain control information but an EIF cannot
    D. An EIF can contain control information but an ILF cannot

20. What is the total function points value for 2 average ILFs, 3 low EIFs, and 4 low ILFs?
    A. 55
    B. 69
    C. **63**[20]
    D. 73

21. Control information:
    A. Is the ability to modify data through an elementary process
    B. Is data that influences an elementary process
    C. Specifies what, when, or how data are to be processed
    D. **B and C**[21]

22. An elementary process:
    A. Is the smallest unit of activity that is meaningful to the user
    B. Is a cohesive collection of automated procedures and data supporting a business objective
    C. Must be self-contained and leave the business of the application being counted in a consistent state
    D. **A and C**[22]

23. Which categories of data entities are usually identified to satisfy the functional user requirements?
    A. Code Data
    B. Business Data
    C. Reference Data
    D. **B and C**[23]

24. Which categories of data entities are usually identified to satisfy the nonfunctional user requirements?
    A. **Code Data**[24]
    B. Business Data
    C. Reference Data
    D. B and C

25. Providing a code and an explanatory name or description for an attribute of a business object is an example of:
    A. Valid Values Data
    B. **Substitution Data**[25]
    C. Static Data
    D. Constant Data

26. Which of the following may also be referred to as Core User Data or Business Objects?
    A. Code Data
    B. **Business Data**[26]
    C. Reference Data
    D. B and C

27. Data that rarely changes is an example of:
    A. Valid Values Data
    B. Substitution Data
    C. **Static or Constant Data**[27]
    D. None of the above

28. Providing a list of available values for an attribute of one or more business object types is an example of:
    A. **Valid Values Data**[28]
    B. Substitution Data
    C. Static Data
    D. Constant Data

---

[18] Refer to IFPUG, *Function Point Counting Practices Manual* (CPM), Release 4.3, Part 2, page 6-1.

[19] Refer to IFPUG, *Function Point Counting Practices Manual* (CPM), Release 4.3, Part 2, page 6-2.

[20] Refer to IFPUG, *Function Point Counting Practices Manual* (CPM), Release 4.3, Part 2, page 6-8.

[21] Refer to IFPUG, *Function Point Counting Practices Manual* (CPM), Release 4.3, Part 2, page 6-2.

[22] Refer to IFPUG, *Function Point Counting Practices Manual* (CPM), Release 4.3, Part 2, page 6-3.

[23] Refer to IFPUG, *Function Point Counting Practices Manual* (CPM), Release 4.3, Part 3, page 1-4.

[24] Refer to IFPUG, *Function Point Counting Practices Manual* (CPM), Release 4.3, Part 3, page 1-4.

[25] Refer to IFPUG, *Function Point Counting Practices Manual* (CPM), Release 4.3, Part 3, page 1-10.

[26] Refer to IFPUG, *Function Point Counting Practices Manual* (CPM), Release 4.3, Part 3, page 1-4.

[27] Refer to IFPUG, *Function Point Counting Practices Manual* (CPM), Release 4.3, Part 3, page 1-11.

[28] Refer to IFPUG, *Function Point Counting Practices Manual* (CPM), Release 4.3, Part 3, page 1-12.

29. Data stored to support the business rules for the maintenance of the Business Data is an example of:
    A. Code Data
    B. Business Data
    C. Reference Data[29]
    D. None of the above

30. Data that reflects the information that must be stored and retrieved by the functional area addressed by the application is an example of:
    A. Code Data
    B. Business Data[30]
    C. Reference Data
    D. All of the above

31. **Business Data characteristics include which of the following logical characteristics?**
    A. Very dynamic—normal business operations cause it to be regularly referenced and routinely added to, changed, or deleted[31]
    B. Essentially static—only changes in response to changes in the way that the business operates
    C. Less dynamic—occasionally changes in response to changes in the functional area's environment, external functional processes, or business rules
    D. None of the above

32. Reference Data characteristics include which of the following logical characteristics?
    A. Mandatory for the operation of the users' functional area
    B. User identifiable (usually by a business user)
    C. Usually user maintainable (usually by an administrative user)
    D. All of the above[32]

33. Code Data characteristics include which of the following logical characteristics?
    A. Provide business transactions access to improve ease of data entry, improve data consistency, ensure data integrity, etc.
    B. Store the data to support core user activities
    C. Store data to standardize and facilitate business activities and business transactions
    D. A and C[33]

34. Valid Values Data:
    A. Provides a code and an explanatory name or description for an attribute of a business object
    B. Contains data that is basically static
    C. Is implemented to satisfy requirements such as reducing errors and increasing user friendliness[34]
    D. Contains one and only one occurrence regardless of the number of attributes

35. States (e.g., State Code, State Name) are an example of:
    A. Static or Constant Data
    B. Substitution Data[35]
    C. Valid Values Data
    D. None of the above

36. Color (e.g., all valid values for the attribute color of a business object) is an example of:
    A. Static or Constant Data
    B. Substitution Data
    C. Valid Values Data[36]
    D. All of the above

37. Examples of Business or Reference Data that should not be considered Code Data include:
    A. Tax Rate Ranges for a Progressive Tax System
    B. Currency Exchange Rate Table
    C. Entity Types with Financial Amounts, Exchange Rates, and Tax Rates, if they are not constants
    D. All of the above[37]

38. "User-recognizable" refers to:
    A. A logical group of permanent data seen from the perspective of the user
    B. The border between the software being measured and the user
    C. The functionality that will be included in a particular function point count
    D. Requirements for processes and/or data that are agreed upon, and understood by, both the users and software developers[38]

39. Reference Data:
    A. Reflects the information that must be stored and retrieved by the functional area addressed by the application

---

[29] Refer to IFPUG, *Function Point Counting Practices Manual* (CPM), Release 4.3, Part 3, page 1-5.

[30] Refer to IFPUG, *Function Point Counting Practices Manual* (CPM), Release 4.3, Part 3, page 1-4.

[31] Refer to IFPUG, *Function Point Counting Practices Manual* (CPM), Release 4.3, Part 3, page 1-4.

[32] Refer to IFPUG, *Function Point Counting Practices Manual* (CPM), Release 4.3, Part 3, page 1-5.

[33] Refer to IFPUG, *Function Point Counting Practices Manual* (CPM), Release 4.3, Part 3, page 1-7.

[34] Refer to IFPUG, *Function Point Counting Practices Manual* (CPM), Release 4.3, Part 3, page 1-12.

[35] Refer to IFPUG, *Function Point Counting Practices Manual* (CPM), Release 4.3, Part 3, page 1-11.

[36] Refer to IFPUG, *Function Point Counting Practices Manual* (CPM), Release 4.3, Part 3, page 1-12.

[37] Refer to IFPUG, *Function Point Counting Practices Manual* (CPM), Release 4.3, Part 3, page 1-13.

[38] Refer to IFPUG, *Function Point Counting Practices Manual* (CPM), Release 4.3, Part 2, page 6-3.

B. Is stored to support the business rules for the maintenance of the Business Data[39]

C. May also be referred to as Core User Data or Business Objects

D. Is sometimes referred to as List Data or Translation Data

40. Code Data:

A. Reflects the information that must be stored and retrieved by the functional area addressed by the application

B. Is stored to support the business rules for the maintenance of the Business Data

C. May also be referred to as Core User Data or Business Objects

D. Is sometimes referred to as List Data or Translation Data[40]

41. Business Data:

A. Reflects the information that must be stored and retrieved by the functional area addressed by the application

B. Is stored to support the business rules for the maintenance of the Business Data

C. May also be referred to as Core User Data or Business Objects[41]

D. Is sometimes referred to as List Data or Translation Data

42. The definition of entity independence is:

A. An association between entities that contains attributes

B. An entity that is meaningful or significant to the business, in and of itself without the presence of other entities[42]

C. An entity that is not meaningful or is not significant to the business, in and of itself without the presence of other entities

D. An entity containing attributes that further describe a many-to-many relationship between two other entity types

43. An attribute is:

A. A fundamental thing of relevance to the user about which a collection of facts is kept

B. Included in the count as a RET

C. Generally analogous to a Data Element Type[43]

D. A and C

44. An entity is:

A. A fundamental thing of relevance to the user about which a collection of facts is kept[44]

B. The smallest unit of activity that is meaningful to the user

C. Data that influence an elementary process of the application being measured

D. Is composed of records and data items

45. Entity dependence is:

A. A logically related group of data

B. An entity that is meaningful or is significant to the business, in and of itself without the presence of other entities

C. An entity that is not meaningful or is not significant to the business, in and of itself without the presence of other entities[45]

D. An entity that is not meaningful or significant in and of itself without the presence of another entity linked to it via a relationship

46. A file system is composed of:

A. Technical attributes

B. A cohesive collection of automated procedures and data supporting a business objective

C. Records and data items[46]

D. None of the above

---

[39] Refer to IFPUG, *Function Point Counting Practices Manual* (CPM), Release 4.3, Part 3, page 1-5.

[40] Refer to IFPUG, *Function Point Counting Practices Manual* (CPM), Release 4.3, Part 3, page 1-6.

[41] Refer to IFPUG, *Function Point Counting Practices Manual* (CPM), Release 4.3, Part 3, page 1-4.

[42] Refer to IFPUG, *Function Point Counting Practices Manual* (CPM), Release 4.3, Part 3, page 2-12.

[43] Refer to IFPUG, *Function Point Counting Practices Manual* (CPM), Release 4.3, Part 3, page 2-6.

[44] Refer to IFPUG, *Function Point Counting Practices Manual* (CPM), Release 4.3, Part 3, page 2-4.

[45] Refer to IFPUG, *Function Point Counting Practices Manual* (CPM), Release 4.3, Part 3, page 2-12.

[46] Refer to IFPUG, *Function Point Counting Practices Manual* (CPM), Release 4.3, Part 3, page 2-4.

Appendix 8

Chapter 5 Sample Exam Answers

1. When compared to an elementary process (EP) already identified, count two similar EPs as the same elementary process if they:
   A. Require the same set of DETs and require the same set of FTRs
   B. Require the same set of FTRs and require the same set of processing logic to complete the elementary process
   C. Require the same set of DETs, require the same set of FTRs, and require the same set of processing logic to complete the elementary process[1]
   D. Require the same set of processing logic to complete the elementary process

2. Identify an elementary process by composing or decomposing the Functional User Requirements into the smallest unit of activity that satisfies which of the following?
   A. Constitutes a complete transaction
   B. Is meaningful to the user
   C. Is self-contained and leaves the business of the application being counted in a consistent state
   D. All of the above[2]

3. Classify each elementary process as an external input (EI), external output (EO), or an external inquiry (EQ) based on:
   A. The smallest unit of activity that is meaningful to the user
   B. Its primary intent[3]
   C. Its processing logic
   D. None of the above

4. Which of the following can be a primary intent of a transactional function?
   A. Altering the behavior of the application
   B. Maintaining one or more ILFs
   C. Presenting information to the user
   D. All of the above[4]

5. The smallest unit of activity that is meaningful to the user is the definition of:
   A. Elementary process[5]
   B. Primary intent
   C. Processing logic
   D. Derived data

6. Which of the following can have a primary intent of maintaining one or more ILFs?
   A. External input[6]
   B. External output
   C. External inquiry
   D. A and B

7. Classify an elementary process as an EQ if it:
   A. Has a primary intent of presenting information to the user
   B. References a data function to retrieve data or control information
   C. Does not satisfy the criteria to be classified as an EO
   D. All of the above[7]

---

[1] Refer to IFPUG *Function Point Counting Practices Manual* (CPM), Release 4.3, Part 2, page 7-11.
[2] Refer to IFPUG, *Function Point Counting Practices Manual* (CPM), Release 4.3, Part 2, page 7-10.
[3] Refer to IFPUG, *Function Point Counting Practices Manual* (CPM), Release 4.3, Part 2, page 7-13.
[4] Refer to IFPUG, *Function Point Counting Practices Manual* (CPM), Release 4.3, Part 2, page 7-13.
[5] Refer to IFPUG, *Function Point Counting Practices Manual* (CPM), Release 4.3, Part 2, page 7-5.
[6] Refer to IFPUG, *Function Point Counting Practices Manual* (CPM), Release 4.3, Part 2, page 7-13.
[7] Refer to IFPUG, *Function Point Counting Practices Manual* (CPM), Release 4.3, Part 2, page 7-13.

8. Processing logic is defined as:
   A. The smallest unit of activity that is meaningful to the user
   B. The functionality that will be included in a particular function point count
   C. Requirements specifically requested by the user to complete an elementary process[8]
   D. The ability to modify data through an elementary process

9. Converting equivalent values is a form of processing logic that can be done by which of the following transactions?
   A. External input
   B. External output
   C. External inquiry
   D. All of the above[9]

10. Which of the following forms of processing logic cannot be performed by an external inquiry?
    A. Update an ILF[10]
    B. Sort or arrange a set of data
    C. Analyze conditions to determine which are applicable
    D. Validations

11. Processing logic:
    A. Is any of the requirements specifically requested by the user to complete an elementary process
    B. Can include validations, algorithms, or calculations
    C. Can include reading or maintaining a file
    D. All of the above[11]

12. Data created by transforming existing data to create additional data is considered to be:
    A. Processing logic
    B. Control information
    C. External input
    D. Derived data[12]

13. Presenting information to a user can be done by which of the following transaction types:
    A. External input
    B. External output
    C. External inquiry
    D. All of the above[13]

---

[8] Refer to IFPUG, *Function Point Counting Practices Manual* (CPM), Release 4.3, Part 2, page 7-5.
[9] Refer to IFPUG, *Function Point Counting Practices Manual* (CPM), Release 4.3, Part 2, page 7-8.
[10] Refer to IFPUG, *Function Point Counting Practices Manual* (CPM), Release 4.3, Part 2, page 7-8.

[11] Refer to IFPUG, *Function Point Counting Practices Manual* (CPM), Release 4.3, Part 2, page 7-5.
[12] Refer to IFPUG, *Function Point Counting Practices Manual* (CPM), Release 4.3, Part 2, page 7-6.
[13] Refer to IFPUG, *Function Point Counting Practices Manual* (CPM), Release 4.3, Part 2, page 7-4.

Appendix 9

Chapter 6 Sample Exam Answers

1. To maintain one or more ILFs and/or alter the behavior of the system is the primary intent of an:
   A. External input[1]
   B. External output
   C. External inquiry
   D. B and C

2. A File Type Referenced (FTR) can be:
   A. An Internal Logical File read by a transactional function
   B. An Internal Logical File maintained by a transactional function
   C. An External Interface File read by a transactional function
   D. All of the above[2]

3. FTR guidance for an external input includes which of the following:
   A. Count an FTR for each ILF maintained
   B. Count an FTR for each ILF or EIF read during the processing of the external input
   C. Count only one FTR for each ILF that is both maintained and read
   D. All of the above[3]

4. The primary intent of an external inquiry is:
   A. To maintain an ILF or alter the behavior of the system
   B. To present information to a user through the retrieval of data or control information[4]

C. To hold data referenced through one or more elementary processes within the boundary
   D. To hold data maintained through one or more elementary processes of the application being measured

5. Transactional functions include which of the following:
   A. Internal Logical Files
   B. External Interface Files
   C. External inquiries[5]
   D. B and C

6. The primary intent of an external output is:
   A. To maintain an ILF or alter the behavior of the system
   B. To present information to a user through processing logic other than, or in addition to, the retrieval of data or control information[6]
   C. To hold data referenced through one or more elementary processes within the boundary
   D. To hold data maintained through one or more elementary processes of the application being measured

7. DET guidance for an external input includes which of the following:
   A. Count one DET for each unique user-recognizable, nonrepeated attribute that crosses (enters and/or exits) the boundary during the processing of the transactional function
   B. Count only one DET per transactional function for the ability to send an application response message even if there are multiple messages

---

[1] Refer to IFPUG *Function Point Counting Practices Manual* (CPM), Release 4.3, Part 2, page 7-3.

[2] Refer to IFPUG, *Function Point Counting Practices Manual* (CPM), Release 4.3, Part 2, page 7-14.

[3] Refer to IFPUG, *Function Point Counting Practices Manual* (CPM), Release 4.3, Part 2, page 7-15.

[4] Refer to IFPUG *Function Point Counting Practices Manual* (CPM), Release 4.3, Part 2, page 7-3.

[5] Refer to IFPUG, *Function Point Counting Practices Manual* (CPM), Release 4.3, Part 2, page 7-1.

[6] Refer to IFPUG, *Function Point Counting Practices Manual* (CPM), Release 4.3, Part 2, page 7-3.

C. Count only one DET per transactional function for the ability to initiate actions even if there are multiple means to do so

D. All of the above[7]

8. DET guidance for an external output includes which of the following:

A. If a DET both enters and exits the boundary, count it twice for the elementary process

B. Do not count literals such as report titles, screen or panel identifiers, column headings, and attribute titles as DETs[8]

C. Count paging variables or system-generated stamps as one DET

D. All of the above

9. Count only one DET per transactional function for the ability to send an application response message even if there are multiple messages is a DET guidance for which type(s) of transaction(s):

A. External output

B. External input

C. External inquiry

D. All of the above[9]

10. Count only one DET per transactional function for the ability to initiate actions even if there are multiple means to do so is a DET guidance for which type(s) of transaction(s):

A. External output

B. External input

C. External inquiry

D. All of the above[10]

11. Which of the following is used to determine the complexity of a transaction:

A. FTRs and RETs

B. DETs and RETs

C. FTRs and DETs[11]

D. FTRs, DETs, and RETs

12. Do not count attributes generated within the boundary by a transactional function and saved to an ILF without exiting the boundary is a DET guidance of which type(s) of transaction(s):

A. External input

B. External output

C. External inquiry

D. All of the above[12]

13. Which of the following is true for an external inquiry:

A. Count one DET for each unique user-recognizable, nonrepeated attribute that crosses (enters and/or exits) the boundary during the processing of the transactional function[13]

B. Count literals as DETs

C. Count paging variables or system-generated stamps as DETs

D. B and C

14. What is the total number of function points for 5 high EIs, 2 low EOs, 3 average EIs, and 2 average EQs:

A. 48

B. 63

C. 61

D. 58[14]

15. A low EO is worth how many function points:

A. 3

B. 4[15]

C. 5

D. 6

16. A low EQ is worth how many function points:

A. 3[16]

B. 4

C. 5

D. 6

17. An average EI is worth how many function points:

A. 3

B. 4[17]

C. 5

D. 6

18. What is the total number of function points for 2 average EIs, 1 low EIF, and 2 high ILFs:

A. 44

B. 43[18]

C. 23

D. 41

[7] Refer to IFPUG, *Function Point Counting Practices Manual* (CPM), Release 4.3, Part 2, page 7-15.

[8] Refer to IFPUG, *Function Point Counting Practices Manual* (CPM), Release 4.3, Part 2, page 7-18.

[9] Refer to IFPUG, *Function Point Counting Practices Manual* (CPM), Release 4.3, Part 2, pages 7-14, 7-16, and 7-17.

[10] Refer to IFPUG, *Function Point Counting Practices Manual* (CPM), Release 4.3, Part 2, pages 7-14, 7-16, and 7-18.

[11] Refer to IFPUG, *Function Point Counting Practices Manual* (CPM), Release 4.3, Part 2, page 7-14.

[12] Refer to IFPUG, *Function Point Counting Practices Manual* (CPM), Release 4.3, Part 2, pages 7-16 and 7-18.

[13] Refer to IFPUG, *Function Point Counting Practices Manual* (CPM), Release 4.3, Part 2, page 7-17.

[14] Refer to IFPUG, *Function Point Counting Practices Manual* (CPM), Release 4.3, Part 2, page 7-20.

[15] Refer to IFPUG, *Function Point Counting Practices Manual* (CPM), Release 4.3, Part 2, page 7-20.

[16] Refer to IFPUG, *Function Point Counting Practices Manual* (CPM), Release 4.3, Part 2, page 7-20.

[17] Refer to IFPUG, *Function Point Counting Practices Manual* (CPM), Release 4.3, Part 2, page 7-20.

[18] Refer to IFPUG, *Function Point Counting Practices Manual* (CPM), Release 4.3, Part 2, page 7-19; Part 2, page 6-8.

19. The main difference between the transactional function types is:
    A. Their elementary process
    B. Their primary intent[19]
    C. Their processing logic
    D. None of the above

20. An elementary process that sends data or control information outside the application's boundary and includes additional processing beyond that of an external inquiry is what type(s) of transactional function(s):
    A. External output[20]
    B. External input
    C. External inquiry
    D. A and C

21. An elementary process that processes data or control information sent from outside the boundary is what type(s) of transactional function(s):
    A. External output
    B. External input[21]
    C. External inquiry
    D. A and C

22. Which is true of transactional functions:
    A. They are defined as external inputs, external outputs, and external inquiries
    B. They are defined as Internal Logical Files and External Interface Files
    C. They are elementary processes that provide functionality to the user to process data
    D. A and C[22]

23. Processing logic is defined as:
    A. The smallest unit of activity that is meaningful to the user
    B. The functionality that will be included in a particular function point count
    C. Requirements specifically requested by the user to complete an elementary process[23]
    D. The ability to modify data through an elementary process

24. Preparing and presenting information outside of the boundary can be done by which of the following transactions:
    A. External input
    B. External output
    C. External inquiry
    D. All of the above[24]

25. Converting equivalent values is a form of processing logic that can be done by which of the following transactions:
    A. External input
    B. External output
    C. External inquiry
    D. All of the above[25]

26. Which of the following forms of processing logic cannot be performed by an external inquiry:
    A. Update an ILF[26]
    B. Resort or rearrange a set of data
    C. Analyze conditions to determine which are applicable
    D. Validations

27. Which of the following is FTR guidance for both external outputs and external inquiries:
    A. Count one FTR for each ILF maintained
    B. Count an FTR for each ILF or EIF read[27]
    C. Count only one FTR for each ILF that is both maintained and read
    D. None of the above

28. Which of the following is true about the function "altering the behavior of the system":
    A. It is the primary intent of an EI[28]
    B. It is the primary intent of an EQ
    C. It is not allowed by an EO
    D. A and C

29. Processing logic:
    A. Includes any of the requirements specifically requested by the user to complete an elementary process
    B. Can include validations, algorithms, or calculations
    C. Can include reading or maintaining a data function
    D. All of the above[29]

---

[19] Refer to IFPUG, *Function Point Counting Practices Manual* (CPM), Release 4.3, Part 2, page 7-4.
[20] Refer to IFPUG, *Function Point Counting Practices Manual* (CPM), Release 4.3, Part 2, page 7-3.
[21] Refer to IFPUG, *Function Point Counting Practices Manual* (CPM), Release 4.3, Part 2, page 7-3.
[22] Refer to IFPUG, *Function Point Counting Practices Manual* (CPM), Release 4.3, Part 2, page 7-1.
[23] Refer to IFPUG, *Function Point Counting Practices Manual* (CPM), Release 4.3, Part 2, page 7-5.
[24] Refer to IFPUG, *Function Point Counting Practices Manual* (CPM), Release 4.3, Part 2, page 7-8.
[25] Refer to IFPUG, *Function Point Counting Practices Manual* (CPM), Release 4.3, Part 2, page 7-8.
[26] Refer to IFPUG, *Function Point Counting Practices Manual* (CPM), Release 4.3, Part 2, page 7-8.
[27] Refer to IFPUG, *Function Point Counting Practices Manual* (CPM), Release 4.3, Part 2, page 7-17.
[28] Refer to IFPUG, *Function Point Counting Practices Manual* (CPM), Release 4.3, Part 2, page 7-4.
[29] Refer to IFPUG, *Function Point Counting Practices Manual* (CPM), Release 4.3, Part 2, page 7-8.

30. Data created by transforming existing data to create additional data is considered to be:
    A. Processing logic
    B. Control information
    C. External input
    D. Derived data[30]

---

[30]Refer to IFPUG, *Function Point Counting Practices Manual* (CPM), Release 4.3, Part 2, page 7-6.

Appendix 10

Chapter 7 Sample Exam Answers

1. Methods of sharing data include which of the following:
    A. Via online screens (e.g., screen scraping)
    B. Via Web applications
    C. Via on-line, real-time information requests
    D. All of the above[1]

2. The term "copy" means:
    A. To copy computer instructions or data from external storage to internal storage
    B. To read data from a source, leaving the source data unchanged, and to write the same data elsewhere in a physical form that may differ from that of the source[2]
    C. Multiple files with the same data elements are consolidated into a single file
    D. A and B

3. Accessing another application's screen transactions to reference/obtain data or to update that application's data is called:
    A. Image copy
    B. Screen scraping[3]
    C. Image load
    D. Merging

4. Application B requires (for performance, etc.) the ability to access a portion of File X in Application A for validation and reference only. Application A sends a physical table within a logical file to Application B. The existing view of that physical table in Application B is "refreshed" each time with the copy. What is counted for Application A and Application B?
    A. Application A, an ILF; Application B, an EIF[4]
    B. Application A, an ILF; Application B, an ILF
    C. Application A, an EIF; Application B, an EIF
    D. Application A, an EIF; Application B, an ILF

5. Application B requires the ability to access file X in Application A for validation and reference only. Application B requires (for performance, etc.) that Application A send a complete file to Application B. The existing data store in Application B is refreshed each time with the copy. What is counted for Application A and Application B?
    A. Application A, an ILF; Application B, an EIF[5]
    B. Application A, an ILF; Application B, an ILF
    C. Application A, an EIF; Application B, an EIF
    D. Application A, an EIF; Application B, an ILF

6. A transaction processed by Application B, requires information from a data store maintained within Application A. Application B is responsible for accessing the data in Application A, and Application B maintains the software for that access. What is counted for Application A and Application B?
    A. Application A, an ILF; Application B, an ILF
    B. Application A, an ILF; Application B, an EIF and an FTR in the transactional function[6]
    C. Application A, an EIF and an FTR in the transactional function; Application B, an EIF
    D. Application A, an EIF; Application B, an ILF

---

[1] Refer to IFPUG, *Function Point Counting Practices Manual* (CPM), Release 4.3, Part 3, page 3-2.

[2] Refer to IFPUG, *Function Point Counting Practices Manual* (CPM) Release 4.3, Part 3, page 3-3.

[3] Refer to IFPUG, *Function Point Counting Practices Manual* (CPM) Release 4.3, Part 3, pages 3-6 and 3-17.

[4] Refer to IFPUG, *Function Point Counting Practices Manual* (CPM) Release 4.3, Part 3, page 3-13.

[5] Refer to IFPUG, *Function Point Counting Practices Manual* (CPM) Release 4.3, Part 3, page 3-11.

[6] Refer to IFPUG, *Function Point Counting Practices Manual* (CPM) Release 4.3, Part 3, page 3-7.

7. Both Application A and Application B maintain the same ILF. Each has its own unique view of the data. There are some common data elements, and some that are unique to each application. What is counted for Application A and Application B?
   A. Application A, an ILF; Application B, an EIF
   B. Application A, an ILF; Application B, an ILF[7]
   C. Application A, an EIF; Application B, an EIF
   D. Application A, an EIF; Application B, an ILF

8. Application A produces a transaction file of changes (File Z) that is loaded into Application B. The records are usually of more than one type. Application B processes the input transactions according to the transaction type on the File Z records, prior to updating the records on internal File Y. The DETs on Application A File X and Application B File Y are different. Processing includes transaction types Add, Change, and Delete. What is counted for Application A and Application B?
   A. Application A, an ILF and EO/EQ; Application B, an EIF
   B. Application A, an ILF; Application B, an ILF and EI
   C. Application A, an ILF and EO/EQ; Application B, an ILF
   D. Application A, an ILF and EO/EQ; Application B, an ILF and three EIs[8]

9. Application B "reads" the content of an inquiry screen in Application A and uses that data in the processing of a transactional function. For Application B, count:
   A. An EIF
   B. An EIF and EQ[9]
   C. An EIF and EI
   D. An EIF and EO

10. Data stored in two applications (Application A and Application B) is image copied and merged to form one file that is loaded into a third application (Application C). Multiple files with the same data elements are being consolidated into a single file. What ILFs and EIFs are counted for the three applications?
    A. Application A, an ILF; Application B, an ILF; Application C, an ILF
    B. Application A, an EIF; Application B, an EIF; Application C, an EIF
    C. Application A, an ILF; Application B, an ILF; Application C, an EIF[10]
    D. Application A, an EIF; Application B, an ILF; Application C, an EIF

11. The process of recreating a set of data to make it current with its source is the definition of:
    A. Copy
    B. Load
    C. Merge
    D. Refresh[11]

12. To read data from a source, leaving the source data unchanged, and to write the same data elsewhere in a physical form that may differ from that of the source is what is meant by:
    A. Copy[12]
    B. Load
    C. Merge
    D. Refresh

13. An exact replication of another object, file, or table usually created through a utility is the definition of:
    A. Image[13]
    B. Copy
    C. Merge
    D. Refresh

---

[7] Refer to IFPUG, *Function Point Counting Practices Manual* (CPM) Release 4.3, Part 3, page 3-18.

[8] Refer to IFPUG, *Function Point Counting Practices Manual* (CPM) Release 4.3, Part 3, page 3-20.

[9] Refer to IFPUG, *Function Point Counting Practices Manual* (CPM) Release 4.3, Part 3, page 3-17.

[10] Refer to IFPUG, *Function Point Counting Practices Manual* (CPM) Release 4.3, Part 3, page 3-15.

[11] Refer to IFPUG, *Function Point Counting Practices Manual* (CPM) Release 4.3, Part 3, page 3-3.

[12] Refer to IFPUG, *Function Point Counting Practices Manual* (CPM) Release 4.3, Part 3, page 3-3.

[13] Refer to IFPUG, *Function Point Counting Practices Manual* (CPM) Release 4.3, Part 3, page 3-3.

Chapter 8 Sample Exam Answers

1. A definition of adaptive maintenance is:
   A. Software maintenance performed to make a computer program usable in a changed environment[1]
   B. The reactive modification of a software product performed after delivery to correct discovered problems
   C. Modification of a software product after delivery to detect and correct latent faults in the software product before they are manifested as failures
   D. None of the above

2. A definition of corrective maintenance is:
   A. The reactive modification of a software product performed after delivery to correct discovered problems[2]
   B. The modification of a software product performed after delivery to keep a software product usable in a changed or changing environment
   C. Software maintenance performed to improve the performance, maintainability, or other attributes of a computer program
   D. None of the above

3. The enhancement project functional size measures the project's modifications to the existing installed application that:
   A. Add user functions
   B. Change user functions
   C. Delete user functions
   D. All of the above[3]

4. Which of the following is true of perfective maintenance?
   A. It provides enhancements for users, improvement of program documentation, and recoding to improve software performance, maintainability, or other software attributes
   B. It is a modification of a software product after delivery to detect and correct latent faults in the software product before they are manifested as failures
   C. The modification repairs the software product to satisfy requirements
   D. A and B[4]

5. Suggested steps for performing an enhancement project functional size can include which of the following:
   A. Determine complexity of the function prior to change
   B. Determine complexity of the function after change
   C. Identify and evaluate any conversion or one-time functionality required to implement this enhancement
   D. All of the above[5]

6. Which of the following is a valid condition for a data function to be counted as a changed function?
   A. If the change involves only the addition of new records to a logical file or new values in an existing attribute within that logical file
   B. If a data function is changed because an attribute is added and that attribute is not used by the application being measured

---

[1] Refer to IFPUG *Function Point Counting Practices Manual* (CPM), Release 4.3, Part 3, page 4-20.
[2] Refer to IFPUG *Function Point Counting Practices Manual* (CPM), Release 4.3, Part 3, page 4-20.
[3] Refer to IFPUG, *Function Point Counting Practices Manual* (CPM), Release 4.3, Part 3, page 4-2.
[4] Refer to IFPUG, *Function Point Counting Practices Manual* (CPM), Release 4.3, Part 3, page 4-21.
[5] Refer to IFPUG, Function Point Counting Practices Manual (CPM), Release 4.3, Part 3, page 4-13.

C. **If a data function is structurally altered (e.g., adding or removing an attribute or changing the characteristics of the attribute)[6]**

D. All of the above

7. Which of the following is true for measuring transactions in an enhancement project?

A. **When processing logic has been altered within an application to meet business requirements, the elementary process that embodies that logic should be identified and counted as being changed[7]**

B. A single change in processing logic always affects all related transactions

C. When an edit or validation change is made to input processing logic and Add, Delete, Update and Implied Inquiry transactions exist, all four transactions (Add, Update, Delete, and Implied Inquiry) are counted for the enhancement

D. All of the above

---

[6] Refer to IFPUG, *Function Point Counting Practices Manual* (CPM), Release 4.3, Part 3, page 4-2.

[7] Refer to IFPUG, *Function Point Counting Practices Manual* (CPM), Release 4.3, Part 3, page 4-3.

Appendix 12

Chapter 9 Sample Exam Answers

1. Which of the following is true of conversion functionality?
   A. It consists of functions used after software installation to satisfy the ongoing business needs of the user
   B. Conversion of application data is based on the user view of the data[1]
   C. It is determined by using the 14 General System Characteristics to rate the application functional complexity
   D. None of the above

2. Which of the following should not be counted as conversion functionality?
   A. Migration of an application to a new platform
   B. Software upgrades due to the installation of a revised version of vendor packages
   C. Conversion of data accomplished via an existing load utility
   D. All of the above[2]

3. Which of the following is true of conversion functionality?
   A. The new or enhanced application's ILF(s) are populated by the converted data, and its user requirements dictate what is required from the old application(s) to meet the Functional User Requirements of the project
   B. The elementary process includes any exception reports, error reports, conversion reports, or control reports required to ensure the integrity of the data being converted

   C. If an EIF for the application being measured is changed, count it as conversion functionality
   D. A and B[3]

4. The view of the conversion process is based on:
   A. The original application
   B. The logical files being converted
   C. The data requirements of the new application
   D. All of the above[4]

5. An enhancement project requires populating new data attributes in an ILF of a system and producing control and error reports for this population process. What is counted as conversion functionality?
   A. One EI and two EQs
   B. One EI and one EQ
   C. One EI[5]
   D. Nothing is counted

[1] Refer to IFPUG, *Function Point Counting Practices Manual* (CPM), Release 4.3, Part 3, page 5-2.
[2] Refer to IFPUG, *Function Point Counting Practices Manual* (CPM), Release 4.3, Part 3, page 5-4.
[3] Refer to IFPUG, *Function Point Counting Practices Manual* (CPM), Release 4.3, Part 3, page 5-2.
[4] Refer to IFPUG, *Function Point Counting Practices Manual* (CPM), Release 4.3, Part 3, page 5-2.
[5] Refer to IFPUG, *Function Point Counting Practices Manual* (CPM), Release 4.3, Part 3, page 5-3.

Appendix 13

Chapter 10 Sample Exam Answers

1. Which of the following is the correct formula for calculating development project functional size?
   A. EFP = ADD + CHGA + CFP + DEL
   B. DFP = ADD + CFP[1]
   C. AFP = ADD
   D. AFPA = (AFPB + ADD + CHGA) − (CHGB + DEL)

2. Which of the following is the correct formula for calculating an application functional size from a measurement after the development project or at any time during the application's life cycle?
   A. EFP = ADD + CHGA + CFP + DEL
   B. DFP = ADD + CFP
   C. AFP = ADD[2]
   D. AFPA = (AFPB + ADD + CHGA) − (CHGB + DEL)

3. Which of the following is the correct formula for calculating an application functional size after an enhancement project?
   A. EFP = ADD + CHGA + CFP + DEL
   B. DFP = ADD + CFP
   C. AFP = ADD
   D. AFPA = (AFPB + ADD + CHGA) − (CHGB + DEL)[3]

4. Which of the following is the correct formula for calculating an enhancement project functional size?
   A. EFP = ADD + CHGA + CFP + DEL[4]
   B. DFP = ADD + CFP
   C. AFP = ADD
   D. AFPA = (AFPB + ADD + CHGA) − (CHGB + DEL)

---

[1] Refer to IFPUG, *Function Point Counting Practices Manual* (CPM), Release 4.3, Part 1, page 20

[2] Refer to IFPUG, *Function Point Counting Practices Manual* (CPM), Release 4.3, Part 1, page 20; Part 3, Chapter 4, page 4-18.

[3] Refer to IFPUG, *Function Point Counting Practices Manual* (CPM), Release 4.3, Part 1, page 21; Part 3, Chapter 4, page 4-19.

[4] Refer to IFPUG, *Function Point Counting Practices Manual* (CPM), Release 4.3, Part 1, page 21; Part 3, Chapter 4, page 4-17.

Appendix 14

Chapter 11 Sample Exam Answers

1. The Degree of Influence (DI) for each General System Characteristic ranges on a scale of:
   A. 0 to 4
   B. 1 to 5
   C. 0 to 5[1]
   D. 1 to 4

2. The degree to which the rate of business transactions influenced the development of the application is which General System Characteristic:
   A. Heavily Used Configuration
   B. Performance
   C. Operational Ease
   D. Transaction Rate[2]

3. Which of the following are characteristics of Operational Ease:
   A. The application minimizes the need for tape mounts or remote data access requiring human intervention
   B. Conversion and Installation Ease are characteristics of the application
   C. Start-up, back-up, and recovery processes were provided, but human intervention is required
   D. A and C[3]

4. A score of 2 for Degree of Influence indicates:
   A. Incidental influence
   B. Moderate influence[4]
   C. Average influence
   D. Significant influence

5. What is the Degree of Influence if an application has provided a Flexible Query and Report facility that can handle requests of average complexity and has Business Control Data kept in tables that are maintained by the user with on-line interactive processes, and the changes take effect immediately:
   A. 1
   B. 2
   C. 3
   D. 4[5]

6. The formula for Value Adjustment Factor is:
   A. VAF = (TDI × 0.01) + 0.65[6]
   B. VAF = TDI + 0.65
   C. VAF = TDI × 0.01
   D. None of the above

7. When applied, the Value Adjustment Factor adjusts the unadjusted functional size:
   A. ±30% to produce the adjusted functional size
   B. ±35% to produce the adjusted functional size[7]
   C. ±60% to produce the adjusted functional size
   D. ±65% to produce the adjusted functional size

8. Multiple Sites describes:
   A. The degree to which the computer resource restrictions influenced the development of the application
   B. The degree to which the application has been developed for different hardware and software environments[8]

---

[1] Refer to IFPUG *Function Point Counting Practices Manual* (CPM), Release 4.3, Part 5, Appendix C, page C-6.
[2] Refer to IFPUG, *Function Point Counting Practices Manual* (CPM), Release 4.3, Part 5, Appendix C, page C-15.
[3] Refer to IFPUG, *Function Point Counting Practices Manual* (CPM), Release 4.3, Part 5, Appendix C, page C-25.
[4] Refer to IFPUG *Function Point Counting Practices Manual* (CPM), Release 4.3, Part 5, Appendix C, page C-6.

[5] Refer to IFPUG, *Function Point Counting Practices Manual* (CPM), Release 4.3, Part 5, Appendix C, page C-29.
[6] Refer to IFPUG, *Function Point Counting Practices Manual* (CPM), Release 4.3, Part 5, Appendix C, page C-4.
[7] Refer to IFPUG, *Function Point Counting Practices Manual* (CPM), Release 4.3, Part 5, Appendix C, page C-4.
[8] Refer to IFPUG, *Function Point Counting Practices Manual* (CPM), Release 4.3, Part 5, Appendix C, page C-27.

C. The degree to which the application transfers data among physical components of the application

D. The degree to which computer resource restrictions influenced the development of the application

9. What is the Degree of Influence if the needs of more than one installation site were considered in the design, the application is designed to operate under different hardware or software environments, and the documentation and support plan are provided and tested to support the application at multiple installation sites and the application:
   A. 1
   B. 2
   C. 3
   D. 5[9]

10. Which of the following are characteristics of End-User Efficiency:
    A. Batch jobs submitted from on-line transactions
    B. Drop-down list box
    C. Flexible query
    D. A and B[10]

11. Multilingual support counts as how many items:
    A. 1
    B. 2
    C. 4
    D. 6[11]

12. An application would receive a score of 3 for On-Line Data Entry if:
    A. 1 to 7% of transactions are interactive
    B. 8 to 15% of transactions are interactive
    C. 16 to 23% of transactions are interactive[12]
    D. 24 to 30% of transactions are interactive

13. Sensitive control or application-specific security processing is a characteristic of:
    A. End-User Efficiency
    B. On-Line Update
    C. Complex Processing[13]
    D. Reusability

14. What is the Value Adjustment Factor if the total Degree of Influence is equal to 45:
    A. 1.00
    B. 1.10[14]
    C. 1.05
    D. .95

15. The total Degree of Influence is between:
    A. 0 and 70[15]
    B. .65 and 1.35
    C. 0 to 5
    D. 1 to 5

16. The Value Adjustment Factor (VAF):
    A. Is the measure of the functionality provided to the user by the project or application
    B. Rates the general functionality of the application being measured
    C. Is calculated based on an assessment of the 14 General System Characteristics for an application
    D. B and C[16]

17. Which of the following formulas is used to calculate the adjusted application functional size after enhancement:
    A. aAFP = ADD × VAF
    B. aEFP = [(ADD + CHGA + CFP) × VAFA] + (DEL × VAFB)
    C. aAFPA = [(AFPB + ADD + CHGA) − (CHGB + DEL)] × VAFA[17]
    D. aDFP = DFP × VAF

18. Which of the following formulas is used to calculate the adjusted development project functional size:
    A. aAFP = ADD × VAF
    B. aEFP = [(ADD + CHGA + CFP) × VAFA] + (DEL × VAFB)
    C. aAFPA = [(AFPB + ADD + CHGA) − (CHGB + DEL)] × VAFA
    D. aDFP = (ADD + CFP) × VAF[18]

---

[9] Refer to IFPUG, *Function Point Counting Practices Manual* (CPM), Release 4.3, Part 5, Appendix C, page C-27.

[10] Refer to IFPUG, *Function Point Counting Practices Manual* (CPM), Release 4.3, Part 5, Appendix C, page C-17.

[11] Refer to IFPUG, *Function Point Counting Practices Manual* (CPM), Release 4.3, Part 5, Appendix C, page C-17.

[12] Refer to IFPUG, *Function Point Counting Practices Manual* (CPM), Release 4.3, Part 5, Appendix C, page C-16.

[13] Refer to IFPUG, *Function Point Counting Practices Manual* (CPM), Release 4.3, Part 5, Appendix C, page C-20.

[14] Refer to IFPUG, *Function Point Counting Practices Manual* (CPM), Release 4.3, Part 5, Appendix C, page C-4.

[15] Refer to IFPUG, *Function Point Counting Practices Manual* (CPM), Release 4.3, Part 5, Appendix C, page C-4.

[16] Refer to IFPUG, *Function Point Counting Practices Manual* (CPM), Release 4.3, Part 5, Appendix C, page C-4.

[17] Refer to IFPUG, *Function Point Counting Practices Manual* (CPM), Release 4.3, Part 5, Appendix C, page C-44.

[18] Refer to IFPUG, *Function Point Counting Practices Manual* (CPM), Release 4.3, Part 5, Appendix C, pages C-32 and C-36.

19. Which of the following formulas is used to establish the initial adjusted application functional size:
    A. **aAFP = ADD × VAF**[19]
    B. aEFP = [(ADD + CHGA + CFP) × VAFA] + (DEL × VAFB)
    C. aAFPA = [(AFPB + ADD + CHGA) − (CHGB + DEL)] × VAFA
    D. aDFP = DFP × VAF

20. Which of the following formulas is used to calculate the adjusted enhancement project functional size:
    A. aAFP = ADD × VAF
    B. **aEFP = [(ADD + CHGA + CFP) × VAFA] + (DEL × VAFB)**[20]
    C. aAFPA = [(AFPB + ADD + CHGA) − (CHGB + DEL)] × VAFA
    D. aDFP = DFP × VAF

21. CHGB in the formula aAFPA = [(AFPB + ADD + CHGA) − (CHGB + DEL)] × VAFA:
    A. Is the size of the functions being deleted by the enhancement project
    B. Is the size of the functions being changed by the enhancement project (as they are/were before the project commenced)

C. **Is the size of the functions being changed by the enhancement project (as they are/will be after implementation)**[21]
    D. Is the size of the functions being added by the enhancement project

22. CHGB in the formula aAFPA = [(AFPB + ADD + CHGA) − (CHGB + DEL)] × VAFA:
    A. Is the size of the functions being deleted by the enhancement project
    B. **Is the size of the functions being changed by the enhancement project (as they are/were before the project commenced)**[22]
    C. Is the size of the functions being changed by the enhancement project (as they are/will be after implementation)
    D. Is the size of the functions being added by the enhancement project

23. In the formula aAFPA = [(AFPB + ADD + CHGA) − (CHGB + DEL)] × VAFA, the lower case "a":
    A. Denotes "application"
    B. Denotes "after"
    C. **Denotes "adjusted"**[23]
    D. None of the above

[19] Refer to IFPUG, *Function Point Counting Practices Manual* (CPM), Release 4.3, Part 5, Appendix C, page C-43.
[20] Refer to IFPUG, *Function Point Counting Practices Manual* (CPM), Release 4.3, Part 5, Appendix C, page C-38.
[21] Refer to IFPUG, *Function Point Counting Practices Manual* (CPM), Release 4.3, Part 5, Appendix C, page C-44.
[22] Refer to IFPUG, *Function Point Counting Practices Manual* (CPM), Release 4.3, Part 5, Appendix C, page C-44.
[23] Refer to IFPUG, *Function Point Counting Practices Manual* (CPM), Release 4.3, Appendix C, page C-1.

Appendix 15

Practice Exam 1 Answers

Part 1. Definitions and Rules

1. Steps in the function point counting procedure include:
   A. Gather the available documentation
   B. Document and report
   C. Calculate the functional size
   D. All of the above[1]

2. The following guidance applies when counting FTRs for EQs:
   A. Count one FTR for each ILF maintained
   B. Count one FTR for each ILF or EIF read[2]
   C. Count only one FTR for each ILF that is both maintained and read
   D. All of the above

3. An associative entity is:
   A. An entity type that further describes one or more characteristics of another entity type
   B. Often created by the data modeler to resolve some of the business rules required to relate two separate entities
   C. Used to associate two or more entities as a way of defining the many-to-many relationship
   D. B and C[3]

4. The application boundary
   A. Acts as a "membrane" through which data processed by transactions pass into and out from the application
   B. Is independent of technical and/or implementation considerations
   C. Is a conceptual interface between the software under study and its users
   D. All of the above[4]

5. Application functional size:
   A. Measures an installed application[5]
   B. Includes the functionality that will be measured in the initial application function point count, as well as any functionality required for data conversion
   C. Measures modifications to existing applications
   D. A and B

6. Functional User Requirements are:
   A. Detailed design specifications
   B. Requirements that specify what the software will do in terms of tasks and services
   C. A subset of the user requirements
   D. B and C[6]

7. Business Data may also be referred to as:
   A. Core Data
   B. Business Objects
   C. List Data
   D. A and B[7]

8. Code Data are sometimes referred to as:
   A. List Data
   B. Core Data

---

[1] Refer to IFPUG, *Function Point Counting Practices Manual* (CPM), Release 4.3, Part 2, page 2-2.

[2] Refer to IFPUG, *Function Point Counting Practices Manual* (CPM), Release 4.3, Part 2, page 7-17.

[3] Refer to IFPUG, *Function Point Counting Practices Manual* (CPM), Release 4.3, Part 3, page 2-34.

[4] Refer to IFPUG, *Function Point Counting Practices Manual* (CPM), Release 4.3, Part 2, page 5-4.

[5] Refer to IFPUG, *Function Point Counting Practices Manual* (CPM), Release 4.3, Part 2, page 4-3, and Part 5, page G-1.

[6] Refer to IFPUG, *Function Point Counting Practices Manual* (CPM), Release 4.3, Part 2, page 1-3.

[7] Refer to IFPUG, *Function Point Counting Practices Manual* (CPM), Release 4.3, Part 3, page 1-4.

C. Translation Data

D. A and C[8]

9. Entity independence is:

A. An entity that is meaningful or significant to the business, in and of itself without the presence of other entities[9]

B. A fundamental thing of relevance to the user, about which a collection of facts is kept

C. An entity that is not meaningful or is not significant to the business, in and of itself without the presence of other entities

D. A and C

10. A refresh is:

A. The process of recreating a set of data to make it current with its source[10]

B. Activity associated with mapping data or programs from one format to another

C. Initiated by business requests to add, change, or delete business functionality

D. To read data from a source, leaving the source data unchanged, and to write the same data elsewhere in a physical form that may differ from that of the source

11. A data function:

A. Represents functionality provided to the user to meet internal and external data storage requirements

B. Represents functionality provided to the user to create internal data storage requirements

C. Is either an Internal Logical File or an External Interface File

D. A and C[11]

12. The smallest unit of activity that is meaningful to the user is the definition of:

A. Functional size

B. Function point

C. Processing logic

D. An elementary process[12]

13. The two types of subgroups for Record Element Types are:

A. Mandatory and logical

B. Mandatory and optional[13]

C. Optional and logical

D. Mandatory and operational

14. Software maintenance performed to correct faults in hardware or software is the definition of:

A. Adaptive maintenance

B. Perfective maintenance

C. Corrective maintenance[14]

D. Preventive maintenance

15. Software maintenance performed to improve the performance, maintainability, or other attributes of a computer program is the definition of:

A. Adaptive maintenance

B. Perfective maintenance[15]

C. Corrective maintenance

D. Preventive maintenance

16. Business Data:

A. May also be referred to as Core User Data or Business Objects

B. Reflects the information needed to be stored and retrieved by the functional area addressed by the application

C. Usually represents a significant percentage of the entities identified

D. All of the above[16]

17. Which of the following defines the set of functional requirements to be included in the function point count?

A. Elementary process

B. Purpose of the count

C. Counting scope[17]

D. Scope creep

18. An application:

A. Is a cohesive collection of automated procedures and data supporting a business objective

B. Consists of one or more components, modules, or subsystems

C. Is a group of related items treated as a unit

D. A and B[18]

[8] Refer to IFPUG, *Function Point Counting Practices Manual* (CPM), Release 4.3, Part 3, page 1-6.

[9] Refer to IFPUG, *Function Point Counting Practices Manual* (CPM), Release 4.3, Part 3, page 2-12.

[10] Refer to IFPUG, *Function Point Counting Practices Manual* (CPM), Release 4.3, Part 3, page 3-3.

[11] Refer to IFPUG, *Function Point Counting Practices Manual* (CPM), Release 4.3, Part 2, page 6-4.

[12] Refer to IFPUG, *Function Point Counting Practices Manual* (CPM), Release 4.3, Part 1, page 14; Part 5, page G-3.

[13] Refer to IFPUG, *Function Point Counting Practices Manual* (CPM), Release 4.3, Part 2, page 6-7.

[14] Refer to IFPUG, *Function Point Counting Practices Manual* (CPM), Release 4.3, Part 3, page 4-20.

[15] Refer to IFPUG, *Function Point Counting Practices Manual* (CPM), Release 4.3, Part 3, page 4-20.

[16] Refer to IFPUG, *Function Point Counting Practices Manual* (CPM), Release 4.3, Part 3, page 1-4; Part 5, page G-2.

[17] Refer to IFPUG, *Function Point Counting Practices Manual* (CPM), Release 4.3, Part 2, page 5-3; Part 5, page G-2.

[18] Refer to IFPUG, *Function Point Counting Practices Manual* (CPM), Release 4.3, Part 2, page 4-3; Part 5, page G-1.

19. An elementary process that processes data or control information sent from outside the boundary is an:
    A. **EI**[19]
    B. EO
    C. EQ
    D. All of the above

20. Which of the following is true about an external output?
    A. **It is an elementary process that sends data or control information outside the application's boundary and includes additional processing beyond that of an external inquiry**[20]
    B. The primary intent is to present information to a user through the retrieval of data or control information
    C. The processing logic contains no mathematical formula or calculation
    D. A and B

21. A File Type Referenced is:
    A. A unique, user-recognizable, nonrepeated attribute
    B. An elementary process that provides functionality to the user to process data
    C. **A data function read and/or maintained by a transactional function**[21]
    D. None of the above

22. No prior or subsequent processing steps are needed to initiate or complete the functional requirements is the definition of:
    A. An elementary process
    B. Maintain
    C. Constant Data
    D. **Self-contained**[22]

23. Which of the following statement(s) is true for conversion?
    A. Transactional or data functions provided to convert data
    B. To read data from a source, leaving the source data unchanged, and to write the same data elsewhere in a physical form that may differ from that of the source
    C. Transactional or data functions that provide other user-specified conversion requirements
    D. **A and C**[23]

24. To read data from a source, leaving the source data unchanged, and to write the same data elsewhere in a physical form that may differ from that of the source is the definition of:
    A. Load
    B. **Copy**[24]
    C. Refresh
    D. Image

25. To copy computer instructions or data from external storage to internal storage is the definition of:
    A. **Load**[25]
    B. Copy
    C. Refresh
    D. Image

26. The process of recreating a set of data to make it current with its source is the definition of:
    A. Load
    B. Copy
    C. **Refresh**[26]
    D. Image

27. Which of the following are transactional functions?
    A. EI, EIF
    B. EI, EO, ILF
    C. **EI, EO, EQ**[27]
    D. EI, EO, EIF

28. Which of the following are data functions?
    A. EI, ILF
    B. **ILF, EIF**[28]
    C. EI, EO, EQ
    D. EI, EIF

29. What type of data provides a list of available values for an attribute of one or more business object types?
    A. Business Data
    B. Constant Data
    C. Reference Data
    D. **Valid Values Data**[29]

---

[19] Refer to IFPUG, *Function Point Counting Practices Manual* (CPM), Release 4.3, Part 2, page 7-3; Part 5, page G-3.

[20] Refer to IFPUG, *Function Point Counting Practices Manual* (CPM), Release 4.3, Part 2, page 7-3; Part 5, page G-4.

[21] Refer to IFPUG, *Function Point Counting Practices Manual* (CPM), Release 4.3, Part 2, page 7-14; Part 5, page G-4.

[22] Refer to IFPUG, *Function Point Counting Practices Manual* (CPM), Release 4.3, Part 1, page 7; Part 5, page G-7.

[23] Refer to IFPUG, *Function Point Counting Practices Manual* (CPM), Release 4.3, Part 3, page 5-2; Part 5, page G-2.

[24] Refer to IFPUG, *Function Point Counting Practices Manual* (CPM), Release 4.3, Part 3, page 3-3.

[25] Refer to IFPUG, *Function Point Counting Practices Manual* (CPM), Release 4.3, Part 3, page 3-3.

[26] Refer to IFPUG, *Function Point Counting Practices Manual* (CPM), Release 4.3, Part 3, page 3-3.

[27] Refer to IFPUG, *Function Point Counting Practices Manual* (CPM), Release 4.3, Part 2, page 7-1; Part 5, page G-7.

[28] Refer to IFPUG, *Function Point Counting Practices Manual* (CPM), Release 4.3, Part 2, page 6-1; Part 5, page G-3.

[29] Refer to IFPUG, *Function Point Counting Practices Manual* (CPM), Release 4.3, Part 3, page 1-12.

30. What type of data are stored to support the business rules for the maintenance of the Business Data?
    A. Code Data
    B. Constant Data
    C. Reference Data[30]
    D. Valid Values Data

31. What type of data rarely change?
    A. Code Data
    B. Constant Data[31]
    C. Reference Data
    D. Valid Values Data

32. What type of data provides a list of valid values that a descriptive attribute may have?
    A. Code Data[32]
    B. Constant Data
    C. Reference Data
    D. Business Data

33. An enhancement project:
    A. Is a project to develop and deliver the first release of a software application
    B. Is a project to develop and deliver adaptive maintenance[33]
    C. Includes repair, minor enhancement, conversion, user support, and preventive maintenance activities
    D. B and C

34 Maintenance activities include:
    A. Defect removal
    B. Hardware or software upgrades
    C. Optimization or quality improvement
    D. All of the above[34]

35. Any of the requirements specifically requested by the user to complete an elementary process, such as validations, algorithms, or calculations, and reading or maintaining a file, is the definition of:
    A. Maintenance
    B. Control information
    C. Conversion
    D. Processing logic[35]

36. A Data Element Type is:
    A. A unique, user-recognizable, nonrepeated attribute[36]
    B. A data function read and/or maintained by a transactional function
    C. A user-recognizable subgroup of Data Element Types within a data function
    D. None of the above

37. A Record Element Type is:
    A. A unique, user-recognizable, nonrepeated attribute
    B. A data function read and/or maintained by a transactional function
    C. A user-recognizable subgroup of Data Element Types within a data function[37]
    D. None of the above

38. A File Type Referenced is:
    A. A unique, user-recognizable, nonrepeated attribute
    B. A data function read and/or maintained by a transactional function[38]
    C. A user-recognizable subgroup of Data Element Types within a data function
    D. None of the above

39. The features or capabilities of an application as seen by the user is the definition of:
    A. Attribute
    B. User view
    C. Elementary process
    D. Function[39]

40. Which of the following is true of an External Interface File?
    A. It is a user-recognizable group of logically related data or control information that is referenced by the application being measured but which is maintained within the boundary of another application
    B. The primary intent is to hold data referenced through one or more elementary processes within the boundary of the application measured
    C. An EIF counted for an application must be in an ILF in another application
    D. All of the above[40]

---

[30] Refer to IFPUG, *Function Point Counting Practices Manual* (CPM), Release 4.3, Part 3, page 1-5.

[31] Refer to IFPUG, *Function Point Counting Practices Manual* (CPM), Release 4.3, Part 3, page 1-11.

[32] Refer to IFPUG, *Function Point Counting Practices Manual* (CPM), Release 4.3, Part 3, page 1-6.

[33] Refer to IFPUG, *Function Point Counting Practices Manual* (CPM), Release 4.3, Part 5, page G-3.

[34] Refer to IFPUG, *Function Point Counting Practices Manual* (CPM), Release 4.3, Part 5, page G-5.

[35] Refer to IFPUG, *Function Point Counting Practices Manual* (CPM), Release 4.3, Part 2, page 7-5; Part 5, page G-6.

[36] Refer to IFPUG, *Function Point Counting Practices Manual* (CPM), Release 4.3, Part 2, pages 6-5 and 7-14; Part 5, page G-2.

[37] Refer to IFPUG, *Function Point Counting Practices Manual* (CPM), Release 4.3, Part 2, page 6-7; Part 5, page G-6.

[38] Refer to IFPUG, *Function Point Counting Practices Manual* (CPM), Release 4.3, Part 2, page 7-14; Part 5, page G-4.

[39] Refer to IFPUG, *Function Point Counting Practices Manual* (CPM), Release 4.3, Part 5, page G-4.

[40] Refer to IFPUG, *Function Point Counting Practices Manual* (CPM), Release 4.3, Part 2, page 6-2.

41. Which of the following is true of an external output?
    A. It may maintain one or more ILFs and/or alter the behavior of the system[41]
    B. It may not contain derived data
    C. It may not contain calculations
    D. It may not maintain one or more ILFs and/or alter the behavior of the system

42. Data in an ILF or EIF that exists because the user requires a relationship with another ILF or EIF is the definition of:
    A. Foreign key[42]
    B. Primary key
    C. Secondary key
    D. None of the above

43. The unique ID of an entity is the definition of:
    A. Foreign key
    B. Primary key[43]
    C. Secondary key
    D. None of the above

44. The definition of primary intent is:
    A. The smallest unit of activity that is meaningful to the user
    B. An elementary process that provides functionality to the user to process data
    C. Intent that is first in importance[44]
    D. Requirements for processes and/or data that are agreed upon, and understood by, both the user(s) and software developer(s)

45. Adaptive maintenance:
    A. Is the modification of a software product, performed after delivery, to keep a software product usable in a changed or changing environment
    B. Provides enhancements necessary to accommodate changes in the environment in which a software product must operate
    C. Changes are those that must be made to keep pace with the changing environment
    D. All of the above[45]

46. Quality includes:
    A. Usability
    B. Reliability
    C. Efficiency
    D. All of the above[46]

47. The result of a normalization process that transforms groups of data so they have a unique identifier, one or more attributes, and no repeating attributes is:
    A. First normal form[47]
    B. Second normal form
    C. Third normal form
    D. None of the above

48. Entity dependence is:
    A. An entity that is meaningful or significant to the business, in and of itself without the presence of other entities
    B. A fundamental thing of relevance to the user, about which a collection of facts is kept
    C. An entity that is not meaningful or is not significant to the business, in and of itself without the presence of other entities[48]
    D. A and B

49. A group of related items that is treated as a unit is a:
    A. Record[49]
    B. File
    C. File system
    D. Function

50. The activity of sequencing attributes in a transactional function is the definition of:
    A. Sorting
    B. Loading
    C. Refreshing
    D. Arranging[50]

Part 2. Implementation

1. How many DETs are counted on an external output that has a pie chart with a category label and a numerical equivalent in a graphical output?
    A. 1
    B. 2[51]
    C. 0
    D. 3

[41]Refer to IFPUG, *Function Point Counting Practices Manual* (CPM), Release 4.3, Part 2, page 7-8; Part 5, page G-4.
[42]Refer to IFPUG, *Function Point Counting Practices Manual* (CPM), Release 4.3, Part 5, page G-4.
[43]Refer to IFPUG, *Function Point Counting Practices Manual* (CPM), Release 4.3, Part 3, page 2-23.
[44]Refer to IFPUG, *Function Point Counting Practices Manual* (CPM), Release 4.3, Part 1, page 6; Part 5, page G-6.
[45]Refer to IFPUG, *Function Point Counting Practices Manual* (CPM), Release 4.3, Part 3, page 4-20; Part 5, page G-1.
[46]Refer to IFPUG, *Function Point Counting Practices Manual* (CPM), Release 4.3, Part 1, page 5; Part 2, page 1-4.
[47]Refer to IFPUG, *Function Point Counting Practices Manual* (CPM), Release 4.3, Part 5, page G-4.
[48]Refer to IFPUG, *Function Point Counting Practices Manual* (CPM), Release 4.3, Part 3, page 2-12.
[49]Refer to IFPUG, *Function Point Counting Practices Manual* (CPM), Release 4.3, Part 3, page 2-5.
[50]Refer to IFPUG, *Function Point Counting Practices Manual* (CPM), Release 4.3, Part 1, page 2; Part 5, page G-1.
[51]Refer to IFPUG, *Function Point Counting Practices Manual* (CPM), Release 4.3, Part 2, page 7-17.

2. An external input that has six DETs and two FTRs has how many function points?
   A. 3
   B. 4[52]
   C. 5
   D. 6

3. What is the application functional size of an application that has five low external inputs, one high external output, three average external inquiries, and one average Internal Logical File?
   A. 40
   B. 42
   C. 44[53]
   D. 49

4. Which of the following would be a high complexity?
   A. An external input with 3 FTRs and 4 DETs
   B. An external output with 4 FTRs and 5 DETs
   C. An external inquiry with 3 FTRs and 19 DETs
   D. None of the above[54]

5. An enhancement project added a low external input, deleted an average external inquiry, and added two average external outputs. What is the enhancement project functional size?
   A. 13
   B. 17[55]
   C. 19
   D. 20

6. Put the following steps in the function point counting procedure in order:
      a. Determine counting scope and boundary and identify Functional User Requirements
      b. Document and report
      c. Measure data functions
      d. Measure transactional functions
      e. Calculate the functional size
      f. Gather the available documentation
   A. b, f, a, c, d, e
   B. f, b, d, c, a, e
   C. f, a, c, d, e, b[56]
   D. f, b, c, d, e, b

7. Application A and Application B both modify the same ILF. Application A added four fields to this ILF. Application A populates these new fields by changing an existing external input to include these four fields. There was no impact to transactions in Application B. What is counted?
   A. A changed ILF for Applications A and B; a changed transaction for Application A
   B. A changed ILF and a changed transaction for Application A[57]
   C. A changed ILF for Applications A and B; a changed transaction for Applications A and B
   D. A changed transaction for Application A

8. Currency Exchange-Rate Table (Country and Current Exchange Rate) is an example of what type of data?
   A. Code Data
   B. Constant Data
   C. Reference Data[58]
   D. Valid Values Data

9. Airport code and airport name are examples of what type of data?
   A. Code Data[59]
   B. Constant Data
   C. Reference Data
   D. Valid Values Data

10. Application A has added two external inputs (add employee and change employee), each having two record types (employee basic information and employee address information). How many external inputs are counted?
    A. 4
    B. 2[60]
    C. 1
    D. 3

11. An application's function points before an enhancement is 200. The enhancement added three low EIs, two high EIs, four average EQs, and one average EO. What is the enhancement project functional size?
    A. 242
    B. 42[61]
    C. 246
    D. 46

[52] Refer to IFPUG, *Function Point Counting Practices Manual* (CPM), Release 4.3, Part 2, page 7-19.

[53] Refer to IFPUG, *Function Point Counting Practices Manual* (CPM), Release 4.3, Part 2, pages 6-8 and 7-20.

[54] Refer to IFPUG, *Function Point Counting Practices Manual* (CPM), Release 4.3, Part 2, page 7-19.

[55] Refer to IFPUG, *Function Point Counting Practices Manual* (CPM), Release 4.3, Part 3, page 4-17.

[56] Refer to IFPUG, *Function Point Counting Practices Manual* (CPM), Release 4.3, Part 2, page 2-2.

[57] Refer to IFPUG, *Function Point Counting Practices Manual* (CPM), Release 4.3, Part 2, Chapters 6 and 7.

[58] Refer to IFPUG, *Function Point Counting Practices Manual* (CPM), Release 4.3, Part 3, page 1-13.

[59] Refer to IFPUG, *Function Point Counting Practices Manual* (CPM), Release 4.3, Part 3, page 1-6.

[60] Refer to IFPUG, *Function Point Counting Practices Manual* (CPM), Release 4.3, Part 2, Chapter 7.

[61] Refer to IFPUG, *Function Point Counting Practices Manual* (CPM), Release 4.3, Part 3, pages 4-14 to 4-17.

12. Which of the following formulas is used to calculate an enhancement project functional size?
    A. DFP = ADD + CFP
    B. EFP = ADD + CHGA + CFP + DEL[62]
    C. AFPA = (AFPB + ADD + CHGA) − (CHGB + DEL)
    D. None of the above

13. DETs that cross the boundary include:
    A. Attributes the user enters via a screen as well as those displayed on a report or screen
    B. Attributes in an electronic file that enter or exit the boundary
    C. Attributes that enter the application boundary and are required to specify when, what, and/or how the data is to be retrieved or generated by the elementary process
    D. All of the above[63]

14. Which of the following are not counted as DETs on a transaction?
    A. Attributes generated within the boundary by a transactional function and saved to an ILF without exiting the boundary
    B. Attributes retrieved or referenced from an ILF or EIF for participation in the processing without exiting the boundary
    C. Attributes provided by, or presented to, the user of the transactional function
    D. A and B[64]

15. Which of the following types of transactions may alter the behavior of the application?
    A. EI
    B. EO
    C. EQ
    D. A and B[65]

16. Which of the following is/are a form of processing logic?
    A. Sorting or arranging a set of data
    B. Conditions are analyzed to determine which are applicable
    C. Validations are performed
    D. All of the above[66]

17. In an enhancement project, the size of the functions being added is 10, the size of the functions being deleted is 10, the size of the functions being changed as they are/will be after implementation is 20, and the size of the functions being changed as they are/were before the project commenced is 15. What is the enhancement project functional size?
    A. 55
    B. 45
    C. 40[67]
    D. 35

18. An invoice data function has a header section of the customer information (customer name; account number; purchase order number; billing street address, city, state, and Zip Code; shipping street address, city, state, and Zip Code; phone number; e-mail address; fax number) and line items of the purchases (item number; description; price; weight; color; quantity ordered). The invoice data store is updated in the application being measured. What is the size of this data function?
    A. 5
    B. 7
    C. 10[68]
    D. 15

19. A transaction whose primary intent is maintaining an ILF is being added to an application. This transaction has 15 unique DETs, updates one ILF, and reads two EIFs. What is the functional size of this transaction?
    A. 4
    B. 5
    C. 6[69]
    D. 7

20. The ability to initiate a transactional function can be done by the clicking on the enter key, the PF2 key, or the OK button. How many DETs are counted for initiating the action?
    A. 0
    B. 1[70]
    C. 2
    D. 3

21. Presenting information to a user is the primary intent of which transaction(s)?
    A. External input
    B. External output

---

[62] Refer to IFPUG, *Function Point Counting Practices Manual* (CPM), Release 4.3, Part 3, page 4-17.

[63] Refer to IFPUG, *Function Point Counting Practices Manual* (CPM), Release 4.3, Part 2, pages 7-14 to 7-18.

[64] Refer to IFPUG, *Function Point Counting Practices Manual* (CPM), Release 4.3, Part 2, page 7-15.

[65] Refer to IFPUG, *Function Point Counting Practices Manual* (CPM), Release 4.3, Part 2, page 7-4.

[66] Refer to IFPUG, *Function Point Counting Practices Manual* (CPM), Release 4.3, Part 2, page 7-8.

[67] Refer to IFPUG, *Function Point Counting Practices Manual* (CPM), Release 4.3, Part 3, page 4-17.

[68] Refer to IFPUG, *Function Point Counting Practices Manual* (CPM), Release 4.3, Part 2, pages 6-4 to 6-8.

[69] Refer to IFPUG, *Function Point Counting Practices Manual* (CPM), Release 4.3, Part 2, pages 7-4, 7-19, and 7-20.

[70] Refer to IFPUG, *Function Point Counting Practices Manual* (CPM), Release 4.3, Part 2, page 7-14.

C. External inquiry

D. B and C[71]

22. Transforming existing data to create additional data is a form of which processing logic?
   A. Equivalent values are converted
   B. Sorting or arranging a set of data
   C. Derived data[72]
   D. Mathematical formulas and calculations are performed

23. Classify an elementary process as an EI if:
   A. It has a primary intent of either maintaining one or more ILFs or altering the behavior of the application
   B. It has the primary intent of presenting information to the user
   C. It includes processing logic to accept data or control information that enters the application boundary
   D. A and C[73]

24. Functional User Requirements may include which of the following?
   A. Data transformation[74]
   B. Quality constraints
   C. Environmental constraints
   D. None of the above

25. Which of the following formulas is used to calculate an application functional size after an enhancement project?
   A. DFP = ADD + CFP
   B. EFP = ADD + CHGA + CFP + DEL
   C. AFPA = (AFPB + ADD + CHGA) − (CHGB + DEL)[75]
   D. AFP = ADD

26. After an enhancement project, the application functional size may be updated to reflect changed functionality. This changed functionality may:
   A. Increase the application functional size
   B. Decrease the application functional size
   C. Have no effect on the application functional size
   D. All of the above[76]

27. The formula DFP = ADD + CFP is used to calculate which of the following?
   A. Application functional size
   B. Development project functional size[77]
   C. Application functional size after an enhancement project
   D. None of the above

28. A transaction to add an employee has the ability to return 10 unique error messages and two unique confirmation messages. How many DETs are counted for the error and confirmation messages?
   A. 12
   B. 11
   C. 2
   D. 1[78]

29. In the formula AFPA = (AFPB + ADD + CHGA) − (CHGB + DEL), CHGB is:
   A. The application functional size before the enhancement project
   B. The application functional size after the enhancement project
   C. The size of the functions being changed by the enhancement project (as they are/will be after implementation)
   D. The size of the functions being changed by the enhancement project (as they are/were before the project commenced)[79]

30. An application functional size before an enhancement project was 100. The enhancement project added two low EIs, deleted one high EO, and changed one EQ from a low to an average. What is the application functional size after the enhancement project?
   A. 100[80]
   B. 107
   C. 113
   D. 104

31. An application functional size before an enhancement project was 100. The enhancement project added two low EIs, deleted one high EO, and changed one EQ from a low to an average. What is the enhancement project functional size?
   A. 16

---

[71] Refer to IFPUG, *Function Point Counting Practices Manual* (CPM), Release 4.3, Part 2, page 7-4.

[72] Refer to IFPUG, *Function Point Counting Practices Manual* (CPM), Release 4.3, Part 2, page 7-6.

[73] Refer to IFPUG, *Function Point Counting Practices Manual* (CPM), Release 4.3, Part 2, page 7-3.

[74] Refer to IFPUG, *Function Point Counting Practices Manual* (CPM), Release 4.3, Part 2, page 1-3.

[75] Refer to IFPUG, *Function Point Counting Practices Manual* (CPM), Release 4.3, Part 3, page 4-19.

[76] Refer to IFPUG, *Function Point Counting Practices Manual* (CPM), Release 4.3, Part 3, page 4-19.

[77] Refer to IFPUG, *Function Point Counting Practices Manual* (CPM), Release 4.3, Part 1, page 20.

[78] Refer to IFPUG, *Function Point Counting Practices Manual* (CPM), Release 4.3, Part 2, pages 7-14 and 7-16.

[79] Refer to IFPUG, *Function Point Counting Practices Manual* (CPM), Release 4.3, Part 3, page 4-19.

[80] Refer to IFPUG, *Function Point Counting Practices Manual* (CPM), Release 4.3, Part 3, page 4-19.

B. 17[81]
C. 10
D. 9

32. A new logon function requires the entry of the fields User Identifier and User Password. When the user logs on, the Security file is read to validate the user identifier and password as well as to determine the windows the user can access and maintain. If the fields do not pass edits, error messages are generated and incorrect fields are highlighted. Two error messages and one confirmation message are included for the security logon transaction. The security logon transactions is counted as an:
    A. EI
    B. EO
    C. EQ[82]
    D. It is not counted

33. During construction of the Payroll application, a requirement for help functionality was added. Help information is not maintained in any application. How is help counted in the Payroll application?
    A. ILF
    B. EIF
    C. EQ
    D. It is not counted[83]

34. A user requires that an application print a monthly report automatically every month. This report lists all employees by department and contains employee name and employee ID. This report is counted as an:
    A. EI
    B. EQ[84]
    C. EO
    D. It is not counted

35. The user requires the ability to perform the following activities:
    ■ Enter a report definition that includes a unique report identifier, a report name, attributes used on the report, and calculations to generate the report.
    ■ Reuse the defined report at any time, changing the definition if necessary.
    ■ View and print a report using the report definition.
    ■ Inquire on existing report definitions by report name or report identifier.

What data functions are counted for these activities?
    A. ILF, EI, EQ
    B. ILF, EI, EO
    C. ILF[85]
    D. EIF

36. A user needs to inquire on report definitions using the report name as the key to finding the desired definition. To satisfy the user requirement, an alternate index is created using the report name as the key. This alternate index is counted as:
    A. An ILF
    B. An EIF
    C. A RET on the report definition ILF
    D. It is not counted[86]

37. The user requires the ability to view a list of states. The list is retrieved from a file containing state code and state description. No other data is stored on the file. The retrieved list is counted as an:
    A. EQ
    B. EI
    C. EO
    D. It is not counted[87]

38. At the end of each day, Application A sends a Daily Check file to Application B listing the check numbers and the amount and date of each check printed for the day. Application B uses the file to update a data function maintained within its boundaries. This transactional function is counted as:
    A. An EQ for Application A and an EQ for Application B
    B. An EQ for Application A and an EI for Application B[88]
    C. An EO for Application A and an EI for Application B
    D. An EQ for Application A and nothing for Application B

39. Application A maintains the following information in the Vendor data function: vendor ID, vendor name, vendor phone number, vendor fax number, and vendor address, which includes floor, street, city, state, and Zip Code. Application B requires the ability to produce

[81] Refer to IFPUG, *Function Point Counting Practices Manual* (CPM), Release 4.3, Part 3, pages 4-14 to 4-17.

[82] Refer to IFPUG, *Function Point Counting Practices Manual* (CPM), Release 4.3, Part 4, pages 2-159 to 2-161.

[83] Refer to IFPUG, *Function Point Counting Practices Manual* (CPM), Release 4.3, Part 2, page 7-13.

[84] Refer to IFPUG, *Function Point Counting Practices Manual* (CPM), Release 4.3, Part 2, pages 7-3 and 7-13.

[85] Refer to IFPUG, *Function Point Counting Practices Manual* (CPM), Release 4.3, Part 2, page 6-2.

[86] Refer to IFPUG, *Function Point Counting Practices Manual* (CPM), Release 4.3, Part 4, page 1-20.

[87] Refer to IFPUG, *Function Point Counting Practices Manual* (CPM), Release 4.3, Part 3, page 1-7.

[88] Refer to IFPUG, *Function Point Counting Practices Manual* (CPM), Release 4.3, Part 3, pages 3-20 to 3-21.

mailing labels for each vendor by retrieving the vendor address from the Vendor data function. The Vendor data function is counted as:

A. An ILF with 5 DETs for Application A and an EIF with 5 DETs for Application B

B. An ILF with 9 DETs for Application A and an EIF with 5 DETs for Application B

C. **An ILF with 9 DETs for Application A and an EIF with 1 DET for Application B**[89]

D. An ILF with 9 DETs for Application A and an ILF with 1 DET for Application B

40. When a user adds a customer record in Application A, a validation is done on the Zip Code by sending the city, state, and Zip Code to Application B. By reading a maintained Zip Code data function, Application B validates that the Zip Code is a valid Zip Code for the city and state and sends a success or failure message back to Application A. If a success message is received, Application A adds the record to the Customer data function. If a failure message is received, Application A does not add the record and sends an error message back to the user that the Zip Code is invalid for the city/state. Identify all of the functions to be counted in this scenario for Application A.

A. An ILF for the Customer data function and an EQ for the Zip Code validation

B. An EI for adding a customer record, an ILF for the Customer data function, and an EQ for the Zip Code validation

C. An ILF for the Customer data function and an EIF for the Zip Code data function

D. **An EI for adding a customer record, an ILF for the Customer data function, and an EIF for the Zip Code data function**[90]

41. A development project has five average complexity EIs and two high complexity EIs; two average complexity EOs; two average complexity EQs and one high complexity EQ; one low complexity ILF and one high complexity ILF; one low complexity EIF; and one average complexity conversion EI. What is the application count after the development project is installed?

A. 85

B. 87

C. 80

D. **83**[91]

42. Which of the following is not considered conversion functionality?

A. Software upgrades due to the installation of a revised version of vendor packages

B. An enhancement project requires the addition of a DET to an existing ILF and the new DET will be populated with a specific default value

C. A changed EIF for the application being measured

D. **All of the above**[92]

43. Identify the transactional functions in the following scenario: A batch feed of new customer data from another application must be accepted. The customer data must be validated and saved to the Customer file; an error report is produced containing any identified errors. The business office is notified via e-mail with processing summary data.

A. One EI, one EO, and one EQ

B. One EI and two EQs

C. One EI and one EO

D. **One EI only**[93]

44. An enhancement project adds six high complexity EIs and two average complexity EQs, deletes one high complexity EQ, and changes three EOs from low to high complexity. If the application count is 1000 before the enhancement, what is the value of the enhancement count?

A. 1059

B. 1047

C. **71**[94]

D. 62

45. The user requires the ability to delete a customer from the Customer ILF. Via an online screen, the user enters the customer ID and clicks on the delete button. If the customer ID is invalid, an error message is returned and the Customer ILF is not updated. If the customer ID is valid, the status field on the Customer ILF is updated with an "I," the system date is entered in the Effective Date on the Customer ILF, and a confirmation message is returned. What is counted for this transactional function?

A. An EI with 1 FTR and 5 DETs

B. An EI with 1 FTR and 6 DETs

C. **An EI with 1 FTR and 3 DETs**[95]

D. An EI with 1 FTR and 4 DETs

---

[89]Refer to IFPUG, *Function Point Counting Practices Manual* (CPM), Release 4.3, Part 4, pages 1-29 to 1-36.

[90]Refer to IFPUG, *Function Point Counting Practices Manual* (CPM), Release 4.3, Part 4, pages 1-29 to 1-36.

[91]Refer to IFPUG, *Function Point Counting Practices Manual* (CPM), Release 4.3, Part 1, pages 20 and 23, and Part 2, pages 6-8 and 7-20.

[92]Refer to IFPUG, *Function Point Counting Practices Manual* (CPM), Release 4.3, Part 3, page 5-4.

[93]Refer to IFPUG, *Function Point Counting Practices Manual* (CPM), Release 4.3, Part 4, pages 2-41 to 2-46.

[94]Refer to IFPUG, *Function Point Counting Practices Manual* (CPM), Release 4.3, Part 3, pages 4-14 to 4-17.

[95]Refer to IFPUG, *Function Point Counting Practices Manual* (CPM), Release 4.3, Part 2, Chapter 7.

46. Application A generates a Monthly PO file at the end of each month and sends it to Application B. During the creation of the Monthly PO file, the total number of purchase orders and the total dollar amount of those purchase orders for the month are calculated. Application B uses this file to update a data function within its boundaries. What transactional functions are counted?
    A. An EQ for Application A and an EI for Application B
    B. An EO for Application A and an EI for Application B[96]
    C. An EQ for Application A; nothing for Application B
    D. An EO for Application A; nothing for Application B

47. A development project has two low complexity EIs, two average complexity EIs, two low complexity EOs, two high complexity EQs, two low complexity ILFs, and one low complexity conversion EI. What is the development count?
    A. 49
    B. 50
    C. 51[97]
    D. 53

48. An application's functional size before an enhancement is 100. The enhancement added two low EIs and deleted one average EO. What is the application size after the enhancement project is delivered?
    A. 100
    B. 101[98]
    C. 110
    D. 111

49. The user has requested that an ILF (or part of an ILF) be populated from an ILF in another application. Validation is required against yet another ILF from a third application. This processing is specified as a one-time process and the data referenced in the third application will not be utilized in the future. What is counted for the conversion functionality?
    A. An EIF and an EI with two FTRs[99]
    B. An ILF and an EI with one FTR

C. An ILF only
D. An ILF, an EQ, and an EI with one FTR

50. Application A generates an image copy with no additional processing logic and sends it to Application B; Application B loads a copy with no additional processing logic. What is counted?
    A. An ILF for Application A and an ILF for Application B
    B. An EIF for Application A and an EIF for Application B
    C. An ILF for Application A and an EIF for Application B[100]
    D. An ILF for Application A and an EI for Application B

Part 3. Case Studies
Case Study 1

An Employee batch file enters Application A with three attributes (Employee ID, Employee Hire Date, and Employee Job Assignment). There are two transaction types: Add Employee and Update Employee. The Employee Job Assignment attribute on the input record is validated against the Job Assignment logical file maintained in Application C; this is the only attribute accessed in the Job Assignment logical file by Application A; however, the Job Assignment logical file has 51 attributes within Application C. If the validation passes, the Employee logical file is updated in Application A; a total of 12 fields are maintained and/or referenced in the Employee logical file within Application A. If the validation fails, no update is made and an error report is produced.

Identify the functional complexity of the possible function types by choosing the correct radio buttons in Table A15.1.

Table A15.1

Names of Possible Function Types	Enter Complexity			
	Low	Average	High	N/A
Add Employee	●	○	○	○
Update Employee	●	○	○	○
Error Listing	○	○	○	●
Employee ILF	●	○	○	○
Job Assignment EIF	●	○	○	○

---

[96] Refer to IFPUG, *Function Point Counting Practices Manual* (CPM), Release 4.3, Part 2, Chapter 7.

[97] Refer to IFPUG, *Function Point Counting Practices Manual* (CPM), Release 4.3, Part 1, pages 20 and 23; Part 2, pages 5-3, 6-8 to 6-9, and 7-19 to 7-20.

[98] Refer to IFPUG, *Function Point Counting Practices Manual* (CPM), Release 4.3, Part 3, pages 4-16 to 4-19.

[99] Refer to IFPUG, *Function Point Counting Practices Manual* (CPM), Release 4.3, Part 3, page 5-3.

[100] Refer to IFPUG, *Function Point Counting Practices Manual* (CPM), Release 4.3, Part 3, page 3-13 to 3-14.

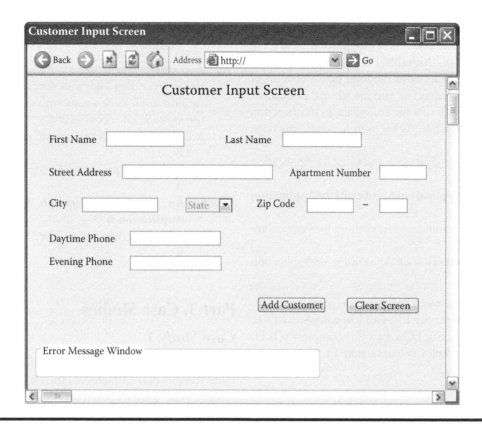

Figure A15.1 Customer input screen.

Case Study 2

Use the screen in Figure A15.1 to identify the functions present (see Table A15.2). Note that the "Add Customer" button causes the Customer Data maintained inside the application boundary to be updated with the fields entered by the user. The "Clear Screen" button causes all of the fields to be erased. The "Error Message Window" displays any errors associated with validations performed against an externally maintained Zip Code Data file after the "Add Customer" button is pressed.

Table A15.2

Names of Possible Function Types	Identify the Function Used					
	ILF	EIF	EI	EO	EQ	N/A
Add Customer	O	O	●	O	O	O
Clear Screen	O	O	O	O	O	●
Error Message Window	O	O	O	O	O	●
Customer Data	●	O	O	O	O	O
Zip Code Data	O	●	O	O	O	O

Case Study 3

A retail store has developed a new application, Frequent Buyer Program (FBP), to track customer purchases. The customer fills out a paper application and gives it to the store clerk. The clerk then adds the customer's information online. The clerk can also list customers, view a customer's detailed information, and change a customer's information. A report is produced daily listing customers that were added with their addresses.

Identify the functions of the FBP application by choosing the correct radio buttons in Table A15.3.

Case Study 4

Use the data flow diagram in Figure A15.2 to identify the functions in the HR application and the Mail Distribution application (see Table A15.4).

Case Study 5

SME is implementing a Customer Relations Management (CRM) application. The Web Info (WI) application, an existing application, will be required to send information to the CRM each evening by retrieving all Requests for Information (RFI) submitted that day and currently maintained in the

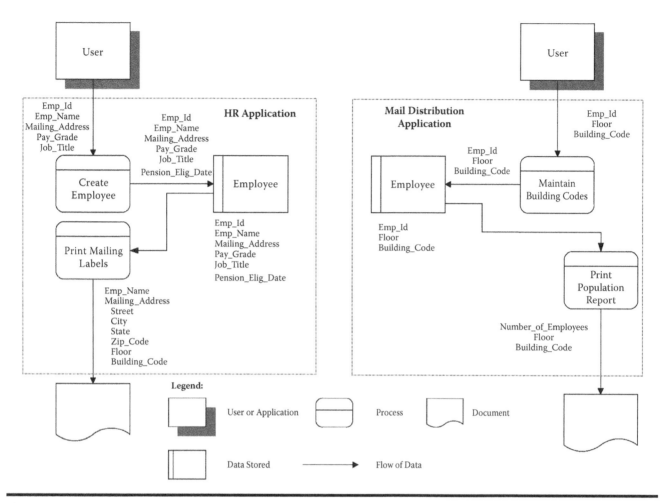

Figure A15.2 HR and mail distribution applications.

RFI logical file within the WI application. The following information is sent on this daily feed: requestor ID; requestor's first, middle, and last name; requestor's organization; requestor's address (street address, city, state, and Zip Code); date of request; requested items; and quantities for requested items. The CRM application will validate and process the daily feed into a new Potential Customer logical file.

Separate reports by state will be generated each morning by the CRM application and delivered to state sales coordinators. The printout will contain all of the information on the Potential Customer logical file as well as a total number of requests for information, which is calculated at the time the report is produced. The state code and state name, retrieved from a code table, will also be printed on each report.

Table A15.3

Names of Possible Function Types	Identify the Function Used					
	ILF	EIF	EI	EO	EQ	N/A
Add Customer	O	O	●	O	O	O
Change Customer's Information	O	O	●	O	O	O
List Customers	O	O	O	O	●	O
View Customer's Detail Information	O	O	O	O	●	O
Customer Report	O	O	O	O	●	O

Table A15.4

Names of Possible Function Types	Identify the Function Used					
	ILF	EIF	EI	EO	EQ	N/A
Create Employee	O	O	●	O	O	O
Print Mailing Labels	O	O	O	O	●	O
Maintain Building Codes	O	O	●	O	O	O
Print Population Report	O	O	O	●	O	O
Employee	●	O	O	O	O	O

Table A15.5

Names of Possible Function Types	Enter Complexity			
	Low	Average	High	N/A
RFI Daily Feed	●	○	○	○
Potential Customer Logical File	●	○	○	○
State Report	●	○	○	○
Retrieve/View Customer Information	●	○	○	○
Update Requested Information	○	●	○	○

Table A15.6

Names of Possible Function Types	Enter Complexity			
	Low	Average	High	N/A
Customer logical file	●	○	○	○
Orders logical file	○	●	○	○
CUSTID logical file	○	○	○	●
Add Bulk Orders	○	●	○	○
Change Bulk Orders	○	●	○	○

Each state sales coordinator will have the ability to retrieve via screen all information maintained in the Potential Customer logical file by entering the requestor ID and action key; hard-coded error messages will be returned if the requestor ID is not found. Using that screen, the state coordinator can revise the requested items and/or quantities using the requestor ID and a preassigned function key; hard-coded error messages may be returned if the newly assigned requested item is not contained in the Inventory logical file maintained by the Inventory application, or a hard-coded confirmation message will occur.

Identify the complexity of the functions for the CRM application by choosing the correct radio buttons in Table A15.5.

Case Study 6

A company is creating a new application called Sales Order System (SOS). This application will have the following logical files:

- CUSTOMER contains the company name; street address, city, state, and Zip Code; customer code; region; sales agent; and billing street address, city, state, and Zip Code.
- ORDERS contains: (a) Record One (Ship to) contains customer code, record ID, "attention to" name (first name, middle initial, last name), street address, city, state, Zip Code, carrier code, and date to be shipped. (b) Record Two (Details) contains customer code, record ID, item code, item quantity, item dollar amount, bulk order discount code, total order dollar amount, tax code, tax amount, and date order placed. (c) Record Three (Billing) contains customer code, record ID, company code, billing street address, city, state, Zip Code, and orderer's name (first name, middle initial, last name).
- CUSTID contains the same information as CUSTOMER but sorted by customer code and is used in processing outputs.

Bulk orders are entered into the SOS via the Bulk Order file from the regional system. The transaction contains 29 attributes and updates the ORDERS logical file. One of the attributes contains an action field with the values A (add) or C (change).

Identify the complexity of the functions for the SOS application by choosing the correct radio buttons in Table A15.6.

Case Study 7

An insurance company offers several product lines, including homeowner's and auto insurance. A new marketing strategy is to offer a discount on the purchase of auto insurance to a policyholder who already has homeowner's insurance with the company. To provide this service, enhancements must be made:

- The Policyholder logical file that is maintained by both the Homeowner's Insurance application and the Auto Insurance application will have two fields added to it: Multipolicy Discount Indicator and Discount Amount.
- Processing logic must be changed in the Auto Insurance application. During the nightly batch processing of new auto policies, the Policyholder logical file must be checked to see if the policyholder has homeowner's insurance with the company. If so, the two new fields in the Policyholder logical file will be updated. In addition, the confirmation report that is produced from the batch process will be changed to include a message that the discount was applied.
- The Homeowner's Insurance application must also be changed. During the nightly batch process of cancelled homeowner's policies, the Policyholder logical file must be checked to see if the policyholder has been receiving the multipolicy discount on auto insurance. If so, the Multipolicy Discount Indicator will be set to "C" for "Cancelled."

Table A15.7

Names of Possible Function Types	Identify the Function Used					
	ILF	EIF	EI	EO	EQ	N/A
Policyholder logical file	●	○	○	○	○	○
New Auto Policy	○	○	●	○	○	○
New Auto Policy Confirmation Report	○	○	○	○	○	●
Cancelled Homeowner's Policy	○	○	●	○	○	○
Policyholder Letter	○	○	○	●	○	○

■ The nightly batch process in the Auto Insurance application must also be changed to check each record on the Policyholder logical file for cancelled homeowner's insurance. If the Multipolicy Discount Indicator is a "C," it will be changed to an "N," the Discount Amount will be set to zero, the new auto insurance premium will be calculated, and a letter outlining the changes will be produced and mailed to the policyholder.

Identify the new and changed functions of the Homeowner's Insurance and Auto Insurance applications by choosing the correct radio buttons in Table A15.7.

Case Study 8

Company XYZ plans to enhance its Accounts Payable (AP) application. The current application interfaces with existing banking, help, and purchase order (PO) applications. This is a menu-driven system. To enter the AP application, the user must make selections from a main menu. The menu has the following options:

■ Invoices
  – Add an invoice
  – Display an invoice
  – Change an invoice
  – Delete an invoice
■ Payments
  – Retrieve payments due
  – Record payments

Invoices and payments are maintained in the Invoice logical file in AP. The enhancement will allow users to maintain Vendor information in the AP application. The following is being added to the AP menu:

■ Vendor
  – Add a vendor
  – Display vendor information
  – Change vendor information

Table A15.8

Names of Possible Function Types	Identify the Function Used					
	ILF	EIF	EI	EO	EQ	N/A
Add Vendor	○	○	●	○	○	○
Change Vendor	○	○	●	○	○	○
Delete Vendor	○	○	○	○	○	●
Display Vendor Information	○	○	○	○	●	○
Vendor logical file	●	○	○	○	○	○

The Vendor information will be maintained in a new Vendor logical file in the AP application.

Identify the enhanced functions of the AP application by choosing the correct radio buttons in Table A15.8.

Case Study 9

A new file is to be passed from the Accounts Payable (AP) application to the Banking application at the close of every business day. This file contains the payment date required, payment amount, PO number, vendor name, and vendor billing street address, city, state, and Zip Code. The Banking application must now be enhanced to process this incoming file and to generate the appropriate checks.

The Banking application will process the incoming file from the AP application without any edits or validation into two user-maintained logical files: Checking Account and Disbursements. The Checking Account logical file previously had 2 RETs and 19 DETs. This change will require the addition of the PO number to the Checking Account logical file. All other attributes were previously included. The Disbursements logical file will not require any changes as a result of this enhancement.

The current process to generate checks to pay invoices is to be modified. Checks now will be generated with the PO number as a separate memo attribute by the banking system. Previously, checks contained the following information: preprinted name and address for the company, preprinted check numbers, payment date, payment amount, payee (same as vendor's name), and payee street address, city, state, and Zip Code. Checks previously did not include a memo attribute. These checks reference only the Checking Account logical file when they are created. The Checking Account logical file is updated internally to indicate payment as part of the check generation elementary process.

A printed report will be generated from the Checking Account logical file if checks were not produced because of an inadequate balance. The Report of Insufficient Funds will contain the following attributes: insufficient funds for

Table A15.9

Names of Possible Function Types	Enter Complexity			
	Low	Average	High	N/A
Payment file from AP	○	●	○	○
Checking Account logical file	○	●	○	○
Disbursement logical file	○	○	○	●
Checks	●	○	○	○
Report of Insufficient Funds	●	○	○	○

payment date, payee, PO number, payment amount, total number of payees, and total payment amount (total attributes are calculated when the report is produced).

Identify the complexity of the enhanced functions for the Banking application by choosing the correct radio buttons in Table A15.9.

Case Study 10

Students enrolling in a course at a local university have the ability to do so online by accessing the Course Registration application. When the student selects File: New, the Course Registration screen shown in Figure A15.3 appears. The student then enters his or her student ID and clicks "Enter." If the entered student ID has no match on the Student logical file, an error message is returned, and the student may either try again or click "Cancel" to exit the application. If a match is found on the student's ID, the student's name is retrieved

from the Student logical file and displayed on the screen. The student then selects a department from the drop-down list box, and a list of all courses offered by that department is retrieved from the Course logical file that is maintained in another application. Displayed on the list are course number, course name, location, start date, and time. To register for a course, the student enters "X" in Column A next to the desired course and clicks "Enter" or "Register." A validation on the Course logical file is made to ensure that the class still has openings. If there are no openings, an error message is displayed on the screen. If there are openings, a validation is made on the Student logical file to ensure that the student is eligible to enroll for the course. If ineligible, an error message is displayed on the screen. Otherwise, the Student logical file is updated, and a confirmation message is displayed. The student can then either register for another course by repeating the process or click on "Exit" to end the process.

Identify the functions for the Course Registration application by choosing the correct radio buttons in Table A15.10.

Table A15.10

Names of Possible Function Types	Identify the Function Used					
	ILF	EIF	EI	EO	EQ	N/A
Student logical file	●	○	○	○	○	○
Course logical file	○	●	○	○	○	○
Register for Course	○	○	●	○	○	○
Department Drop-Down List Box	○	○	○	○	●	○
Cancel	○	○	○	○	○	●

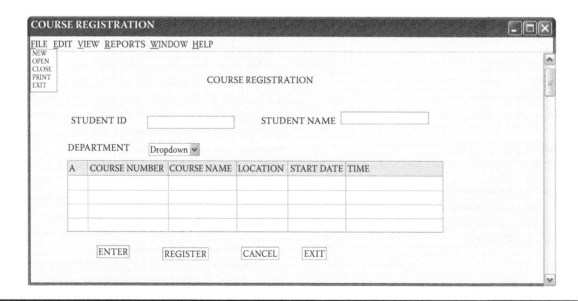

Figure A15.3 Course registration.

Appendix 16

Practice Exam 2 Answers

Part 1. Definitions and Rules

1. Translation Data is sometimes referred to as:
   A. User Metacode Data
   B. Substitution Data
   C. Code Data[1]
   D. None of the above

2. Examples of repair include:
   A. Missing functions that do not result in application failure (external design error)
   B. Errors resulting in a stop-run situation (code error)
   C. Both A and B[2]
   D. Neither A nor B

3. Steps in the Functional Size Measurement Method procedure include:
   A. Gather the available documentation[3]
   B. Report quality metrics
   C. Calculate the technical size
   D. Both A and B

4. The application area:
   A. Acts as a "membrane" through which data processed by transactions pass into and out from the application
   B. Is a general term for a grouping of applications that handle a specific business area
   C. Corresponds to an administrative level for management purposes
   D. Both B and C[4]

5. The smallest unit of activity that is meaningful to the user is the definition of:
   A. An elementary unit
   B. A single function point
   C. An elementary process[5]
   D. A functional unit

6. An elementary process that processes data or control information sent from outside the boundary is an:
   A. EO
   B. EI[6]
   C. EQ
   D. Both A and C

7. Business Data may also be referred to as:
   A. Personal User Data
   B. Core Objects
   C. List Data
   D. None of the above[7]

8. The Value Adjustment Factor (VAF) is:
   A. A measure of the functional vs. technical ratio in a given application
   B. The factor that indicates the general functionality provided to the user of the application
   C. The factor of value delivered to the end user by the application
   D. None of the above[8]

---

[1] Refer to IFPUG, *Function Point Counting Practices Manual* (CPM), Release 4.3, Part 3, page 1-6.

[2] Refer to IFPUG, *Function Point Counting Practices Manual* (CPM), Release 4.3, Part 5, page G-6.

[3] Refer to IFPUG, *Function Point Counting Practices Manual* (CPM), Release 4.3, Part 2, page 2-2.

[4] Refer to IFPUG, *Function Point Counting Practices Manual* (CPM), Release 4.3, Part 5, page G-1.

[5] Refer to IFPUG, *Function Point Counting Practices Manual* (CPM), Release 4.3, Part 2, page 7-5, and Part 5, page G-3.

[6] Refer to IFPUG, *Function Point Counting Practices Manual* (CPM), Release 4.3, Part 2, page 7-3.

[7] Refer to IFPUG, *Function Point Counting Practices Manual* (CPM), Release 4.3, Part 3, page 1-4.

[8] Refer to IFPUG, *Function Point Counting Practices Manual* (CPM), Release 4.3, Part 5, pages C-4 and G-7.

9. Entity subtype:
   A. Is a subdivision of entity type
   B. Inherits all the attributes and relationships of its parent entity type
   C. May have additional, unique attributes and relationships
   D. All of the above[9]

10. The process of recreating a set of data to make it current with its source is the definition of:
    A. Reload
    B. Copy
    C. Refresh[10]
    D. Image Load

11. General System Characteristics (GSCs) are:
    A. A set of 14 questions that quantify the degree of quality for the application
    B. A set of 14 questions that evaluate the overall complexity of the application[11]
    C. Both A and B
    D. None of the above

12. Total Degree of Influence (TDI) is:
    A. ±35%
    B. The sum of the 14 degrees of influence
    C. A score between 0 and 70
    D. Both B and C[12]

13. The two types of subgroups for Record Element Types are:
    A. Obligatory and arbitrary
    B. Mandatory and optional[13]
    C. Optional and indispensable
    D. Compulsory and discretionary

14. Corrective maintenance is:
    A. The modification of a software product performed after delivery to account for scope creep
    B. The modification of a software product performed after delivery to introduce product enhancements
    C. The reactive modification of a software product performed after delivery to correct discovered problems[14]
    D. All of the above

15. Flexible query/report capability is accounted for in which of the following GSCs:
    A. Complex Processing
    B End-User Efficiency
    C. Facilitate Change[15]
    D. Operational Ease

16. Internal Logical Files (ILFs) can:
    A. Be hard coded
    B. Be counted in more than one application[16]
    C. Contain multiple FTRs
    D. Both B and C

17. Counting scope:
    A. Includes the effect of scope creep
    B. Defines the set of Functional User Requirements to be included inside of the application boundary
    C. Defines the set of Functional User Requirements to be included in the function point count[17]
    D. Both A and C

18. An application:
    A. Is a cohesive collection of automated procedures and data supporting a business objective
    B. Consists of one or more components, modules, or subsystems
    C. Is a group of related items treated as a unit
    D. A and B[18]

19. The formula for Value Adjustment Factor is:
    A. VAF = (TDI × 0.01) + 0.65[19]
    B. VAF = TDI + 0.65
    C. VAF = TDI × 0.01
    D. None of the above

20. Which GSC describes the degree to which the application and the code in the application have been specifically designed, developed, and supported to be usable in other applications:
    A. Installation Ease
    B. Operational Ease
    C. Reusability[20]
    D. Multiple Sites

---

[9] Refer to IFPUG, *Function Point Counting Practices Manual* (CPM), Release 4.3, Part 3, page 2-6; Part 5, page G-3.

[10] Refer to IFPUG, *Function Point Counting Practices Manual* (CPM), Release 4.3, Part 3, page 3-3.

[11] Refer to IFPUG, *Function Point Counting Practices Manual* (CPM), Release 4.3, Part 5, pages C-5 and G-4.

[12] Refer to IFPUG, *Function Point Counting Practices Manual* (CPM), Release 4.3, Part 5, pages C-4, C-31, and G-7.

[13] Refer to IFPUG, *Function Point Counting Practices Manual* (CPM), Release 4.3, Part 2, page 6-7; Part 3, pages 2-37 to 2-38.

[14] Refer to IFPUG, *Function Point Counting Practices Manual* (CPM), Release 4.3, Part 3, page 4-20; Part 5, page G-2.

[15] Refer to IFPUG, *Function Point Counting Practices Manual* (CPM), Release 4.3, Part 5, page C-29.

[16] Refer to IFPUG, *Function Point Counting Practices Manual* (CPM), Release 4.3, Part 2, Chapter 6; Part 3, pages 3-18 to 3-19.

[17] Refer to IFPUG, *Function Point Counting Practices Manual* (CPM), Release 4.3, Part 2, page 2-4; Part 5, page G-2.

[18] Refer to IFPUG, *Function Point Counting Practices Manual* (CPM), Release 4.3, Part 2, page 4-3; Part 5, page G-1.

[19] Refer to IFPUG, *Function Point Counting Practices Manual* (CPM), Release 4.3, Part 5, page C-4.

[20] Refer to IFPUG, *Function Point Counting Practices Manual* (CPM), Release 4.3, Part 5, page C-22.

21. A File Type Referenced is:
    A. A data function maintained by an elementary process
    B. A data function maintained by a transactional function
    C. A data function read and/or maintained by a transactional function[21]
    D. None of the above

22. Which of the following can be counted as one or more ILFs in a project:
    A. Application data
    B. Application security data
    C. Control data
    D. All of the above[22]

23. What do most mainframe applications score for the Multiple Sites GSC:
    A. 3
    B. 2
    C. 1
    D. 0[23]

24. On-line applications typically receive a score of _____ for the Data Communications GSC.
    A. 3
    B. 4[24]
    C. 5
    D. None of the above

25. The IEEE definition of load is:
    A. To copy computer instructions or data from external storage to internal storage[25]
    B. To read data from a source, leaving the source data unchanged, and to write the same data elsewhere in a physical form that may differ from that of the source
    C. The process of recreating a set of data to make it current with its source
    D. None of the above

26. The process of recreating a set of data to make it current with its source is the definition of:
    A. Load
    B. Copy

Figure A16.1   Steps in function point counting procedure.

    C. Refresh[26]
    D. Image

27. Which of the following are exclusively transactional functions:
    A. EI, EIF
    B. EI, EO, ILF
    C. ILF, EIF
    D. None of the above[27]

28. Which of the following are data functions:
    A. ILF, ELF
    B. ILF, EIF[28]
    C. EI, EO, EQ
    D. None of the above

Refer to Figure A16.1 for questions 29 through 31.

29. What is the number of the step corresponding to "calculate functional size":
    A. 2
    B. 3
    C. 4
    D. 5[29]

30. What is the number of the step corresponding to "measure data functions":
    A. 2
    B. 3[30]
    C. 4
    D. None of the above

31. The last step of the functional size measurement method procedure labeled 6 in the figure is:
    A. Measure data functions
    B. Calculate functional size
    C. Measure transactional functions
    D. None of the above[31]

[21] Refer to IFPUG, *Function Point Counting Practices Manual* (CPM), Release 4.3, Part 2, page 7-14; Part 5, page G-4.

[22] Refer to IFPUG, *Function Point Counting Practices Manual* (CPM), Release 4.3, Part 2, Chapter 6.

[23] Refer to IFPUG, *Function Point Counting Practices Manual* (CPM), Release 4.3, Part 5, page C-27.

[24] Refer to IFPUG, *Function Point Counting Practices Manual* (CPM), Release 4.3, Part 5, page C-8.

[25] Refer to IFPUG, *Function Point Counting Practices Manual* (CPM), Release 4.3, Part 3, page 3-3; Part 5, page G-5.

[26] Refer to IFPUG, *Function Point Counting Practices Manual* (CPM), Release 4.3, Part 3, page 3-3; Part 5, page G-6.

[27] Refer to IFPUG, *Function Point Counting Practices Manual* (CPM), Release 4.3, Part 2, page 7-1; Part 5, page G-7.

[28] Refer to IFPUG, *Function Point Counting Practices Manual* (CPM), Release 4.3, Part 2, page 6-1; Part 5, page G-3.

[29] Refer to IFPUG, *Function Point Counting Practices Manual* (CPM), Release 4.3, Part 2, page 2-2.

[30] Refer to IFPUG, *Function Point Counting Practices Manual* (CPM), Release 4.3, Part 2, page 2-2.

[31] Refer to IFPUG, *Function Point Counting Practices Manual* (CPM), Release 4.3, Part 2, page 2-2.

32. A score of 2 for degree of influence indicates:
    A. Incidental influence
    B. Moderate influence[32]
    C. Average influence
    D. Significant influence

33. The degree to which the rate of business transactions influenced the development of the application is which General System Characteristic:
    A. Transaction Rate[33]
    B. Heavily Used Configuration
    C. Operational Ease
    D. Performance

34. A project used to develop and deliver adaptive maintenance is:
    A. A development project
    B. An enhancement project[34]
    C. Not measurable using function point analysis
    D. An application function point count

35. Hardware or software upgrades are an example of:
    A. Planned obsolescence
    B. An enhancement project
    C. System upgrades
    D. A maintenance activity[35]

36. When applied, the Value Adjustment Factor adjusts the unadjusted functional size:
    A. ±30% to produce the adjusted functional size
    B. ±35% to produce the adjusted functional size[36]
    C. ±60% to produce the adjusted functional size
    D. ±65% to produce the adjusted functional size

37. A unique, user-recognizable, nonrepeated attribute is:
    A. A Data Element Type[37]
    B. A File Type Referenced
    C. A Record Element Type
    D. None of the above

38. Multilingual support counts as how many items:
    A. 1
    B. 2

C. 4
D. 6[38]

39. The Total Degree of Influence is between:
    A. 0 to 5
    B. 0 to 70[39]
    C. 1 to 5
    D. 0.65 to 1.35

40. What is the Value Adjustment Factor if the TDI is equal to 45:
    A. 0.95
    B. 1.00
    C. 1.05
    D. 1.10[40]

41. Which of the following statements is false:
    A. An ILF is a user-recognizable group of logically related data or control information that is referenced by the application being measured but which is maintained within the boundary of another application[41]
    B. The primary intent of an EIF is to hold data referenced through one or more elementary processes within the boundary of the application measured
    C. An EIF counted for an application must be in an ILF in another application
    D. All of the above are true

42. Processing logic for EIs may include:
    A. Validations are performed
    B. Equivalent values are converted
    C. One or more ILFs are updated
    D. All of the above[42]

43. A record is equivalent to the relational database term:
    A. A row
    B. A column
    C. A tuple
    D. Both A and C[43]

44. Attributes designed to provide fast access to the information is the definition of:
    A. Foreign key
    B. Primary key

---

[32] Refer to IFPUG, *Function Point Counting Practices Manual* (CPM), Release 4.3, Part 5, page C-6.

[33] Refer to IFPUG, *Function Point Counting Practices Manual* (CPM), Release 4.3, Part 5, page C-15.

[34] Refer to IFPUG, *Function Point Counting Practices Manual* (CPM), Release 4.3, Part 1, page 4; Part 3, page 4-20; Part 5, page G-3.

[35] Refer to IFPUG, *Function Point Counting Practices Manual* (CPM), Release 4.3, Part 3, pages 4-20 to 4-22; Part 5, page G-5.

[36] Refer to IFPUG, *Function Point Counting Practices Manual* (CPM), Release 4.3, Part 5, page C-4.

[37] Refer to IFPUG, *Function Point Counting Practices Manual* (CPM), Release 4.3, Part 2, pages 6-5 and 7-14; Part 5, page G-2.

[38] Refer to IFPUG, *Function Point Counting Practices Manual* (CPM), Release 4.3, Part 5, page C-17.

[39] Refer to IFPUG, *Function Point Counting Practices Manual* (CPM), Release 4.3, Part 5, page C-4.

[40] Refer to IFPUG, *Function Point Counting Practices Manual* (CPM), Release 4.3, Part 5, page C-4.

[41] Refer to IFPUG, *Function Point Counting Practices Manual* (CPM), Release 4.3, Part 2, page 6-2.

[42] Refer to IFPUG, *Function Point Counting Practices Manual* (CPM), Release 4.3, Part 2, pages 7-5 to 7-8.

[43] Refer to IFPUG, *Function Point Counting Practices Manual* (CPM), Release 4.3, Part 3, page 2-5.

C. **Secondary key**[44]

D. None of the above

45. When performing function point analysis, it is preferable to analyze the logical data model in:
A. First normal form
B. Second normal form
C. **Third normal form**[45]
D. Fourth normal form

46. An average complexity EIF has a value of:
A. 5
B. **7**[46]
C. 10
D. 15

47. Functional size can be approximated but not measured during what stage:
A. **Proposal**[47]
B. Requirements
C. Design
D. Maintenance

48. An EI can be invoked if the user hits the submit button on the GUI screen, presses the F10 key on the keyboard, or enters an "Add" command on a command line. How many DETs should be counted for these options:
A. **1**[48]
B. 3
C. 0
D. None of the above

49. The Functional User Requirements as perceived by the user is:
A. Requirements view
B. Specification view
C. **User view**[49]
D. Design view

50. A group of related items that is treated as a unit is a:
A. **Record**[50]
B. File
C. File system
D. Function

Sales

4th Qtr 9%
3rd Qtr 10%
2nd Qtr 23%
1st Qtr 58%

Figure A16.2   Sales pie chart.

Part 2. Implementation

1. An application includes 72 occurrences of field level help that are all maintained inside the application boundary. How many transactional functions are counted:
A. 72 EQs
B. 72 EOs
C. No transaction functions are counted
D. **One transaction function**[51]

2. Which of the following is not an example of Reference Data:
A. Job rates
B. Tax tables
C. Discount rates
D. **Airport Codes/Airport Names**[52]

3. Which of the following could be an EQ:
A. A menu screen providing only navigation
B. An output report containing derived data
C. **Help text retrieved from an ILF**[53]
D. An output containing a monthly total not retrieved from a data function

4. Assuming the data shown have been calculated at the time of display, how would you count the pie chart shown in Figure A16.2:
A. 4 EOs
B. 1 EO with 4 DETs
C. **1 EO with 2 DETs**[54]
D. 1 EO with 8 DETs

---

[44] Refer to IFPUG, *Function Point Counting Practices Manual* (CPM), Release 4.3, Part 3, page 2-23.

[45] Refer to IFPUG, *Function Point Counting Practices Manual* (CPM), Release 4.3, Part 3, page 2-6.

[46] Refer to IFPUG, *Function Point Counting Practices Manual* (CPM), Release 4.3, Part 2, page 6-9; Part 5, page A-2.

[47] Refer to IFPUG, *Function Point Counting Practices Manual* (CPM), Release 4.3, Part 2, page 3-8.

[48] Refer to IFPUG, *Function Point Counting Practices Manual* (CPM), Release 4.3, Part 2, page 7-16.

[49] Refer to IFPUG, *Function Point Counting Practices Manual* (CPM), Release 4.3, Part 2, page 3-2; Part 5, page G-7.

[50] Refer to IFPUG, *Function Point Counting Practices Manual* (CPM), Release 4.3, Part 3, page 2-5; Part 5, page G-6.

[51] Refer to IFPUG, *Function Point Counting Practices Manual* (CPM), Release 4.3, Part 4, pages 2-140 to 2-144.

[52] Refer to IFPUG, *Function Point Counting Practices Manual* (CPM), Release 4.3, Part 3, page 1-5 to 1-6.

[53] Refer to IFPUG, *Function Point Counting Practices Manual* (CPM), Release 4.3, Part 2, Chapter 7; Part 4, pages 2-140 to 2-144.

[54] Refer to IFPUG, *Function Point Counting Practices Manual* (CPM), Release 4.3, Part 2, page 7-17.

5. An enhancement project added three low external inputs, deleted two high external inquiries, and changed two average external outputs to low complexity. What is the enhancement project functional size:
   A. 5
   B. 20
   C. 29[55]
   D. None of the above

6. The change in the value of the application functional size for the preceding question is:
   A. −20
   B. −5[56]
   C. 30
   D. 42

7. The function point value of an ILF with 20 DETs and 4 RETs is:
   A. 5
   B. 7
   C. 10[57]
   D. 15

8. An application has a Pantone color table that contains two data elements: color code and color description. This table is an example of what type of data:
   A. Code Data[58]
   B. Constant Data
   C. Reference Data
   D. Valid Values Data

9. Users have requested four tabs on a Web application to accomplish the elementary process of creating a purchase order. What is counted:
   A. 1 EI[59]
   B. 4 EIs
   C. 1 EI and 4 EQs
   D. 4 EIs and 1 EQ

10. In a count of DETs in an EO the following should be counted:
    A. System generated dates in the heading
    B. Calculated totals of sales data retrieved from an ILF[60]
    C. Literals in the heading
    D. Both A and B

11. An ILF is maintained by three separate applications. Where is it counted:
    A. In the application that maintains the most DETs
    B. In all three applications[61]
    C. In the application that accesses the ILF with the greatest frequency
    D. In none of the applications because it cannot be shared

12. Which of the following formulas is used to calculate an enhancement project functional size:
    A. DFP = ADD + CFP
    B. EFP = ADD + CHGA + DEL
    C. AFPA = (AFPB + ADD + CHGA) − (CHGB + DEL)
    D. None of the above[62]

13. Three user-defined groups of data are maintained by the application and exist in the same physical file. How many ILFs are counted:
    A. 0
    B. 1
    C. 2
    D. 3[63]

14. Which of the following cannot be counted as an EQ:
    A. Screens providing only navigation
    B. Reports that contain derived data
    C. A screen displaying data simply retrieved from an ILF
    D. A and B[64]

15. Which of the following types of transactions may perform validations:
    A. EI
    B. EO
    C. EQ
    D. All of the above[65]

16. To be an EI, it is mandatory that you either update at least one ILF or do one of the following:
    A. Sort or arrange a set of data
    B. Perform validations
    C. Create derived data
    D. Alter the behavior of the application[66]

---

[55] Refer to IFPUG, *Function Point Counting Practices Manual* (CPM), Release 4.3, Part 1, pages 21 and 23; Part 3, pages 4-14 to 4-17.

[56] Refer to IFPUG, *Function Point Counting Practices Manual* (CPM), Release 4.3, Part 1, pages 21 and 23; Part 3, pages 4-14 to 4-19.

[57] Refer to IFPUG, *Function Point Counting Practices Manual* (CPM), Release 4.3, Part 1, page 23; Part 2, pages 6-8 to 6-9.

[58] Refer to IFPUG, *Function Point Counting Practices Manual* (CPM), Release 4.3, Part 3, page 1-11.

[59] Refer to IFPUG, *Function Point Counting Practices Manual* (CPM), Release 4.3, Part 2, page 7-21.

[60] Refer to IFPUG, *Function Point Counting Practices Manual* (CPM), Release 4.3, Part 2, pages 7-17 to 7-18.

[61] Refer to IFPUG, *Function Point Counting Practices Manual* (CPM), Release 4.3, Part 2, page 6-10; Part 3, pages 3-18 to 3-19.

[62] Refer to IFPUG, *Function Point Counting Practices Manual* (CPM), Release 4.3, Part 1, page 21; Part 3, page 4-17.

[63] Refer to IFPUG, *Function Point Counting Practices Manual* (CPM), Release 4.3, Part 2, page 6-10; Part 3, pages 2-8 to 2-9.

[64] Refer to IFPUG, *Function Point Counting Practices Manual* (CPM), Release 4.3, Part 2, page 7-3; Part 4, pages 2-129 to 2-133.

[65] Refer to IFPUG, *Function Point Counting Practices Manual* (CPM), Release 4.3, Part 2, page 7-8.

[66] Refer to IFPUG, *Function Point Counting Practices Manual* (CPM), Release 4.3, Part 2, pages 7-3, 7-4, and 7-8.

17. In an enhancement project, the size of the functions being added is 30, the size of the functions being deleted is 15, the size of the functions being changed as they are/will be after implementation is 35, and the size of the functions being changed as they are/were before the project commenced is 20. What is the enhancement project functional size:
    A. 60
    B. 65
    C. 80[67]
    D. None of the above

18. A data function stores customer information (customer name; account number; purchase order number; billing street address, city, state, and Zip Code; shipping street address, city, state, and Zip Code; phone number; e-mail address; fax number). The billing address and shipping address are each treated as a single unit. The customer information store is being updated by the application being measured. What type of data function is this and how many DETs are present:
    A. An EIF with 14 DETs
    B. An EIF with 8 DETs
    C. An ILF with 8 DETs[68]
    D. An ILF with 14 DETs

19. A transaction whose primary intent is maintaining an ILF is being added to an application. This transaction has 15 unique DETs, updates one ILF, and reads one EIF. What is the functional size of this transaction:
    A. 4[69]
    B. 5
    C. 6
    D. 7

20. When determining the Value Adjustment Factor for an enhancement project:
    A. Use the Value Adjustment Factor from the application functional size
    B. Use the Value Adjustment Factor from the most recent enhancement count
    C. Use the constant 1.0 as your Value Adjustment Factor
    D. None of the above[70]

21. Which of the following activities are within the enhancement counting scope:
    A. Correction of production errors
    B. Perfective or preventative maintenance
    C. Platform upgrades, new system software releases
    D. None of the above[71]

22. Which of the following is an EO:
    A. Confirmation messages displayed to the screen
    B. Error messages printed as a report
    C. A report containing derived data requested via an on-line menu[72]
    D. Both B and C

23. Which of the following is not an EQ:
    A. Application level help
    B. A logon screen that does not reference a data function
    C. Navigation screen with no retrieved data
    D. Both B and C[73]

24. Functional user requirements may include which of the following:
    A. Technical constraints
    B. Quality constraints
    C. Environmental constraints
    D. None of the above[74]

25. Which of the following formulas is used to calculate an adjusted development project functional size:
    A. DFP = ADD + CFP
    B. EFP = ADD + CHGA + CFP + DEL
    C. aDFP = DFP × VAF[75]
    D. aDFP = DFP + ADD + CHGA + CFP + DEL

26. After an enhancement project, the application functional size must be updated to reflect changed functionality. This changed functionality may:
    A. Increase the application functional size
    B. Decrease the application functional size
    C. Be unable to be determined
    D. Both A and B[76]

[67] Refer to IFPUG, *Function Point Counting Practices Manual* (CPM), Release 4.3, Part 1, page 21; Part 3, pages 4-14 to 4-17.

[68] Refer to IFPUG, *Function Point Counting Practices Manual* (CPM), Release 4.3, Part 2, pages 6-5 to 6-6.

[69] Refer to IFPUG, *Function Point Counting Practices Manual* (CPM), Release 4.3, Part 2, pages 7-13 to 7-20.

[70] Refer to IFPUG, *Function Point Counting Practices Manual* (CPM), Release 4.3, Part 5, pages C-37 to C-42.

[71] Refer to IFPUG, *Function Point Counting Practices Manual* (CPM), Release 4.3, Part 3, pages 4-20 to 4-22.

[72] Refer to IFPUG, *Function Point Counting Practices Manual* (CPM), Release 4.3, Part 2, Chapter 7; Part 4, pages 2-114 to 2-116.

[73] Refer to IFPUG, *Function Point Counting Practices Manual* (CPM), Release 4.3, Part 2, Chapter 7; Part 4, pages 2-129 to 2-130 and 2-155 to 2-160.

[74] Refer to IFPUG, *Function Point Counting Practices Manual* (CPM), Release 4.3, Part 2, pages 1-3 to 1-4.

[75] Refer to IFPUG, *Function Point Counting Practices Manual* (CPM), Release 4.3, Part 5, page C-32.

[76] Refer to IFPUG, *Function Point Counting Practices Manual* (CPM), Release 4.3, Part 5, page C-44.

```
┌─────────────────────────────────────────────────────────────────────┐
│ COLLEGE CREDITS REPORT                                   [_][□][X]    │
├─────────────────────────────────────────────────────────────────────┤
│ FILE  EDIT  VIEW  REPORTS  WINDOW  HELP                               │
│                                                                       │
│                                                                       │
│                    COLLEGE CREDITS REPORT                             │
│                                                                       │
│      Student          Course Number  Course Date      Credits         │
│      nnnnnnn, nnnnn n.    xxxxxxx     xx/xx/xxxx         xx            │
│      nnnnnnn, nnnnn n.    xxxxxxx     xx/xx/xxxx         xx            │
│      nnnnnnn, nnnnn n.    xxxxxxx     xx/xx/xxxx         xx            │
│      Total Students for Course Number xxxxx:  15                      │
│                                                                       │
│      nnnnnnn, nnnnn n.    xxxxxxx     xx/xx/xxxx         xx            │
│      nnnnnnn, nnnnn n.    xxxxxxx     xx/xx/xxxx         xx            │
│      nnnnnnn, nnnnn n.    xxxxxxx     xx/xx/xxxx         xx            │
│      Total Students for Course Number xxxxx:  15                      │
│                                                                       │
│                                                                       │
│                  STUDENT logical file is referenced                   │
│                                                                       │
└─────────────────────────────────────────────────────────────────────┘
```

Figure A16.3 College credits report.

27. Application A maintains an ILF that is also read by Application B. Application A should:
    A. Get credit for an ILF and an EIF
    B. Get credit for an ILF[77]
    C. Get credit for an EQ
    D. Both B and C

28. In the previous question, Application B should:
    A. Get credit for an EIF and EI
    B. Get credit for an EI
    C. Get credit for an ILF
    D. Get credit for an EIF[78]

29. A transaction to add an employee has the ability to return ten unique error messages and two unique confirmation messages. How many EQs are counted for the error and confirmation messages:
    A. 12
    B. 2
    C. 1
    D. 0[79]

30. An application has three menus to navigate through the system. Each page of navigation contains 25 selections. How many DETs should be counted:
    A. 0[80]
    B. 1

C. 3
D. 75

31. The maximum Total Degree of Influence is:
    A. 35
    B. 65
    C. 70[81]
    D. 135

32. How would you count the College Credits Report shown in Figure A16.3? No totals are stored in the Student logical file.
    A. 1 low EQ
    B. 1 average EQ
    C. 1 low EO[82]
    D. 1 average EO

33. An ILF has 50 DETs and 5 RETs. What is its functional size:
    A. 5
    B. 7
    C. 10[83]
    D. 15

34. A user requires that an application print a monthly report automatically every month. This report lists all employees by department and contains employee name and employee ID. This report is generated automatically by the system, thus no DETs cross the

[77] Refer to IFPUG, *Function Point Counting Practices Manual* (CPM), Release 4.3, Part 3, pages 3-7 and 3-8.

[78] Refer to IFPUG, *Function Point Counting Practices Manual* (CPM), Release 4.3, Part 3, pages 3-7 and 3-8.

[79] Refer to IFPUG, *Function Point Counting Practices Manual* (CPM), Release 4.3, Part 2, pages 7-13 to 7-18.

[80] Refer to IFPUG, *Function Point Counting Practices Manual* (CPM), Release 4.3, Part 4, pages 2-129 to 2-130.

[81] Refer to IFPUG, *Function Point Counting Practices Manual* (CPM), Release 4.3, Part 5, page C-4.

[82] Refer to IFPUG, *Function Point Counting Practices Manual* (CPM), Release 4.3, Part 2, pages 7-13 to 7-19.

[83] Refer to IFPUG, *Function Point Counting Practices Manual* (CPM), Release 4.3, Part 2, pages 6-8 to 6-9.

application boundary to cause the report to print. This report is counted as an:

A. EI

B. EQ[84]

C. EO

D. It is not counted

35. The functional complexity of EQs is determined by:

A. The number of FTRs and RETs

B. The number of DETs and RETs

C. The number of DETs and FTRs[85]

D. None of the above

36. A report is printed with retrieved fields from a single ILF and a single EIF. A different ILF is updated with the time and date when the report was printed. What is counted:

A. 2 EQs and 1 EI

B. 1 EI and 1 EO

C. 1 EQ

D. 1 EO[86]

37. A user-defined customer file is maintained in three database tables. These three tables are customer, address, and a hash table used to accelerate the search for a customer's data. How many ILFs are counted within this single application:

A. 0

B. 1[87]

C. 2

D. 3

38. When counting DETs in an ILF, count:

A. All DETs in the file

B. Only those DETs maintained

C. Only those DETs referenced

D. Only those DETs maintained and/or referenced[88]

39. An Accounts Payable application allows the user to extract information from an ILF and an EIF. The users enters an ID number and presses the submit key. A screen display provides a response screen with 19 retrieved data elements and no derived or calculated fields. What is counted:

A. A low EI and an average EQ

B. A low EI and a high EQ

C. **A high EQ**[89]

D. An average EQ

40. Examples of EIs include:

A. Batch input from another application that adds data to an ILF[90]

B. Control information that initiates the generation of a report

C. Data referenced by another application

D. Both A and B

41. A development project has four average complexity EIs and one high complexity EI; two average complexity EOs; three average complexity EQs and two high complexity EQs; three low complexity ILFs and one high complexity ILF; two low complexity EIFs; and four average complexity conversion EIs. What is the application functional size after the development project is installed:

A. 86

B. 90

C. 102[91]

D. 118

42. For the above question, what is the development project functional size:

A. 90

B. 102

C. 118[92]

D. None of the above

43. A screen containing a drop-down list with items retrieved from an ILF is displayed to the user. This drop-down list should be counted as:

A. An EO only

B. A DET on the count of the screen

C. A EQ and a DET on the screen being counted

D. An EQ only[93]

44. An enhancement project adds six high complexity EIs and two average complexity EQs, deletes one high complexity EQ, changes three EOs from low to high complexity, and adds two high complexity EIs for conversion. If the application functional size is 1000 before the enhancement, what is the value of the conversion functionality:

A. 1059

---

[84] Refer to IFPUG, *Function Point Counting Practices Manual* (CPM), Release 4.3, Part 4, pages 2-149 to 2-150.

[85] Refer to IFPUG, *Function Point Counting Practices Manual* (CPM), Release 4.3, Part 2, pages 7-17 to 7-19.

[86] Refer to IFPUG, *Function Point Counting Practices Manual* (CPM), Release 4.3, Part 2, Chapter 7; Part 4, pages 2-120 to 2-121.

[87] Refer to IFPUG, *Function Point Counting Practices Manual* (CPM), Release 4.3, Part 2, Chapter 6; Part 3, pages 2-8 to 2-10.

[88] Refer to IFPUG, *Function Point Counting Practices Manual* (CPM), Release 4.3, Part 2, pages 6-5 to 6-6; Part 3, pages 2-24 to 2-25.

[89] Refer to IFPUG, *Function Point Counting Practices Manual* (CPM), Release 4.3, Part 2, pages 7-3 to 7-19.

[90] Refer to IFPUG, *Function Point Counting Practices Manual* (CPM), Release 4.3, Part 2, pages 7-3 to 7-18.

[91] Refer to IFPUG, *Function Point Counting Practices Manual* (CPM), Release 4.3, Part 1, pages 19, 20, and 23.

[92] Refer to IFPUG, *Function Point Counting Practices Manual* (CPM), Release 4.3, Part 1, pages 19, 20, and 23.

[93] Refer to IFPUG, *Function Point Counting Practices Manual* (CPM), Release 4.3, Part 4, pages 2-136 to 2-138.

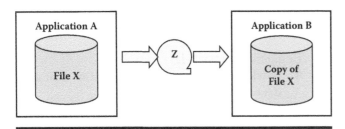

Figure A16.4 Shared data example.

B. 1047
C. 71
D. 12[94]

45. The top right-hand corner of every application contains an "About" link that displays information about the application, including version number, product ID, and copyright information. This information is maintained in an application outside the boundary by a developer tool called Robot_Help. What should be counted for the "About" link:
   A. An EIF and an EQ
   B. Only an EQ
   C. An EI and an EQ
   D. Nothing is counted[95]

46. Figure A16.4, from the IFPUG *Counting Practices Manual*, Release 4.3, illustrates what process:
   A. Screen scraping
   B. Image copy/load[96]
   C. Static image copy
   D. Copy merge "refresh"

47. A development project has three low complexity EIs and four average complexity EIs, three average complexity EOs, four high complexity EQs, one low complexity ILF, and five low complexity conversion EIs. What is the development functional size:
   A. 16
   B. 71
   C. 86[97]
   D. 89

48. An application's functional size before an enhancement is 100. The enhancement added four low complexity EIs, changed three EQs from low to average complexity, and deleted three average complexity EOs. What is

the functional size of the application after the enhancement project is delivered:
   A. 97
   B. 100[98]
   C. 115
   D. 124

49. The user has requested that an ILF (or part of an ILF) be populated from an ILF in another application. Validation is required against yet another ILF from a third application. This is specified as a one-time process, and the data reference in the third application will not be utilized in the future. What is counted for the conversion functionality:
   A. An EIF and an EI with two FTRs[99]
   B. An ILF and an EI with one FTR
   C. An ILF and an EI with three FTRs
   D. An ILF, an EQ and an EI with one FTR

50. To avoid the overhead of Application C having to dynamically search the data from both Application A and Application B, the data is being copied from Application A and Application B and merged into a new data store in Application C. The user requires that the information from Applications A and B be refreshed daily for validation or reference purposes only. Unload, Merge, and Load utilities are used. There is no business processing logic involved. What is counted:
   A. An ILF for Application A, an ILF for Application B, and an EI for Application C
   B. An ILF and EQ for Application A, an ILF and EQ for Application B, and an EI for Application C
   C. An ILF for Application A, an ILF for Application B, and an EIF for Application C[100]
   D. An ILF for Application A, an ILF for Application B, and an EI and EIF for Application C

Part 3. Case Studies

Case Study 1

SME is implementing a Customer Relations Management (CRM) application. The Web Info (WI) application, an existing application, will be required to send information to the CRM each evening by retrieving all Requests for Information (RFI) submitted that day and currently maintained in the RFI logical file within the WI application. The

---

[94] Refer to IFPUG, *Function Point Counting Practices Manual* (CPM), Release 4.3, Part 1, pages 19, 20, and 23; Part 3, page 4-17.

[95] Refer to IFPUG, *Function Point Counting Practices Manual* (CPM), Release 4.3, Part 4, pages 2-155 to 2-156.

[96] Refer to IFPUG, *Function Point Counting Practices Manual* (CPM), Release 4.3, Part 3, page 3-11 to 3-14.

[97] Refer to IFPUG, *Function Point Counting Practices Manual* (CPM), Release 4.3, Part 1, pages 19, 20, and 23.

[98] Refer to IFPUG, *Function Point Counting Practices Manual* (CPM), Release 4.3, Part 1, pages 19, 21, and 23; Part 3, pages 4-14 to 4-19.

[99] Refer to IFPUG, *Function Point Counting Practices Manual* (CPM), Release 4.3, Part 3, page 5-3.

[100] Refer to IFPUG, *Function Point Counting Practices Manual* (CPM), Release 4.3, Part 3, pages 3-15 to 3-16.

following information is sent on this daily feed: requestor ID; requestor's first, middle, and last name; requestor's organization; requestor's address: street address, city, state, and Zip Code; date of request; requested items; and quantities for requested items. The CRM application will validate and process the daily feed into a new Potential Customer logical file.

Separate reports by state will be generated each morning by the CRM application and delivered to state sales coordinators. The printout will contain all of the information on the Potential Customer logical file as well as a Total Number of Requests for Information, which is calculated at the time the report is produced. The state code and state name, retrieved from a code table, will also be printed on each report. Each state sales coordinator will have the ability to retrieve via screen all information maintained in the Potential Customer logical file by entering the requestor ID and action key; hard-coded error messages will be returned if the requestor ID is not found.

Using that screen, the state coordinator can revise the requested items and/or quantities using the requestor ID and a preassigned function key; hard-coded error messages may be returned if the newly assigned requested item is not contained in the Inventory logical file maintained by the Inventory application or a hard-coded confirmation message will occur.

Identify the data functions for the CRM application by choosing the correct radio buttons in Table A16.1.

Case Study 2

A university's Course Registration application is being enhanced so students can view a list of all of the courses for which they have registered in the past. The requirements are:

1. Upon entering the student ID, a list of courses for which that student has registered at any time at that university is retrieved from the Student logical file. A list of course numbers and the corresponding course date is displayed if any records are found; otherwise, a static error message is returned.
2. If a list of courses is returned, the student may view details of the course registration by selecting the course number and course date from the list and clicking the Enter button. The details displayed will be the student's name, student's ID, course number, course name, course date, and course location.

All information is retrieved from the Course Registration logical file (which is maintained in the Course Registration application) and the Student logical file (which is not maintained by the Course Registration application but is maintained in another application). No new attributes were added

Table A16.1

Names of Possible Function Types	Identify the Function Used		
	ILF	EIF	N/A
Potential Customer logical file	●	○	○
RFI	○	○	●
Inventory logical file	○	●	○
Error Messages Table	○	○	●
State Code Table	○	○	●

Table A16.2

Names of Possible Function Types	Enter Complexity			
	Low	Average	High	N/A
List Courses	●	○	○	○
View Course Details	○	●	○	○
Student logical file	○	○	○	●
Course Registration File	○	○	○	●
Error File	○	○	○	●

to Course Registration logical file, and no new attributes were retrieved from the Student logical file as a result of this enhancement.

Identify the complexity of the enhancement functions by choosing the correct radio buttons in Table A16.2.

Case Study 3

Use the data flow diagram in Figure A16.5 to determine the complexity for the functions in the Human Resources application and Mail Distribution application.

Indicate the complexity of the function types by selecting the correct radio buttons in Table A16.3.

Case Study 4

The user requires the Human Resources application to provide the following capabilities:

1. All hourly employees must be paid in U.S. dollars.
2. When the user adds or changes employee information, the Human Resources application must access the Currency application to retrieve a conversion rate. After retrieving the conversion rate, the HR application converts the employee's local standard hourly rate to a U.S.

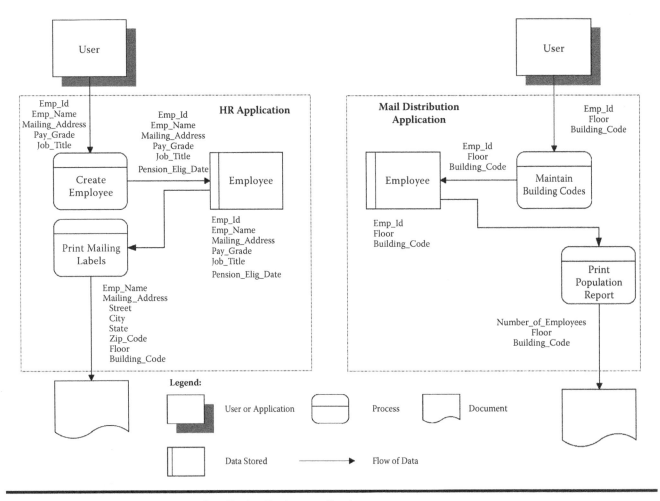

Figure A16.5 Human Resources and Mail Distribution applications.

hourly rate using the following calculation: standard hourly rate ÷ conversion rate = U.S. dollar hourly rate.

Figure A16.6 shows the relationships for this example. The currency conversion rate information includes:

CURRENCY
  Conversion_Rate_To_Base_Currency
  Currency

Identify the data functions for the Human Resources application by choosing the correct radio buttons in Table A16.4.

Case Study 5

The business users have requested a new Payroll Department application to track details of subcontractors' employment. These attributes will be maintained in a logical file called

Table A16.3

Names of Possible Function Types	Enter Complexity			
	Low	Average	High	N/A
Create Employee	●	O	O	O
Maintain Building Codes	●	O	O	O
Employee ILF	●	O	O	O
Print Mailing Labels	●	O	O	O
Print Population Report	●	O	O	O

Table A16.4

Names of Possible Function Types	Identify the Function Used		
	ILF	EIF	N/A
Currency Conversion Rate	O	●	O
Employee	●	O	O
Dependent	O	O	●
Hourly_Employee	O	O	●
Conversion Rate	O	O	●

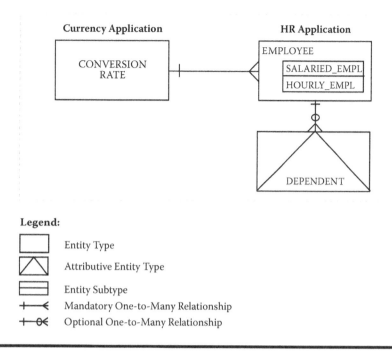

Figure A16.6 Human Resources and Currency applications.

Contractor_Data that will be maintained inside the application boundary. Contractor_Data will include the contractor's first name, last name, home address, Social Security Number, contract number, and ten additional user-specified attributes (not indicated here). An audit requirement has been imposed that requires that the application maintain audit data any time a change will be made to any of these attributes. The date of change, time of change, and User_ID of the user responsible for the change must be recorded together with "before" and "after" copies of the changed attributes. This data will be held in a file inside the application boundary in a table named Audit_Data. An audit report can be generated that will include the date of change, time of change, and User_ID of all changes in the last 30 days.

To place this new application into service, two single-use conversion processes will be run. The first conversion process will load a static attribute of "C" (indicating "Contractor") into one of the ten additional user-specified attributes specified earlier in the application's Contractor Data file. The second conversion process will use the Social Security Number as a primary key to lookup data in a file named Sub_Contractors_Agreements maintained outside of the application boundary and load the returned the Contractor's First_Name, Last_Name, Home Address, and Social Security Number in the application's Contractor Data file.

Select the correct radio buttons in Table A16.5 to indicate the complexity of the function types listed.

Table A16.5

Names of Possible Function Types	Enter Complexity			
	Low	Average	High	N/A
Contractor_Data	○	●	○	○
Audit_Data	○	○	○	●
Audit Report	●	○	○	○
First Conversion	○	○	○	●
Second Conversion	●	○	○	○

Case Study 6

Application A retrieves a transaction file of changes named "Transaction Data" from an Internal Logical File named "Locations"; calculations are performed during the creation of this file. The transaction file contains three transaction types: Add, Change, and Delete; Application B processes the Transaction Data file based on the transaction type in updating its Internal Logical File, also named "Locations." Although they share the same physical name (Locations), the attributes maintained in Application A's Locations and those maintained Application B's Locations are different. Figure A16.7 shows this transfer.

Count the first two questions from Applications A's perspective (Table A16.6). Count the next three questions form Application B's perspective (Table A16.7).

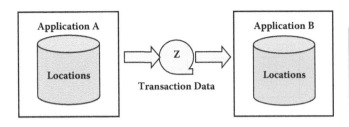

Figure A16.7   Data transfer.

Case Study 7

A data function (Main_Data) is maintained within the application boundary of a Patient Maintenance application. This table has 200 columns of data that store the functional and nonfunctional data used by the application. The Patient Maintenance screen allows the user to add, change, or delete the following attributes of Main_Data:

a. Patient first name
b. Patient middle initial (optional)
c. Patient last name
d. Patient title (optional)
e. Patient ID number
f. Patient street address
g. Patient city
h. Patient state
i. Patient Zip Code
j. Patient home phone
k. Patient work phone
l. Patient blood type
m. Patient is organ donor (1 is stored for yes, 0 is stored for no)
n. Date of last patient checkup (stored as an integer starting from January 1, 1900)
o. Patient date of birth (stored as an integer starting from January 1, 1900)
p. Patient HIV status (1 is stored for positive, 0 is stored for negative)
q. Patient HIPPA consent (1, consent on file; 0 otherwise)

An optional subgroup of information is maintained that contains:

r. Patient advocate name
s. Patient advocate address (as one block of data)
t. Patient advocate phone

Other columns have been set aside for potential future use.

For an Add transaction, all of the attributes supplied by the user are saved in Main_Data; the next available patient ID is calculated at the time of the Add transaction and saved to Main_Data. For a Change transaction, the patient ID and any changed attributes will cross the application boundary. For a Delete transaction, only the patient ID crosses the application boundary.

Table A16.6

Names of Possible Function Types	Identify the Function Used					
	ILF	EIF	EI	EO	EQ	N/A
Locations	●	○	○	○	○	○
Transaction Data	○	○	○	●	○	○

Table A16.7

Names of Possible Function Types	Identify the Function Used					
	ILF	EIF	EI	EO	EQ	N/A
Locations	●	○	○	○	○	○
Transaction Data (Adds and Changes)	○	○	●	○	○	○
Transaction Data (Deletes)	○	○	●	○	○	○

Table A16.8

Names of Possible Function Types	Enter Complexity			
	Low	Average	High	N/A
Patient Maintenance Screen (Add)	○	●	○	○
Patient Maintenance Screen (Delete)	●	○	○	○
Main_Data	○	●	○	○
Initialize Reminders	○	○	○	●
Check-Up List	●	○	○	○

The system clock kicks off an Initialize Reminders process at midnight every day that compares the Date of Last Patient Checkup to the current date and places a one-bit attribute in the DET Send Reminder Card in Main_Data if over one calendar year has passed. The user can generate a report by pressing the "Who Is Due for a Check-Up" button. The report extracts attributes a through i and n from the Main_Data and prints them with a heading and system-generated date and page numbers. The report name is "Check-Up List."

Identify the complexity of the functions by choosing the correct radio buttons in Table A16.8. Assume that there are no additional data functions or data elements used by the Patient Maintenance application for the above functions.

Case Study 8

(Refer to Figures A16.8 through A16.10.) Old Country Bank plans to enhance its on-line banking application. The current application interface allows customers to check balances,

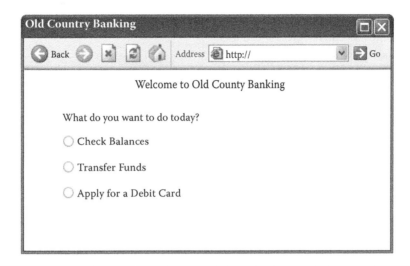

Figure A16.8   Main screen before enhancement.

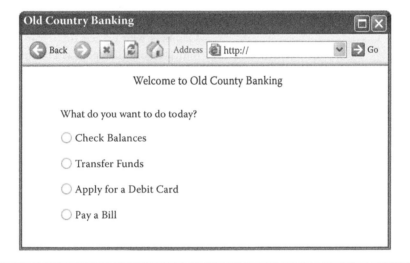

Figure A16.9   Main screen after enhancement.

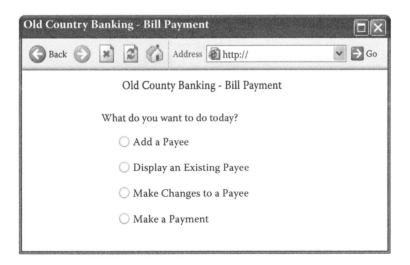

Figure A16.10   Screen added during enhancement.

transfer funds, and apply for a bank debit card. To enter the on-line banking application, the user enters a preassigned user name and password. Once validated, the user gains access to a main menu, which is displayed in Figure A16.8. The bank plans to add a bill-payment option to its available services. After the enhancement, the menu screen will include the option for maintaining payee information and making payments, as displayed in Figure A16.9.

Payee data will be maintained by the on-line banking application in a Payee logical file through Add and Change transactions. Display Payee will retrieve data from the Payee logical file and will not include any calculations. Payment by an Old Country Bank check will be mailed to a designated payee when Make Payment has been selected and submitted; the payment date will be entered into the Payee logical file when the check is created. The functionality shown in Figure A16.10 is being added via the Bill Payment screen.

Identify the new functions of the application by choosing the correct radio buttons in Table A16.9.

Case Study 9

An on-line multilevel marketing company named New Age Distributors has developed an application to maintain profiles of members and record individual member sales. A clerk from New Age sets up a member's profile. The clerk can also list members with their profiles and change a member's information. A monthly customer report is produced that lists all members and calculates their year-to-date sales. Members who exceed total year-to-date sales of $5000 are indicated on the report as Diamond Club members. A copy of the monthly report appears in Figure A16.11.

Identify the functions of the FBP application by choosing the correct radio buttons in Table A16.10.

Table A16.9

Names of Possible Function Types	Identify the Function Used					
	ILF	EIF	EI	EO	EQ	N/A
Add Payee	○	○	●	○	○	○
Change Payee	○	○	●	○	○	○
Make Payment	○	○	○	●	○	○
Display Payee Information	○	○	○	○	●	○
Payee logical file	●	○	○	○	○	○

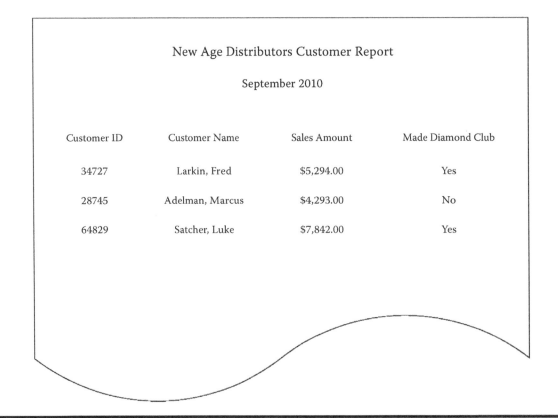

New Age Distributors Customer Report

September 2010

Customer ID	Customer Name	Sales Amount	Made Diamond Club
34727	Larkin, Fred	$5,294.00	Yes
28745	Adelman, Marcus	$4,293.00	No
64829	Satcher, Luke	$7,842.00	Yes

Figure A16.11 New Age Distributors customer report.

Table A16.10

Names of Possible Function Types	Identify the Function Used					
	ILF	*EIF*	*EI*	*EO*	*EQ*	*N/A*
Set Up Member's Profile	O	O	●	O	O	O
Change Member's Information	O	O	●	O	O	O
List Members	O	O	O	O	●	O
Membership logical file	●	O	O	O	O	O
Customer Report	O	O	O	●	O	O

Case Study 10

A building access system sends a batch update with time-card data indicating when employees swipe their ID cards to enter and leave the building. This data enters the company's Time Management application and includes three attributes (employee ID, time of day, and in/out indicator). The employee

Table A16.11

Names of Possible Function Types	Enter Complexity			
	Low	*Average*	*High*	*N/A*
Batch Update	●	O	O	O
Confirmation Message	O	O	O	●
Error Listing	O	O	O	●
Employee Hours ILF	●	O	O	O
Active Employees EIF	●	O	O	O

ID attribute on the input record is validated against an Active Employees logical file maintained in the company's Employee Payroll application. If the validation passes, the Employee Hours logical file is updated in the Time Management application, and a confirmation message is printed. If the validation fails, no update is made, and an error listing is printed.

Identify the functional complexity of the functions in the Time Management application by choosing the correct radio buttons in Table A16.11.

Glossary

Adaptive maintenance: The modification of a software product, performed after delivery, to keep a software product usable in a changed or changing environment. Adaptive maintenance provides enhancements necessary to accommodate changes in the environment in which a software product must operate. These changes are those that must be made to keep pace with the changing environment. For example, the operating system might be upgraded and some changes may be made to accommodate the new operating system (ISO/IEC 14764:2006).

Adjusted functional size: The adjusted functional size is the result of the unadjusted functional size multiplied by the Value Adjustment Factor. The adjusted functional size is calculated using a specific formula for development project, enhancement project, and application.

Application: An application is a cohesive collection of automated procedures and data supporting a business objective; it consists of one or more components, modules, or subsystems.

Application boundary: See Boundary.

Application function point count: The activity of applying the IFPUG Functional Size Measurement (FSM) Method to measure the functional size of an application.

Application functional size: An application's functional size is a measure of the functionality that an application provides to the user, determined by the application function point count by the activity of applying the IFPUG Functional Size Measurement (FSM) Method.

Arranging: The activity of sequencing attributes in a transactional function.

Associative entity type: An entity type that contains attributes which further describe a many-to-many relationship between two other entity types.

Attribute: See Data attribute.

Attribute key: Provides the relationship between one entity and another.

Attributive entity type: An entity type that further describes one or more characteristics of another entity type.

Base functional component (BFC): Elementary unit of Functional User Requirements defined by and used by the FSM Method for measurement purposes (ISO/IEC 14143-1:2007); ILFs, EIFs, EIs, EOs, and EQs are types of BFCs.

Baseline function point count: See Application function point count.

Boundary: The boundary is a conceptual interface between the software under study and its users.

Boundary of application: See Boundary.

Business Data: May also be referred to as *Core User Data* or *Business Objects*. This type of data reflects the information needed to be stored and retrieved by the functional area addressed by the application. Business Data usually represents a significant percentage of the entities identified.

Code Data: The user does not always directly specify Code Data, sometimes referred to as *List Data* or *Translation Data*; in other cases, it is is identified by the developer in response to one or more technical requirements of the user. Code Data provides a list of valid values that a descriptive attribute may have. Typically the attributes of the Code Data are code, description, and/or other standard attributes describing the code (standard abbreviation, effective date, termination date, audit trail data, etc.).

Complex Processing GSC: One of the 14 General System Characteristics describing the degree to which processing logic influences the development of the application.

Consistent state: The point at which processing has been fully executed; the functional user requirement has been satisfied and there is nothing more to be done.

Constant Data: Data that rarely changes.

Contribution: The function type's (ILF, EIF, EI, EO, EQ) contribution to the functional size.

Control information: Control information is data that influences an elementary process by specifying what, when or how data is to be processed.

Conversion functionality: Transactional or data functions provided to convert data and/or provide other user-specified conversion requirements.

Copy: (1) To read data from a source, leaving the source data unchanged, and to write the same data elsewhere in a physical form that may differ from that of the source; for example, to copy data from a magnetic disk onto a magnetic tape. (2) The result of a copy process as in above; for example, a copy of a data file (IEEE).

Corrective maintenance: The reactive modification of a software product performed after delivery to correct discovered problems. The modification repairs the software product to satisfy requirements (ISO/IEC 14764:2006).

Counting scope: The counting scope defines the set of Functional User Requirements to be included in the function point count.

Data attribute: A characteristic of an entity; data attributes are generally analogous to Data Element Types (DETs). Also known as *field*.

Data Communications GSC: One of the 14 General System Characteristics describing the degree to which the application communicates directly with the processor.

Data Element Type (DET): A Data Element Type is a unique, user-recognizable, nonrepeated attribute.

Data entity: See Entity.

Data function: A data function represents functionality provided to the user to meet internal and external data storage requirements. A data function is either an Internal Logical File or an External Interface File.

Degree of Influence (DI): A numerical indicator of the amount of impact of each of the 14 General System Characteristics, ranging from zero to five. These indicators are used to compute the Value Adjustment Factor.

Derived data: Data created as a result of processing that involves steps other than. or in addition to, direct retrieval and validation of information from data functions.

Development project: A development project is a project to develop and deliver the first release of a software application.

Development project function point count: The activity of applying the IFPUG Functional Size Measurement (FSM) Method to measure the functional size of a development project.

Development project functional size: The development project functional size is a measure of the functionality provided to users with the first release of the software, as measured by the development project function point count by the activity of applying the IFPUG Functional Size Measurement (FSM) Method.

Distributed Data Processing GSC: One of the 14 General System Characteristics describing the degree to which the application transfers data among physical components of the application.

Elementary process (EP): An elementary process is the smallest unit of activity that is meaningful to the user.

End-User Efficiency GSC: One of the 14 General System Characteristics describing the degree of consideration for human factors and ease of use for the user of the application measured.

Enhancement project: An enhancement project is a project to develop and deliver adaptive maintenance.

Enhancement project function point count: The activity of applying the IFPUG Functional Size Measurement (FSM) Method to measure of the functional size of an enhancement project.

Enhancement project functional size: The enhancement project functional size is a measure of the functionality added, changed, or deleted at the completion of an enhancement project, as measured by the enhancement project function point count by the activity of applying the IFPUG Functional Size Measurement (FSM) Method.

Entity (or entity type): A fundamental thing of relevance to the user, about which a collection of facts is kept. An association between entities that contains attributes is itself an entity.

Entity-dependent: An entity that is not meaningful or is not significant to the business, in and of itself, without the presence of other entities such that (1) an occurrence of entity X must be linked to an occurrence of entity Y, and (2) the deletion of an occurrence of entity Y results in the deletion of all related occurrences of entity X.

Entity-independent: An entity that is meaningful or significant to the business, in and of itself, without the presence of other entities.

Entity subtype: A subdivision of entity type. A subtype inherits all the attributes and relationships of its parent entity type and may have additional, unique attributes and relationships.

External input (EI): An external input is an elementary process that processes data or control information sent from outside the boundary. The primary intent of an EI is to maintain one or more ILFs and/or to alter the behavior of the system.

External inquiry (EQ): An external inquiry is an elementary process that sends data or control information outside the boundary. The primary intent of an external inquiry is present information to a user through the retrieval of data or control information. The processing logic contains no mathematical formula or calculation and creates no derived data. No ILF is maintained during the processing nor is the behavior of the system altered.

External Interface File (EIF): An External Interface File is a user-recognizable group of logically related data or control information which is referenced by the application being measured but which is maintained within the boundary of another application. The primary intent of an EIF is to hold data referenced through one or more elementary processes within the boundary of the application measured. This means an EIF counted for an application must be in an ILF in another application.

External output (EO): An external output is an elementary process that sends data or control information outside the application's boundary and includes additional processing beyond that of an external inquiry. The primary intent of an external output is to present information to a user through processing logic other than or in addition to the retrieval of data or control information. The processing logic must contain at least one mathematical formula or calculation, create derived data, maintain one or more ILFs, and/or alter the behavior of the system.

Facilitate Change GSC: One of the 14 General System Characteristics describing the degree to which the application has been developed for easy modification of processing logic or data structure.

Field: See Data attribute.

File: For data functions, a logically related group of data, not the physical implementation of those groups of data.

File system: Is composed of records and data attributes.

File Type Referenced (FTR): A data function read and/or maintained by a transactional function.

First normal form: Result of a normalization process that transforms groups of data so they have a unique identifier, one or more attributes, and no repeating attributes.

Foreign key: Data in an ILF or EIF that exists because the user requires a relationship with another ILF or EIF.

Function: The features or capabilities of an application as seen by the user.

Function point (FP): The unit of measure for functional size as defined within the IFPUG Functional Size Measurement (FSM) Method.

Function point analysis: The method for measuring functional size as defined within the IFPUG Functional Size Measurement (FSM) Method.

Function point count: The activity of applying the rules within the IFPUG Functional Size Measurement (FSM) Method to measure the functional size of an application or project. There are three types of function point counts: application, development project, and enhancement project.

Function type: The five base functional components identified in the IFPUG Functional Size Measurement (FSM) Method; also known as *base functional component*. The five function types are external input, external output, external inquiry, Internal Logical File, and External Interface File.

Functional complexity: The specific complexity rating assigned to a function using the rules as defined within the International Standard.

Functional size: Size of the software derived by quantifying the Functional User Requirements (ISO 14143-1:2007).

Functional User Requirements (FURs): A subset of the user requirements specifying what the software shall do in terms of tasks and services (ISO 14143-1:2007).

Functionality: See Function.

General System Characteristics (GSCs): The General System Characteristics are a set of 14 questions that evaluate the overall complexity of the application.

Heavily Used Configuration GSC: One of the 14 General System Characteristics describing the degree to which computer resource restrictions influenced the development of the application.

IFPUG: The International Function Point Users Group is a membership governed, nonprofit organization committed to promoting and supporting function point analysis and other software measurement techniques.

Image: An exact replication of another object, file, or table that is usually created through a utility.

Installation Ease GSC: One of the 14 General System Characteristics describing the degree to which conversion from previous environments influenced the development of the application.

Installed function point count: See Application function point count.

Internal Logical File (ILF): An Internal Logical File is a user-recognizable group of logically related data or control information maintained within the boundary of the application being measured. The primary intent of an ILF is to hold data maintained through one or more elementary processes of the application being measured.

Load: To copy computer instructions or data from external storage to internal storage (IEEE).

Logical file: See Data function.

Maintain: The term maintain refers to the ability to add, change, or delete data through an elementary process.

Maintenance: The effort to keep an application performing according to its specifications, generally without changing its functionality (or functional size). Maintenance includes repair, minor enhancement, conversion, user support, and preventive maintenance activities. Activities include defect removal (see Repair), hardware or software upgrades (see Conversion), optimization or quality improvement (see Preventive maintenance), and user support.

Mandatory subgroup: One of the two types of subgroups for Record Element Types (RETs). Mandatory subgroups mean the user must use one of the subgroups during an elementary process that creates an instance of the data.

Meaningful: Is user-recognizable and satisfies a functional user requirement.

Measure: As a noun, a number that assigns relative value; some examples may include volume, height, function points, or work effort. As a verb, to ascertain or appraise by comparing to a standard.

Merge: Multiple files with the same data elements consolidated into a single file (IEEE).

Multiple Sites GSC: One of the 14 General System Characteristics describing the degree to which the application has been developed for different hardware and software environments.

Normalization: The process by which any data structure can be transformed by a database designer into a set of normalized relations that have no repeating groups.

On-Line Data Entry GSC: One of the 14 General System Characteristics describing the degree to which data is entered or retrieved through interactive transactions.

On-Line Update GSC: One of the 14 General System Characteristics describing the degree to which Internal Logical Files are updated online.

Operational Ease GSC: One of the 14 General System Characteristics describing the degree to which the application attends to operational aspects, such as start-up, back-up, and recovery processes.

Optional subgroup: Optional subgroups are those that the user has the option of using one or none of the subgroups during an elementary process that adds or creates an instance or the data.

Perfective maintenance: Modification of a software product after delivery to detect and correct latent faults in the software product before they are manifested as failures. Perfective maintenance provides enhancements for users, improvement of program documentation, and recoding to improve software performance, maintainability, or other software attributes. Contrast with adaptive maintenance; corrective maintenance (ISO/IEC 14764:2006).

Performance GSC: One of the 14 General System Characteristics describing the degree to which response time and throughput performance considerations influenced the application development.

Preventive maintenance: Changes to hardware or software performed to prevent future defects or failures; for example, restructuring programs or data to improve maintainability or to prevent defects.

Primary intent: Intent that is first in importance.

Primary key (PK): The unique ID of an entity.

Processing logic: Any of the requirements specifically requested by the user to complete an elementary process, such as validations, algorithms, or calculations, and reading or maintaining a data function.

Project: A collection of work tasks with a time frame and a work product to be delivered.

Purpose of the count: The reason for performing the function point count.

Quality: Quality includes conformity to user expectations, conformity to user requirements, customer satisfaction, reliability, level of defects present. Context and policy will decide the best definition for a given situation.

Record: A group of related items that is treated as a unit.

Record Element Type (RET): A Record Element Type is a user-recognizable subgroup of Data Element Types within a data function.

Reference Data: This type of data is stored to support the business rules for the maintenance of the Business Data; for example, in a payroll application it would be the data stored on the government tax rates for each wage scale and the date the tax rate became effective. Reference Data usually represents a small percentage of entities identified.

Refresh: The process of recreating a set of data to make it current with its source.

Relationship: An association of interest between two entities. A relationship does not have attributes and does not count as a RET when counting function points.

Reusability GSC: One of the 14 General System Characteristics describing the degree to which the application and the code in the application have been specifically designed, developed, and supported to be usable in other applications.

Second normal form: Result of a normalization process that transforms groups of data so each non-key attribute depends on the key attribute(s) of the group of data and all parts of the key attribute(s).

Secondary key (SK): Attributes used primarily as an aid to access.

Self-contained: No prior or subsequent processing steps are needed to initiate or complete the functional requirement(s).

Sorting: The activity of sequencing of rows or records in a transactional function.

Static data: See Constant data.

Substitution data: Provides a code and an explanatory name or description for an attribute of a business object.

Subtypes: See Entity subtype.

Support: See Maintenance.

System: See Application.

Technical attribute: Nonfunctional attribute that is a result of a design or implementation consideration.

Technical requirements: Requirements that are related to the technology and environment, for the development, maintenance, support, and execution of the software.

Third normal form: Result of a normalization process that transforms groups of data so each non-key attribute does not depend on any other non-key attribute.

Total Degree of Influence (TDI): The sum of the degrees of influence for the 14 GSCs.

Transaction: See Transactional function.

Transaction Rate GSC: One of the 14 General System Characteristics describing the degree to which the rate of business transactions influenced the development of the application.

Transactional function: A transactional function is an elementary process that provides functionality to the user to process data. A transactional function is an external input, external output, or external inquiry.

Unadjusted function point count (UFP): See Function point count.

Unadjusted functional size: See Functional size.

User: A user is any person or thing that communicates or interacts with the software at any time.

User-recognizable: The term user-recognizable refers to requirements for processes and/or data that are agreed upon and understood by both the user(s) and software developer(s).

User view: A user view is the Functional User Requirements as perceived by the user.

Valid Values Data: Provides a list of available values for an attribute of one or more business object types.

Value Adjustment Factor (VAF): The factor that indicates the general functionality provided to the user of the application. The VAF is calculated based on an assessment of the 14 General System Characteristics (GSCs) for an application.

Index

Printed and bound by CPI Group (UK) Ltd, Croydon, CR0 4YY

22/10/2024

01777634-0020